ARAVINDA

My Autobiography

Aravinda de Silva
with Shahriar Khan

MAINSTREAM
PUBLISHING

EDINBURGH AND LONDON

Thanks to Matthew Bannister of Alston Elliot Ltd
and to Richard Lockwood of *The Cricket Quarterly.*

First published in Great Britain in 1999 by
MAINSTREAM PUBLISHING COMPANY (EDINBURGH) LTD
7 Albany Street
Edinburgh EH1 3UG

ISBN 1 84018 196 6

A catalogue record for this book is available from the British Library

Typeset in Garamond
Printed and bound in Great Britain by Butler & Tanner Ltd

'May my book teach you to care more for yourself than for it,
and then more for all the rest than for yourself.'

André Gide, *Fruits of the Earth*

Foreword

A short drive through the cluttered Colombo streets with Aravinda de Silva helps you understand the way he bats. There's a sense of controlled aggression as he manoeuvres into a narrow space with the same ease that he finds a gap in the field. And then he accelerates quickly, just like his scoring rate.

Aravinda would rank high as a driver but nowhere near his lofty perch among the top batsmen in the world. The first time Aravinda's batting made an impression on me was in Australia during the 1984-85 World Series games. He played a big part in Sri Lanka's only win over the home side when, aged only 19, Aravinda scored 46 from just 37 balls, including a soaring six over the fine-leg fence at a crucial moment as he guided his team home with only four balls to spare. That innings at the MCG suggested that this young man had something special.

There was even more convincing evidence of his abilities when he toured Australia for a Test series in 1989-90 and scored a magnificent century at the Gabba. His hooking was exceptional, hammering Merv Hughes to the boundary behind square-leg, and when the big fast bowler opted for a second fieldsman in the deep, Aravinda dismissively swayed inside the short-pitched deliveries. When Hughes tired of this lop-sided contest and dispensed with the second outfielder, Aravinda immediately resumed hooking him imperiously; it was brilliant stuff as he unveiled his control over the horizontal bat shots. At the time my only doubt about Aravinda was his insistence on hitting the ball at catchable height through the infield. Eradicate that blemish, I thought, and he'll become one of the best.

When Aravinda scored his faultless century in the World Cup final to bring his country the ultimate glory, we witnessed a batsman who had harnessed his talent and was capitalising on his ability. Gone was the fired-up batsman with an urge to belt the ball into oblivion. This was the more relaxed but ultra-aggressive stroke-maker who so often destroyed attacks. A year later he capitalised to the full, with that World Cup hundred preceding an amazing sequence of seven Test centuries in twelve innings; here was a batsman playing at his peak.

Apart from his obvious skill and talent, Aravinda's sport is full of thought and flair. He has a very shrewd cricket brain and if it hadn't been for the competence of Arjuna Ranatunga, Aravinda would've been a good long-term Sri Lankan captain.

Despite his sporting prowess, it would be a mistake to think of Aravinda as a one-dimensional person. He's also been very successful in his business ventures and a lengthy chat with the man unearths an interest in what is happening in his own country as well as around the world. It's no surprise to discover such a well-rounded son after you meet Aravinda's parents.

I first came across Sam (I called him Sammy, but was politely told by his wife Indrani that no one ever referred to him as that) at a fine feast in a Colombo Chinese restaurant. Sam and Upali Mahanama (father of Roshan) combined to provide the entertainment. Sam and Upali had a decent repertoire of songs but my favourite was the verse of 'She'll be coming round the mountain' that referred to 'sucking cookel cuckle'. Sam later told me it means sucking chicken wings. As well as contributing to our entertainment and enjoying his own life to the full, Sam has provided exactly the right amount of support and encouragement for his son, without smothering his sporting career.

The better a man is, the more he dares and Aravinda dares plenty. Aravinda is a rare sportsman who has been given a great gift. He has made the most of his talent while still remaining a humble, decent human being. That in itself is remarkable.

Ian Chappell

PROLOGUE

A four through the covers took me to my century, and a boundary off the last ball of that over brought the scores level. The Lahore crowd roared. Australian heads slumped into their shoulders. But for a long time they had known they were going to lose. At the turn-around between overs, Ian Healy came up to Arjuna and said, 'There won't be time afterwards, so I'll say it now – well played, mate.'

Arjuna and Healy had 'history' between them going back several years, most recently to the 1995-1996 World Series Cup in Australia just two months before. During the Sydney final, bruised and battered, breathless with the pain of a pulled hamstring, Arjuna had appealed for a runner to the umpires. From behind the stumps Healy said that it wasn't Arjuna's hamstring that was the problem, it was his waistline. The umpires sided with Healy, and Arjuna didn't get his runner. I had never seen Arjuna so angry. We lost that game and, with it, the tournament. It had been a difficult tour for us. We'd suffered humiliating defeats in the Test matches, been stunned at the labelling of our off-spinner Muralitharan as a 'chucker', and endured a battle-weary trek to the finals of the World Series where we had to confront Australian competitiveness at its most abrasive.

Two months later, in Pakistan, we had a chance for revenge and a greater glory. Healy's gracious closing words at the end of a stormy World Cup final were received by Arjuna in the spirit they were intended. From one fierce competitor to another: an acknowledgement of a better performance. You invariably have to be at your best to beat Australia and in this match, indeed throughout the whole tournament, each Sri Lankan had been simply irresistible at one time or another.

Healy was right about there not being any time afterwards. As soon as Arjuna had glided Glenn McGrath down to the third-man boundary for the winning runs, Arjuna and I embraced in the middle of the wicket like two brothers who finally find each other after years of searching. Our team-mates ran on to the pitch, we hugged and danced a jig of triumph, the start of a party that went on for days and days. We had won the World Cup. Sri Lanka were champions of the world.

CHAPTER ONE

Whenever a child is born into a Buddhist family in Sri Lanka objects of devotion are arranged in the time-honoured tradition and placed around the house and local temple to give thanks to, and receive the blessing of, the household spirits. My father put a new twist on this custom. His over-riding ambition for his son's future was that I should be 'a cricket player' and from the beginning of my life he did everything he could to help me on this path. Family legend has it that my father put a bat and ball in my crib soon after I was born. If there were household gods with an eye for cricket, putting the leather and willow by my side made it more likely that at least a little cricketing ability would find me.

As a very young boy, my father began to feed me 'imaginary' balls to hit. I'd be coached in moving back and across, back and across, to 'hook' these phantom balls. For a long time the hook shot was the only one I knew and this thing my father called 'cricket' simply meant moving my feet and swinging a plastic bat in a certain way. I must have enjoyed it. But 'cricket' to my father meant something a whole lot more. Cricket meant moral and social standards, good conduct, civility, fraternity. The understanding was that playing cricket made someone a better person. My father's Buddhist soul saw in cricket a reflection of Buddhism's principles of self-sublimation, good conduct, mental discipline and honest endeavour. Buddhism makes small distinction between religious activity and the acts of every day: the religious ceremony is life itself. Cricket with its rites and regulations, its practices and precepts, its ethic of individuality within a team framework, really appealed to my father. He was a great collector of sayings and mottoes, which the schoolmaster element in him would delight in slipping into conversation. One of his favourite quotes was from someone called Lord Harris, who soon assumed a rather mythical stature in my life – I still don't know exactly who Lord Harris was, apart from the fact that he played cricket for England in the 19th century, but I do know that of cricket he said – 'to play it keenly, honourably, self-sacrificingly is a moral lesson in itself'. The game has changed a great deal in the past fifteen years let alone in the past one hundred and fifty, but the essential truths have remained the same. Cricket is a great definer of character. This game with so many possibilities for failure, tests just how much one is prepared to go the distance in order to prevail. It was never my father's overriding ambition to turn me into a national cricketer, when I was born no one could have imagined that Sri Lanka would even be a Test-playing nation sixteen years later. My father simply wanted me to learn the game well enough so that I could fully participate in the games at school as a growing child, and thus be able to absorb all the lessons the game had to offer.

In his own college days in Calcutta, where he went to study commerce just after Partition, my father's sporting talents ran to athletics with him becoming an exceptional miler and 880 yards-runner. He played plenty of football and cricket too, and he really devoted himself to developing his fitness and physique. Small and wiry, as a collegian he put himself on a strict milk and protein diet and embarked on a vigorous exercise regime. He might not have been a great natural athlete but his competitiveness must have made him a tough adversary. Pretty soon he was lifting twice his body-weight. Now near to seventy years old, his appetite for life remains legendary and he has the energy and strength of a young man. And the voice of an opera-singer. Ready to celebrate most things with a song – a Sri Lankan victory, a wedding, a birthday, the simple fact of being alive and in good company – he loves to sing our local 'bailas' (calypso songs) like the 'portuguesikaraya' originally sung by the Portuguese settlers of the island, who apparently believed that any war could be won by writing the right songs for it and not losing your sense of humour. Life is ready to be a party whenever Sam de Silva's around.

Sam de Silva is actually two people in one: one is his public image – the swinger, the singer, the larger-than-life ring-a-ding dinger; the other is the serious professional, the father, the friend, the devout moralist. The façade of fun and mantle of laughs is worn lightly on the frame of a lifetime of hard-earned experience. He wants everyone to be happy because he knows just how difficult life can be. When he believes something, he dramatises what he believes. When I was a child he impressed upon me in the most vivid and fun-filled manner that my cricket bat was not just a toy to be picked up and put down like any other. It was more: something akin to a musical instrument, something which if I carried I would have to master. To my father, being an athlete meant not just having physical skill but having completeness of person (physical, spiritual, intellectual ability), and the passion to prevail. He never let me forget that sharpness of mind was a person's most valuable asset. He would encourage me to think about my game and emphasised the need to always stay alert to the possibility of doing something better. All this he would do gently and encouragingly, not at the cricket-field but on the drives and walks to and from a day's play and at the dinner table. He would leave my actual performance on the field to me and my coaches, who themselves were made to feel as though they were caught up in the cause of bringing me along the rightful cricketing path. My father has a remarkable capacity to transmit his cheerful strength to others, to allow those who hear his message to begin to feel it and to take part in it. He never let me forget that I had it in me to be a good cricketer and a good human being. That was pretty inspiring.

From the very first time I was given a cricket bat to hold, my father says he fed me on a diet of fundamentals and fresh milk. I was taught the sideways-on stance early and guided in how to hit the ball as hard as possible. I think that my first cricket bat became a part of me: I couldn't walk without it. Tennis balls, seven/eight at a time, were thrown at me from all angles by my father, fast and slow, high and low, from near and far. The foundations of whatever hand-eye co-ordination I have, must have been developed in these sessions. It's still true to this day: I might not be the quickest in the field (do allow me my occasional understatement) but I can position my hands and feet properly to take a catch. I drank milk like it was a soft drink. It was fed to me as a nutritional building block, my father figuring that if it worked for him in his days as an athlete it would work for me too. He must have been determined to give me every chance to compensate for my smallness by giving me the strength to handle all physical demands. I always had to finish whatever was on my plate, for my sake and for those who were not fortunate enough to be able to eat as well as I.

During those days of childhood cricket my friends and I would gather after school and play until we virtually couldn't see the ball. At which point my father would come to take me back home, remind me I had homework to do, and distribute some ice-creams to all the players. He always had sweets in his pocket and a smile on his face. He never treated me or any of my friends with any condescension and had time for everyone: they called him 'Uncle Sam'. Sometimes I could sense just a hint of envy of my companions against me, because I was perceived as having all the breaks – an indulgent father who lavished affection, cricket gear and all the goodies a boy could want. And the fact that it was my bat and my ball that was used every day probably had something to do with me getting a game whenever I wanted. But my friends didn't envy me my cricket gear or abilities, they envied the fact that I had a father who was so supportive of me.

My father developed my English and my knowledge of cricket by means of a *Readers Digest Encyclopaedia*. With text and diagrams it showed the proper way to grip a bat and hold the ball for various deliveries. It described what a hook shot was, with small drawings of the footwork and body-position required to execute the stroke, defined the cover drive, the leg-glance, the position of hands and fingers on the ball for the outswinger, the leg-break and so much more. Everything in black and white, everything easily understood. During my first few school holidays he would have me copy out the cricket section of the *Encyclopaedia* so that I could refresh my knowledge of the game and practise my handwriting at the same time. The basis of my father's fascination for the game was that as you are in life you are as a cricketer. His conversation to this day is spiced with cricketing metaphors: 'playing it straight' means being honest or displaying integrity; 'meeting it on the full' means boldly facing up to difficult or tricky situations. He showed me the virtue of courage at a very early age. It has been said that courage is a man's chief virtue because it makes all other virtues possible. I believe that to be true. Whatever success I have had as a cricketer and as a human being has simply been due to my having the courage of my convictions. Examine the lives of people who have established themselves as the best competitors and you will see that their success hasn't been achieved by being like anybody else, but by being themselves. They have simply had the guts to be individuals. Life takes guts. If you don't take chances you don't succeed.

To this day the respect my father and my mother have earned reflects on me, empowers me and subtly alters others' perceptions of who I am, of what I can do. No scandal can stick to my name, at a time when scandal-mongering is at a peak, because people know that I would never do anything to embarrass my parents or my Buddhist faith. The simple fact that my parents have always been popular people helped me get noticed in cricketing circles when I was a boy. Mr Abu Fuard was the first to really notice my talent at an early age – he had been Sri Lanka's top off-spinner in the 1960s and had been a very tough competitor on the field. A family friend, legend has it that Mr Fuard came to dinner one night when I was six, at a time when I was striding around whacking the furniture, my elder sister, the maid and just about anyone who came in reach, with my plastic cricket bat. Something about Mr Fuard must have stopped me in my tracks. I probably sensed that, like my father, he didn't look like someone who laughed indulgently at being wantonly smacked by a cricket bat. Mr Fuard chose to test out my ball-hitting, rather than my welt-inflicting, prowess by bouncing a tennis ball at me which I then proceeded to straight-drive back at him. With correct footwork, my head over the ball and good timing. My father had taught me well. Mr Fuard's reaction on seeing this was to say in an aside to my parents that I had the makings of a fine batsman, and that I should be sent to a good coach immediately. When I was a little older, on further visits Mr Fuard would always present me with new cricket balls which I would keep at home and carry around with me, flicking them from hand to hand whenever I had a free moment, simply to get used to the feel of a cricket ball. It was initially very heartening to find Mr Fuard managing the Sri Lankan team on my entry into the national side fourteen years later.

As a boy I was encouraged to play all sports, and was taken to all the big sporting occasions – schools matches, games against touring cricket teams and rugby finals (rugby being another Lankan passion). I loved watching cricket most of all, and my first sporting heroes were the batsmen Duleep Mendis and Roy Dias. Indeed they were idolised by everyone for their big-hitting and fast-scoring. I wanted to play like them. Everyone did. They were carrying on the tradition of bold, dynamic island batting as demonstrated by Derrick de Saram, 'Sargo' Jayawickrema, his nephew Mahes Rodrigo (the island's Ranjitsinhji and Duleepsinhji), Vernon Prins, C.H. and C.I. Gunasekera, Mahadevan Sathasivam, Stanley Jayasinghe and Michael Tissera, just to name a few legends. Cricket in Sri Lanka is so intensely remembered because it is so intensely watched. In the days before televisions were common in Sri Lanka (and television has only really started being seen across the island since the 1970s) the big matches and big names would draw huge crowds. Games became social occasions where the very best that Lankan cricket had to offer would be on display for people to celebrate and relish. Colombo was the big centre for island cricket in those days. And the top Colombo schools were considered the sole breeding grounds for top cricketers. The outlying provinces and other Colombo schools were reckoned to be backwaters which couldn't produce players of sufficient standard or style or technique. In recent years, however, the selection monopoly formerly held by the elite schools and clubs has been shattered and cricketers from lesser known schools and provinces have had chances in the national team. Just about everyone in the national team of the 1990s has benefited from this policy, as has Lankan cricket generally.

The two most prominent schools in Colombo, the Eton and Harrow of Sri Lanka, are Royal College and St Thomas' College, and once I reached school-going age my parents applied for my admission. Entry's tough into these schools, you have either to be demonstrably very bright, a good cricketer, of the right sort (i.e. a son of a former alumnus) or live within a two-mile radius of the school. Obviously, at the age of five, living on the other side of town and with a father who was educated at St Aloysius' College in Galle, I was very apparently none of the above. It is my enduring good fortune that being turned down for admission into both Royal and St Thomas', I became a D.S. Senanayake pupil. The 'old school-tie' network is prominent in Sri Lanka and my father heard of the efforts in 1967 of one of St Aloysius' former pupils, Mr Ralph Alles, to start a new school in Colombo to be named in honour of the first Prime Minister of independent Sri Lanka, Don Stephen Senanayake. Mr Alles had been chosen by the then Minister of Education to start a parallel school to Royal College and was allotted a dozen acres of undeveloped (i.e. jungle) land to put up some tin-roofed schoolhouses. My father heard of Mr Alles' efforts, enlisted as unofficial bursar, and put me forward to be one of the new school's pupils once I was old enough. Other parents followed suit, and in my first year, 1971, we were about a hundred pupils. As we grew older, the school grew with us too, every year bringing forth a fresh batch of five-year-olds. Now, after all the efforts and sacrifices of parents and teachers and so many volunteers in those early years, the school has 5,000 pupils, its own cricket pitch, nets, air-conditioned buildings and a huge school hall which has already developed an aura of tradition and history. Everyone who has been to D.S. Senanayake is proud of their association with the school.

When I first started playing competitive cricket, Sri Lanka was not a Test-playing nation, and all thoughts of Test cricket were far away for all of us. I myself never had any great cricketing ambitions as a child, apart from hoping that it would never rain on a day I was due to play. But I guess my father looked further ahead. He never spoke of his hopes; they were deeper than that. There was always an expectation that I would do something. I can't explain it, but I was always aware that there was this high expectation factor for me. People always seemed to look at me expecting me to make something happen, to do something big. True enough, take enough small steps and pretty soon you outdistance your competition.

Typically, the forward defensive is the first stroke a batsman is taught, and the first stroke he forgets. This wasn't true in my case. I just couldn't bring myself to learn the forward defensive at a time when the satisfying sting of belting a bouncing ball was on offer. But my first formal cricket coaches, Mr Charlie Warnakulasuriya and Mr W.A.N. Silva were instrumental in developing my game. They had a great deal of patience and had a way of helping me without being patronising. 'You were bowled because your bat wasn't straight, Aravinda, and you're going to keep getting bowled until it is.' There always was a 'why' to their 'how'. Mr Warnakulasuriya showed me how to bowl too, and more than just working with me on developing a run-up and action, he taught me all about attacking batsmen's weaknesses. And just by looking at my game, I knew that batsmen had plenty. Playing under their eyes, in organised nets with real wickets, I heard close up for the first time the sound a cricket ball makes as it cannons into stumps. It really was a shock to the system. Cricket had a downside apparently. I continued to hear those clunky-clacks behind me many times more. But by nature Mr Silva and Mr Warnakulasuriya were great technique and confidence builders, and all my mistakes were dismissed as temporary faults which could be easily corrected. Every time you give young people a 'well done', they go on to do better. Under their guidance my love and respect for the game deepened.

By the time a cricketer has been playing for four or five years, he is no longer evaluated by what he might be but by his actual accomplishments and weight of runs and wickets. Even though I was initially considered to have possibilities as an attacking off-spinner, my friends and I were all predominantly batting all-rounders in those days. Only a few of us found that bowling actually offered possibilities of a series of glorious rewards for the effort of running up in the heat to bowl ball after ball. None of us really focused on bowling because batting seemed to be the most glamorous activity; batsmen were the national heroes and the sporting role-models. Bowlers were seen as serving batsmen's interests. As we all grew older and established distinctive playing characteristics and, most importantly, exposed ourselves to a widening circle of competition, many of us found our seemingly open-ended potential replaced by limitations and fast-receding possibilities. It became harder to win. It became harder to be the best and to shine. I've read the book, seen the film, lived the life and know that there is no such thing as being 'The Natural'. Every feature of your game on top of having good reflexes, co-ordination and a decent physique is the product of an acquired skill. Everything is learned. Anything can be learned by asking the right questions of yourself. Many of my friends and peers peaked as 14-year-olds. It is hard to say exactly why their talents didn't develop beyond a certain point. Natural ability gets you to a certain level and good coaching can take you further, but after a point you have to keep digging deeper and deeper into yourself to progress. You have to really want to be good at this game, if you want to be good at this game.

After-hours at school, while I waited for my father to take me home after he'd finished attending various school committee meetings, I used to hang around the older boys' net practices and 'casually' field out in the deep to those shots that were hit past the bowlers. To all intents and purposes I'd just be killing time, but I'd be looking closely at their techniques and dreaming of doing damage to the best bowlers when I was old enough. Buddhists say 'when you are ready, the teacher will appear' and, fortunately for me, at just the right time as a young teenager I came to the attention of Mr Walter Perera, the first XI coach at school. It was Mr Perera who said to all those (including me) who were worried about my chances, that I was good enough as a slip of a 13-year-old to play against young men of 18 and 19. As much as there was concern for my form and confidence against these fully-grown hurlers of hard leather cricket balls, there was also genuine fear for my well-being. I could well get smacked on the head, break a finger, be bruised all over. I wasn't fully convinced about my ability to cope with either, but Mr Perera thought I could do well and that I really did need to move up a few levels to develop as a batsman. And he was right. Early on in my first XI days, trying to hook a ball, I was hit smack between the eyes by the fastest delivery I had yet faced, but I survived. Having survived, fear disappeared. I knew I could overcome the worst that a bowler could do.

Coaching under Mr Silva at school continued apace. He was involved with the national team as well at the time and to get a player's technique perfect according to the tried and tested fundamentals of the game was his ideal. I learned from him to do things as elegantly and as simply as I possibly could. He had the infinite and loving patience which distinguishes the great from the competent coach. From day one we were taught to play straight, never to play across the line. For this the leading hand had to be in control. We did thousands of bat drills with a bat held only with the top hand so that we would get used to using the top hand as the primary force for the bat, playing straight and not controlling the bat with the bottom hand. On no account were across-the-line hoicks to the leg-side tolerated. Another thing that was emphasised was that cricket was a sideways game. When batting, you approached and played the ball in a sideways manner, and even while bowling you kept yourself sideways on for as long as possible. It was all about making the shoulders move in the same direction. Mr Silva was always highly pleased when he saw a perfect off-drive or an outswinger, because it meant you had stayed sideways for as long as possible. The look on his face whenever one of us cover-drove an outswinger! As a youngster you always looked for that kind of approval from an elder. It proved you were really doing all right. And he was always quick to encourage a bowler who had been bested in spite of bowling a good-ball. 'That was the batsman's moment. Just a moment. Keep bowling that kind of ball and you'll end up the hero in the scorebook.'

Learning these new lessons called for concentration, patience and persistence. It was something we teenagers really had to work at. It wasn't so much that we were motivated by dreams of playing Test cricket or even becoming famous cricketers in Sri Lanka, Mr Silva inspired us youths to love practising the fundamentals by pricking our pride. We had to practise hard, repeatedly rehearsing what we thought we already knew, because we understood that any slip would show us as still too young to be trusted with responsibility for our own destinies. And what a teenager wants more than anything, of course, is to be trusted to be master of his own life.

Looking back, I understand now just how vital it was for Mr Silva to put into perspective all that we did. It wasn't just that the good performances of his pupils in the nets would translate into good performances in match conditions, he would always emphasise the need to build a solid foundation to our game. As a batsman, for all your eye, reflexes, talent, and appetite for the game, you were not going to get very far without a proper defensive technique. And as a coach associated in those days with the national team, Mr Silva knew just what it took to succeed against international competition. He would tell us, 'If you have a good defence now, you'll have it forever, and you will be able to develop attacking strokes as you get bigger and stronger.' In fact the Sri Lankan standard method of coaching could be said to be textbook MCC coaching with a 'twist'. We were all taught to use our wrists to control the strokes and place the ball where we wanted it to go – 'Hit through the ball, not at it. Aim for the gaps. Don't aim for the boundary-line first,' Mr Silva would say. We would devote plenty of time to drills where without a ball, and with just the top hand holding the bat, we would practise turning the wrist at the point of impact to direct the ball where we wanted it to go, so that it would become second nature. Again, I was very lucky. Whereas it has now become the trend amongst batsmen to 'visualise' their game, whereby a batsman pictures in his mind's eye his responses to every kind of delivery, thus refreshing his reflexes, rehearsing his strokes and conditioning himself for action, I was introduced to this method as a schoolboy and have relied on it ever since.

When we became a little older a great deal of emphasis was placed on rhythm and timing. Again it was a matter of having hours and hours of throwdowns so that it would become an embedded part of our game. These throwdowns were quite often used to highlight technical deficiencies and point out opportunities where a player could be doing better. As a little youth and even littler child, I would watch bigger boys thump the ball all over the nets or the park and long to do the same. I certainly hated it when they would do that to my bowling. But all Mr Silva would say to the batsman as he observed these whacking strokes was, 'your front elbow is dropping' or, 'you are just thumping it with your bottom hand, and will be found wanting when the ball is swinging or seaming'. Defence in the service of attack was the foundation of his teaching. Mr Silva believed that spinners should be attacked in all instances by going down the wicket, with the caveat that strokes against them should always be hit along the ground and not in the air. In his view this applied all the time when you were batting, because hitting the ball in the air simply gave the fielding side an extra opportunity of getting you out. At that time, I couldn't quite figure out what the fuss was about when the bigger lads were hitting the ball so hard and such a long way. It was always difficult to resist the temptation to hit the ball as hard as one possibly could; not that I was a paragon of virtue in this respect, but some of us never ever resisted indulging ourselves. They are the ones who have given up competitive cricket. Big hits over the boundary can only take you so far. And Mr Silva positively discouraged hooking for being a stroke that lost more wickets than it scored runs. Instead, to the short-pitched ball he would recommend the kind of disdainful swaying of the body that Martin Crowe would later do so well, whereby one would simply lean forward or back, maintaining one's sideways-on position, keeping both eyes on the ball as the ball passed harmlessly across one's body.

I was a devoted follower of all of Mr Silva's precepts, but I disobeyed him on two things. I had to. There was nothing I could do. Something inside me, when presented with a ball in my 'slots', simply said 'hit it high wide and handsome'. I loved hooking. I loved pulling. I loved hitting the ball over the top. Popular myth has it that I don't like to unnecessarily run for anything. It's not a myth. It's true. I'll always go up and down the pitch in order to notch runs for me or my batting partners, but I don't really see the point in pushing ones and twos when the opportunity to strike a four or a six presents itself. I also liked using bats perhaps a little too heavy for someone only gently threatening to grow past five foot in length. As it was, I knew that if I timed the ball well enough (and that was all I was interested in, timing the ball), even if I slightly mis-hit the drives I intended to hit along the ground by playing just a fraction too early, all that leverage and heft would probably see that the ball flew over any fielders. This ingrained attitude led to a famous miscalculation against Australia in 1992, however, and it probably caused us to lose that particular Test match. And caused me considerable anguish.

In the early days I was constantly being underestimated. I would play several age-groups above my year in school matches and thus would find myself looking even smaller than normal. I guess there was something about seeing someone they considered a roly-poly kid come gambolling up to the wicket that put opposing captains and bowlers at ease. How could someone who looked and played like me be a threat? Someone that is, who took a horizontal bat to anything on a length, chipping over the infield at every opportunity. So attacking fields would greet me, as my opponents expected a short life for me at the crease. I loved to disappoint them. I think there's always been some degree of scepticism about me because of the 'unathletic' way I look. With a tendency to put on weight quicker than those who double-cross the Mafia put on concrete boots, I certainly have put on a 'few' more kilos since my youth. But, irrespective of any perceived bulk of belly and backside, my shoulders have always been broader than my trunk! And from the start I have been hitting the ball with all my weight moving solidly forward. Those cribbed strokes with an imaginary ball naturally meant that from the very beginning I was swinging through the ball, not at it. It has led to me being able to hit the ball as hard as I like, with pretty good timing. In fact I was able to hit the ball harder, with more whip and zip, when I was younger and spindlier. What has improved with age is shot selection and stroke-making, and that has come about through self-knowledge and experience.

People think I'm small, too. I'm surprised when they say it, because I have always been tall enough to do just what I want. Being a batsman of unusual height, however, bowlers initially find it hard to know what length to bowl to me. A good-length ball to a batsman of average height is a short ball to me. Rather in the way that a bowler has to adjust their line whenever both left-handed and right-handed batsmen are partners, so bowlers find that with me being five to ten inches shorter than most batsmen, they have to adjust their idea of a good length. Because of my height, my first encounters with bowlers can mean that they have their usual rhythms and patterns upset and, following an attack on them, their mental composure can be upset too. In that period I am at a distinct advantage. Certainly at junior level, where bowlers hadn't developed the experience to be able to deal with someone like me, I was really able to tailor things to my advantage. Anything short of a half-volley was pullable, and once I had learned to play the cut, I was really able to indulge myself. I didn't always succeed of course, but if I failed it was always on my terms – mistiming a drive, being caught on the boundary – always as the result of an attacking stroke. I never ever had to feel that someone had bested me.

Irrespective of all the runs I scored and all the mentions I received in newspaper dispatches of schools' cricket in Sri Lanka, and all the pats on the back I received, Mr Silva was different from everyone else who observed me because, rather than take my continuing development as a given, he would keep on telling me that only if I really perfected my technique would I really have a chance of being a top cricketer. I respected him so much because he saw through me. Mr Silva knew that all those drills and rehearsals without a ball stultified my soul. I did them because they were necessary, but I would much rather have been out in the middle stroking some real runs. And when I finally faced some real bowling I just went crazy. I delighted in hitting boundaries. That was all that batting meant to me. I didn't always come off, and I didn't always play strokes in the approved manner. I batted like a man indiscriminately quenching his thirst on juicy bowling, simply because practice had whetted my appetite for boundaries. In spite of all his lessons and my practices, I didn't always present a pretty picture, but Mr Silva saw me for what I was, and he had the good grace to let me be. Practice was the work, performance was the pleasure. When a coach holds back your natural instincts, you lose your feeling for the game. It stops being fun. But Mr Silva and Mr Perera never let me forget that, while in the world of schoolboys the talented succeed, amongst the grown-ups other qualities were needed.

CHAPTER TWO

Colombo was just starting to develop its suburbs when I was a child, and near where I lived there were vast tracts of undeveloped land which afforded plenty of scope for adventures. It was an outdoors life and my friends and I threw ourselves into physical challenges at every opportunity. We were always testing each other's daring and 'manhood': climbing trees, jumping fences, playing intensely competitive games and occasionally scrapping in fights where no one ever got punched but much was somehow decided by a few seconds of rolling around in the dirt. Going crazy was my all-purpose self-defence technique, and I was rarely troubled by the bigger boys because of my reputation for going wild when cornered. Fearlessness got me far, and as long as I had a bat in my hand I felt the equal of anybody. Everyone has a goal, an ideal picture of how they would like to see themselves. Expectation is so much the promise of achievement. All I've ever wanted to do since I was a young boy was to keep playing cricket. With me, everything was just a continuation of what had come before. I don't really know why I'm a cricketer. I just know it's the only thing that makes me happy.

As a youth I started to build a reputation for playing flamboyant shots no one else would, and for not necessarily staying too long at the crease. My aim from the first ball I faced was to assert myself, make an impression, dominate the bowling. The nearby RABS playground was where local boys would gather after school and the afternoon siesta to play softball cricket, or touch-rugby if conditions were too damp. These occasions were an opportunity to play with and against schoolboys from rival schools, to compare and contrast the relative merits of our schools when no school officials were watching. These games were really hard fought. The Royal and St Thomas boys had all the best facilities at their schools, and all the august coaching. The games of us other boys were just a little rougher around the edges. Rivalry was such that we all felt a need to prove ourselves the better of each other, especially now that we were batting for ourselves and not for our schools. We were playing specifically for each other's approval and recognition. As schoolboys our only form of individual identity was our sporting ability and our academic prowess. I had no distinguishing academic marks to speak of, so my identity was established with cricket. This need to stand out amongst the herd, this need to compete in a crowd, to battle for the edge, led me to think that the most effective strategy would be to develop the unexpected: to develop shots that were fundamentally different from the usual methods of putting the ball out of reach of the fielders. Our parents had their jobs, their positions in society, their cars, clubs and houses to distinguish them; grown-ups had cards, drink and pleasures of society for recreation. We kids had very little of our own. But there in the RABS ground we could act free of inhibitions and, by being spectacular, rise against the rules and regulations of our lives. Some bowlers had pace, others the ability to turn a ball a mile, some batsmen oozed style and could hit over the top with arrogant ease. My school's motto was 'Country Before Self', echoing Buddhist precepts of the subjugation of personal ego, but away from school, where it really was a contest between individuals, you competed very hard. Nothing beat the feeling of a triumphant walk home after a good day's play as you relived every good shot you played, every step of the way.

Anyone who thought themselves a batsman had their own way of going about things: by their strokes they were known. The shots that began as tactics for scoring soon became my calling cards, and how I came to be distinguished from my peers. Cricket at this level could be a hazardous business. These batting tracks, when we weren't using them, were used for grazing local goats and cows and for soccer and rugby. The bounce was unpredictable, and the bigger boys could sure make the ball kick viciously. The most important asset was quickness of eye and feet to cope with the unpredictability of the pitch and the delivery which suddenly reared off the ground or shot along the ground. You learnt to keep bat and pad close together for as long as possible for self-preservation's sake, but there never seemed to be much point in playing too defensively.

Back then a short innings didn't really bother me because the thrill of the shots or the applause and respect of my peers whenever I hit the winning boundaries in run-chases (everything was a run-chase in those days), did away with the need for me to examine my game too closely. I was young, dumb and full of the joys to come the next day. And if I didn't get any runs one day, I'd have a chance to get more the next. I was an adrenaline junkie living from ball to ball, innings to innings, looking for that thrill to transmit itself up my arm from bat meeting ball, the thrill that said I had made a sweet hit. On rainy days, and Sri Lanka has plenty of those, a friend and I would stay at home and, with a hard plastic ball on the cement driveway of my house, throw zingy bouncers at each other in an attempt to duplicate fast-bouncer bowling conditions. Such teenage practices have been instrumental in establishing my ease with the short-pitched ball. And just to keep busy in solitary moments I would bat a golf ball back and forth against a wall using the metal ruler from my sister's schoolbag, all the while keeping up a running commentary in the way I'd heard being done on the radio.

From the mid-1980s to the mid-1990s a whole batch of us all roughly the same age – Arjuna Ranatunga, Roshan Mahanama, Hashan Tillekeratne, Asanka Gurusinha and myself – embedded ourselves in the Sri Lanka team. We've all known each other since we were kids. We've played hundreds of games of cricket together for Sri Lanka. We've won the World Cup together. We've lived as a team, a family, and a band of brothers. The older we became the more we played for each other. The question why we made it when no one else who was being coached alongside us did is at the same time easy and difficult to answer. First, only eleven can play at any one time. All of us played up and down the batting order early in our career, wherever we could fit in. Hashan played primarily as a wicketkeeper for a time, Asanka played as an all-rounder, as did Arjuna, and I played in every position from opener to No. 8 until I finally found a home at No. 4 in the line-up. Initially we played anywhere the selectors would put us. There were only so many positions open to newcomers and the unestablished. To be selected you had to be very good and very lucky with form and fitness. Secondly, playing cricket for the national team paid hardly anything, and waiting around to be selected paid even less. You had to go out and find a job to support yourself and many talented cricketers took the career route as young men. Essentially the easiest distinction between us and the rest: we were the best young cricketers in Sri Lanka. Why we were better than the rest is difficult to answer. It wasn't talent, reflexes or innate ability that saw us all progress tenaciously through schools, colts, club and representative teams. It was desire. It was self-belief. It was hunger. It wasn't just that we didn't want anyone to be better than us, we didn't ever want to fall short of what we thought we should be. We (and our parents) made huge sacrifices in order for us to represent Sri Lanka. All of us can point to people we played with at school and in clubs who were the equal of us when it came to volume of runs scored. All of us had as many failures as successes, but we kept going where other youngsters didn't. We saw only possibility. And just as significant was competition amongst ourselves in domestic cricket. Arjuna was the greatest competitor amongst us. If Arjuna made runs while any of us were playing against him, we'd want to do the same when it came to our turn to bat. If Asanka took wickets whenever he bowled, then Arjuna would want to do so too. If Roshan made runs while I was fielding, I'd want to make at least the same number as him and vice-versa. Our definition of playing success back then was to be doing better than your best friend. We spurred each other on to compete at greater and greater heights until we became self-assured enough to stop competing against each other and instead concentrated on competing with our international opponents.

Sri Lankan youngsters when they're not playing school matches typically play on matting wickets and on dirt strips pock-marked by the various doings of livestock, mostly with a tennis ball, cricket balls being too expensive to replace and too dangerous to contend with when you haven't got the full range of protective gear. Balls trampoline steeply off taut matting; back-foot shots predominate. It doesn't take much imperfection on the 'wicket' to make any pitched ball deviate unpredictably. You learn to keep bat close to the body, play late and watch the ball ever so closely. To thrive you improvise. The kind of cricket we played day in day out as youngsters was the same as the kind of game played by Indian, Pakistani and West Indies youngsters, the kind of game they'd been displaying to the world decades before Sri Lanka's arrival on the international scene.

All batsmen are different. Very good ones are very different. Batting is very nearly unteachable but it thrives on confidence. Most highly competitive athletes give off a tangible scent of their ego and drive; it is impossible to be around them without feeling their ambition or watching them stake out their territory. When people like Arjuna and Asanka were at the crease taking guard, snuffling and rooting and displacing dirt, it was like they were tangibly staking their claim to occupy the crease. They would reach the middle after the inevitable fall of a lesser individual, look around the field, take their time to get comfortable and then fiercely look the bowlers in the eye and dare them to do their worst. It was as if they couldn't contemplate giving up their wicket until they had filled their boots, until they had shown what they could do. I have always cut a more shambolic figure, and would rely on my strokes rather than my physical presence to impress myself on the opposition. Indeed the more reckless and insane my batting appeared, the more irresistible and exhilarating I found it. This willingness to challenge opponents on our own individual terms – when you played as much cricket as we did, for so many different sides, everyone became an opponent eventually – separated those who went onto full representative honours, from the rest. We all wanted to dominate the bowling sooner or later. Of course you have to know the rules before you break them, you have to school yourself. To begin to make even a small impression you have to learn the rules, you have to know about technique, about the principles of the game, enough to know that your unorthodoxy has merit.

Since the time I was shoulder-high to a snooker table, I had been accompanying my father to the Airport Club, a men's club near our house, where my father was the club treasurer. There, as Sam de Silva's son, I was given the opportunity to indulge in a couple of soft drinks on my visits and make use of the billiards-room. The angles of snooker and billiards, the precision of stroke needed in order to maintain a break fascinated me, and I spent many hours trying to master the game. I'd make use of a certain wooden box kept behind the bar on these trips to the Airport Club so that, by standing the box next to the tables, I could raise myself to the necessary height in order to play a shot. At this point it's worth mentioning that the Airport Club was a place my mother didn't approve of. She understood the need for my father to be a social animal after working hours, but she didn't like me being in the company of men who drank, smoked and had 'loose' ways. It was certainly true that from the sanctity of the billiards-room, I could observe certain people for whom it could be said that work got in the way of their drinking and gambling. Many Sri Lankan men do lead lives as colourful as their sarongs. Ours is a hot, sticky climate and plenty of hanky-panky goes on. But my youth and innocence and the fact that my father was never too far away saved me from any indulgences myself.

Around one's early teens while other people burst into long trousers, I kind of crept up on them. But I had actually entered into the grown-ups' world much earlier than the other children. From boyhood I was used to talking with older people and accustomed to their way of thinking. It is to their credit that my father's friends, my 'uncles', never treated me as a junior and would allow me to sit with them soaking up their sportsmen's tales. I learnt a hell of a lot about the game and people in those hours. Pretty soon I was invited to play cricket with them too. Batting down the order at No. 8 or No. 9 gave me plenty of scope to observe the way grown-ups played the game and to hear detailed talk of incidents, tactics and strategy. No game was ever forgotten. Everybody had once played with somebody who had been a 'great'. I came to realise that the worst possible crime a man can commit is that of being boring. To me it seemed that these old-timers (people in their thirties and above) had a breathtaking self-confidence. And horse-sense. As one of these uncles once said about hooking, 'the risks are great but they're much greater if you think about them'. Whatever maturity I had as a youngster came from acting in the way the grown-ups did.

These old-timers had all been legends of a sort in their heyday, before the demands of making money and grown-up responsibilities had taken them off the cricket-pitches, only to return each weekend. Stout in forearm and thigh, they all had strength and power and amazing eyes, but yorkers were their weakness. For some reason, and perhaps it had something to do with the broadening of their bellies not allowing for a straight downswing, in spite of batting like titans, they would all eventually succumb to yorkers. It was only a matter of time. So they made hay while the sun shone. They didn't like to let a ball go past them unmolested. If they felt particularly conscious of their mortality to the yorker, they'd take guard outside the crease and gradually inch forward as they got their eye in. Fast bowlers' usual gauges of length could well be upset, and they'd be forced into bowling just that little bit shorter or fuller, which played into these old-timers' hands as they smote the ensuing long-hops and full-tosses to all parts. They were using their heads, getting the bowlers to give them balls they could hit. They played short balls directed at their bodies in two ways. They either stepped outside leg stump and hit them over third man for six, or stepped outside off stump and hit them over fine leg for six. These shots weren't totally controlled but they got the job done and satisfied their sense of themselves. The old-timers of the greatest age wouldn't always give a full swing of the bat. Nudgers and deflectors, they were cunning and knew what to leave alone. But give them a ball to hit and they would smack it with the flourish of a musketeer.

Watching these 'veteran' cricketers as they came to terms with their reduced responsibilities and talents, I saw that it wasn't one's reflexes that went first, nor was it one's hand-eye co-ordination, the first sign of waning ability was a loss of proper footwork. Either because they'd reached a certain age, or because they'd stopped conditioning themselves to simultaneously move feet, body, arms, hands and wrists in response to the bowlers' deliveries, you knew and they knew that they had weaknesses which would defeat them sooner or later. Their heads wouldn't consistently get over the ball, nor could they always get to the pitch. It would still need good bowling to dismiss them, but it was only a matter of time before any good bowler would find them out. Back then, these prospects were far away for me. I thought I would be young and improving forever or at least for five or ten years, which came to the same thing. Having played against men of all ages as a boy, I now realise that I have witnessed the arc of a cricketer's life in its entirety. It has been a truly invaluable experience. Nowadays, I devote the bulk of my practice time to conditioning myself physically so that I can put off for as long as possible my inevitable decline.

Schooldays would mean waking up at 5.30 in the morning in order to get to school in enough time to fit in a couple of hours of playground cricket with other fanatics before classes. My target, my daily challenge, was to score a 100 before the first bell summoned us to lessons. From the school-office end the leg-side boundary was quite short, so I would always look to score as many runs on that side as possible: mows, pulls and hooks, mows, pulls and hooks. However, a shot square of the wicket at the RABS field where I played after school wasn't really an option. That ground was long and narrow, with houses beyond the boundary square of the wicket. A hit into someone's back garden meant 'six and out'. To stay in you had to play straight. So again through circumstance, I found a way to develop a particular kind of shot. Day in day out we might have been playing on wickets of dubious quality, with school bags and bricks as wickets, with ragged balls and battered bats, barefoot or in sandals, but we learnt how to play shots and how to survive. During school holidays until the time came to gather with all the other local cricket-crazy boys, a neighbouring boy (a certain Roshan Mahanama), his brother, another local friend and I would play epic matches – 2 against 2 in a vacant plot in our street. We had elaborate rules and variations to keep the game interesting. We were incredibly competitive. I would invariably find ways of getting out but Roshan could never be shifted; he was a master of improvisation. He was also distinguished by having a particularly fine bat, heavy but with a well-balanced pick-up and a sweet middle. Whenever I had a big game to play and Roshan wasn't using it, I would nip over to his house and borrow that bat. Sometimes I even asked his permission.

As a teenager, with me devoting every possible moment out of school to cricket and my time at school being spent in playing games, my mother asked my father to stop encouraging my passion for cricket. My mother felt I just wasn't spending enough time at my studies, though she did encourage me to play tennis at every opportunity. In her opinion anybody who played tennis was a good sort, and rather chic too. But to my father cricket was my education and off the cricket field, once he had established that I could read, write and do arithmetic to a sufficient standard, he was satisfied. He knew I might never be an accountant like him but he had me do mental arithmetic all the time, on journeys in his car and even at the dinner table. It's a knack that has certainly come in useful during run-chases. And he would always have me count my blessings. Traditionally, in Sri Lanka, cricketing ability has been seen as a passport to getting a good job. And perhaps my father could rest easy regarding my future because of this. But for my mother, academic ability was the key to getting a good job. A good job meant a good income meant a good house meant a good wife meant a good life etc etc etc. Any kind of proper success had to do with education in my mother's opinion. She has the highest expectations and the highest standards of anyone I've ever met; 'a good name is worth more than diamonds or gold' she has always said. You have it drilled into your head: job, money, security. Wanting to be a cricketer as a young man doesn't chime with any of that. Fame is a vapour, popularity is an accident and money takes wings. The only thing that endures on your permanent record in society is education. In Asia, scholastic achievement has traditionally been seen as the means to a life of dignity and honour, of ease and universal respect. With my grades at school, all that didn't look too likely! Cricket and

Wisden have rescued me from a lifetime of oblivion, and for that I am deeply thankful. Now there is a permanent record to the tenor of my life. I have done hardly anything of consequence in the grand scheme of things, but I have done something from which others may derive pleasure.

My sister Araliya, five years older than me, was always under more pressure to study than I was. Her attitude to life has always been, and I quote, 'that if life is not about passionate poetic celestial incredible aching thrilling totally beautiful things, then life is not worth living'. And until her inevitable rebellion against what she thought to be the boring rules of her school, her academic brilliance certainly deflected attention away from my own fecklessness. My mother didn't want me to stop playing cricket, she just wanted me to pay some attention, any attention, to my studies. My father and his encouraging indulgence of my passion had to stop. So my mother wrote to my headmaster, Mr Alles, enlisting his help. It was a long impassioned letter, asking for him to enforce proper study hours on me, asking him to schedule fewer schools matches for me. She called on his wisdom, his compassion for her plight as a concerned mother who wants only the best for her son's future well-being, she called upon his feelings as a parent himself. By all accounts it was a masterpiece of passionate pleading. My mother then gave it to my father to deliver to Mr Alles. Naturally, my father didn't.

I am not sure whether my mother's letter would have had the effect she desired, for Mr Alles was an out-and-out cricket fan too. Headmasters are typically forbidding, distant characters; Mr Alles, however, was forgiving, patient and kind. D.S. Senanayake school had literally been raised from the ground by his fund-raising efforts and the efforts of dozens and dozens of schoolboys and their parents chipping into help with painting and decorating during the school holidays. I didn't add anything to its academic reputation of course, but I was able to contribute something to putting it on the map by my schools cricket exploits. In school I had the feeling I would have been forgiven everything except insolence and bad manners. In fact, the acts of a vandal, my wanton and wilful destruction of school property, were easily forgiven by Mr Alles. Beyond one of the boundaries on the school pitch were the newly erected offices and Mr Alles's residence with their slate–tiled roofing. And every lofted straight drive, if I caught it just right, would deposit a cricket ball on to the roof and along with the descending ball would often come a shattered slate tile or two. I just couldn't resist going for the shots. I was a punk with a cricket bat. I cost Mr Alles a tidy sum of money I'm sure, but he never complained. 'I would rather encourage his talent than stifle it,' he told my father as the cost of repairs mounted up.

In my last two years at school I was playing cricket every possible day either for my school or for Nondescripts C.C., a Colombo club team. I supported Nondescripts in all the Colombo tournaments and was very much encouraged by how they treated juniors amongst whom Ravi Ratnayeke, Rumesh Ratnayake and Ranjan Madugalle were coming to the fore. Actually I was allowed to play for Nondescripts only because Mr Ranjit Fernando promised my mother he'd look after me – in the company of sporting men, I needed the protection of a noble man. The Airport Club had been one thing, but as a fully-fledged teenager there was even more scope for me to be 'influenced' by clubhouse mores. A family friend, Mr Fernando, had been Sri Lanka's hard-hitting opening batsman/wicketkeeper during the 1970s. By the time I came under his wing he had largely retired from the game in order to concentrate on his commodities business, but from the times I saw him play I could see that his style, like that of most short strong men, though practical rather than beautiful, was essentially correct. It gave me confidence to think that people like he and Duleep Mendis had made a success of the game and had gone on to the highest honours for Sri Lanka, for they were the people whose game most resembled mine.

Ranjit Fernando has been kind enough to say that by the time I came to him I was already a 'complete cricketer' but his greatest gift to me was the gift of reassurance, at a time when, between the age of 15 and 18, I was just bedding in my unorthodox tendencies for the world to see. Bad style in those days still could be grounds to exclude a cricketer from the very highest consideration. He gave me the confidence to play my natural game. Ranjit Fernando focused on me the mental side of the game – how you build an innings, the need to maintain concentration, the need to forget about the previous ball that might have dismissed you or might have been hit for a boundary. For the first time in my life I started to attempt to systematically build an innings, instead of machine-gunning shots in all directions. I was starting to play games that didn't end at sunset, when you went home for dinner, but continued on to the next day. With refreshed bowlers.

Even though I managed to pass my O-levels to my mother's satisfaction, I didn't want any further education and the ensuing 9 to 5, Monday to Friday kind of lifestyle that would keep me away from the things I loved most – long days of fun and games and cricket whenever possible. A proper job-related life called for planning, budgeting and the taking of infinite pains. I knew I couldn't be any good at that. I thought my father had it great, in being able to work and play hard, but I sensed that I just didn't have his kind of energy. No one does. I really thought life should be about a search for daily meaning as well as daily bread, for recognition as well as money, for excitement rather than boredom; in short, for a sort of life rather than a Monday through Friday sort of living.

What did I want of life? Nothing grand. Just passionately to be a cricketer for as long as possible, to enjoy what I thought cricketers enjoyed – each other's company, big crowds, a chance to entertain, and the opportunity to bring honour to one's family and school. Nothing over the top. Just the most ordinary, the most common and the most precious things. I was trying to avoid responsibilities, eager to live a life of endless possibility; that's why I became a cricketer.

The Sri Lankan press makes schoolboy cricketers the heroes of their times with Royals and Thomians being at the top of the tree, and even though I wasn't at one of the elite schools I was coming to the notice of national youth selectors. The school games were often played before packed houses of 10,000 and more, at grounds that would just a few years later host Test matches. The fans were fanatical in their loyalty, the rivalries ancient and passionate. Tickets to the century-old Royal College vs St Thomas' were more expensive and in more demand than those for Tests for quite some time. Newspapers carry daily homilies on the Corinthian spirit of the game, on the virtues of playing correctly with proper technique and deportment for personal, team and social satisfaction. After a player's first success, which becomes national news courtesy of the sports pages, audience friendliness gradually gives way to audience challenge. Fed on a diet of dashing stroke-makers since the game came to the island, the crowds bay for bowlers' blood to be shed at every opportunity. Sometimes when batting in front of a Sri Lankan crowd I really do feel like a gladiator, with the bowler as my target. The crowds want nothing less than Sri Lankan batsmen to put bowlers to the sword and are disapproving of anyone who doesn't execute strokes with rapidity.

At this stage in my life, pre-national team, but being talked about as a potential star of the future, the most powerful factor in my pleasure in the game was my own skill. I loved to do what I did well, and having done it well, I loved to do it better. It was all self-reinforcing. Good coaching and encouragement were vital in my progress. What with all the schools games, club games and representative games, I had been dropped into a world that fitted me as water fits a fish. It was a world that demanded no real effort from me. It just asked me to do what I wanted to do. There were no responsibilities beyond enthusiasm. I needed to do nothing else than to remain as I always had been – excited, excitable, an eager pupil, a devoted practitioner. Stakes were low then in comparison to now but it was still important to win, still important to feel you'd done your best. The more prominent my performances became, the more advice I received from all kinds of quarters – other teams' coaches, former national players, just about anyone who'd ever swung a bat and wanted the best for Sri Lankan cricket. It was just the same for Roshan and Arjuna and all those who were tipped for the top as youngsters. Having seen many coaches in action over the years, I've found that the best way to offer advice to a cricketer is to exercise the mind of the player concerned and to make him go away and think about his game for himself. Constructive criticism is the only form of criticism worth paying attention to. You're never too old or too good to learn something useful. Critics who only deal in negatives: don't even bother to ignore them. I remember Ranjit Fernando telling me that, 'It's better to learn from other people's mistakes than from your own'. Mistakes at the level of club cricket were rarely of technique, but more of application. The wrong shot was played at the wrong time. Batsmen didn't always value their time at the wicket high enough. I knew this fault well. You could even say that for many years I was its major international practitioner. It took me a long time, too long, to see the error of my ways.

At that time, however, my excuse for 'irresponsibility' would have been that even though it was the highest level of domestic cricket Sri Lanka had to offer, a game for Nondescripts was only a club game, and that my performance in the midst of all the more established players didn't really matter. It's a dangerous attitude; an attitude born of arrogance, overweening self-confidence and deep-down laziness. Having worked so hard to get to the level of 'National Team Prospect', with Sri Lanka about to break through into full-Test status, I didn't see the need to make any further adjustments to my game. I've already pointed to reasons why so many of my talented peers have fallen by the wayside, but this attitude if anything explains why people don't develop beyond a certain point. Once things become tougher than expected, requiring just a little extra concentrated effort, so many of us slip into performing a little less well than expected; we do things which on the whole we would rather not have done, and then, when our careers are finished, it turns out that our lives have fallen well short of their potential. To succeed as a top cricketer, as a top sportsman, to succeed in whatever field of life you choose, you need talent. You need discipline. You need drive. But most of all you have to want it.

CHAPTER THREE

When facing fast bowlers in the West Indies they used to say that 'if you want to drive, go get a car'. Ever since I can remember I have loved the idea of driving cars. The faster the better. I love a lot of high-speed turns, turns where you have to force yourself to go fast, turns where there's something telling your foot to lift off the gas, and it's invigorating when you get that feeling and you just drive on. Danger was my turn-on. When I wasn't occupied with cricket, I was dreaming of being behind the wheel of a fast car. Going through gaps, overtaking other cars, going wheel to wheel on a racetrack, taking long curves in the road at top-speed . . . speed was the thrill. The thing about racing drivers, I realised, was that more than reflexes, you need courage. If you're scared, you're not going to drive fast. If you're scared, you're not going to take the chequered flag. I'm passionately in love with motor-racing and watch races and television broadcasts and racing movies whenever I can. All those reading this book will have seen me bat and know the outward manifestations of my strokeplay, but if you want to know what goes through my head the very second I'm hitting the ball it would be something like what goes through Tom Cruise's character's head in the racing film *Days of Thunder* when he has to blindly drive at top speed through a cloud of smoke in order to squeeze through the narrowest gap available between the concrete walls of the oval racetrack and the burning car in front of him. Take the safe option, slow down and steer left, and he doesn't win. Only if he is positive and trusts his ability completely can he get ahead. So he drives flat out through the smoke and comes through victorious to the other side. My batting is like that; out in the middle I never think of the things that could go wrong, only what I should do to make things go right. (If you have a lot of cameras on you, you may as well play like a movie star). Of course sometimes you consciously take risks you don't really want to and many attacking strokes are actually calculated gambles. For sure, you may not always succeed, but the trick is to get the odds on your side stacked as high as possible.

I would love to have started on the long and winding road to driving in Grand Prix, but my father wouldn't let me leave home at 16 and enrol in the European driving schools. However, he did let me have a motorbike while I was still at school and life became a great deal more fun for me. And noisy for the neighbours. I chose my motorbike with three criteria in mind: it had to have monster tyres, the most awesome acceleration and yet still be of a size to be straddled. It was one of the few times in my life I've wished I was taller; I got a Honda 250. Well after I was playing for Sri Lanka I kept that bike and would travel to games with bat and pads strapped together on my back, kit bag strapped to the pillion. I would break in new pairs of batting gloves by using them while riding, getting the leather and grip soft and supple to the curve of my hands. Any rumours that I would do wheelies down the seven miles of the Galle Road, challenging myself each time to go on a little further without having to put the front wheel down, are only partially true.

I played quite a bit of tennis in my teens but, notwithstanding my ambitions to be a racing driver, cricket dominated my life. I'd get up early and sleep late, in between it was just bat and ball the live-long day. Some enterprising wags procured home-recorded videotapes from Australia of World Series Cricket highlights when Australia played a triangular series of SuperTests and one-dayers against the West Indies and the Rest of the World. Roshan and I and other friends would watch together, awestruck by the brilliance of the talents on display. Viv Richards, Barry Richards, the Chappell brothers, Clive Lloyd, Andy Roberts, Imran Khan, Dennis Lillee, Jeff Thomson – the fastest bowlers, the best batsmen. The very best possible cricket action at the very highest level to which to aspire. I soaked it all up, absorbing whatever I could. I started collecting data.

Sri Lankan cricket wasn't yet in the world's consciousness but the world's best cricketers were household names in Sri Lanka. All those of us who saw these superstars in action on television would ask each other how they had got to be the way they were and played the way they did. We were always eager to discover new facts about them, about their legendary exploits in the past. From whatever issues of England's *The Cricketer* magazine we could find, we learned what our heroes had been up to at various stages in their career. I remember seeing a close-up picture of the bat Viv Richards had used throughout his 1976 Tests when against Australia first and then England, he blasted something like 1,000 runs. The bat was riddled with small cracks and had splinters coming out of it, its surface was golden brown as if it had been soaked in honey, and just where the bat's 'middle' would have been was a depression the size of the Bay of Bengal. The meat of the bat had literally been battered back into itself. He must have used the bat like a weapon against the very best the world could throw at him. When it came to Viv, the whole world kept being reminded what greatness really is. He became my hero. As a youngster, I couldn't imagine ever playing against Viv Richards, but I did want to be something like him. That our careers did actually overlap to the point when we did play against each other several times proved to be a mixed blessing. Viv once destroyed Sri Lanka in a 1987 World Cup match when he made the then World Cup record one-day score, 181. Off only 125 deliveries. I was fielding at deep mid-wicket and would watch in regret, awe and sheer delight, as the ball kept flying over my head. No matter where we bowled at him he had a stroke for it. One stroke in particular stands out in the memory: coming down the wicket to Ravi Ratneyeke, Viv found himself a little short of the ideal driving position so, checking himself in mid-stride and using only his wrists and a swivel of hip and shoulder, he flicked a ball that was half a yard outside off-stump so that it ended up carrying sixty yards over on the leg-side!

As a teenager I might watch Viv Richards on television one night and then next day attempt to play some shots like him, stepping away to leg to hit through off when faced with a packed leg-side field, for example. Other days I would try to play like Sunil Gavaskar with his balance and poise and economy of effort. Initially of course, my on-driving didn't compare with Sunil's. I'd aim towards mid-on and find the ball going through square-leg. I was trying to hit the ball too hard without quite the proper footwork. It really took a long-time to get it right. I was experimenting all the time, attempting to find out for myself what it felt like to play in the particular style of a top batsman. In all these top players from all around the world, for all their differences, I could recognise one thing which united them: their pride in their performance. The same names would feature prominently in the press time and time again. I saw how small the world of cricket really was – only a hundred or so people in the whole world played Test cricket at any one time. To be one of them must be something really special.

If by the time I started playing international cricket, I had all the strokes (including the forward defensive), and was technically sound, what I didn't have was any mental depth. It took me another ten years or so to be fundamentally sound in the mental aspects of the game purely because I had to start from scratch. Just like every other Sri Lankan. Sri Lanka as ICC champions had played with some pluck in the 1975 World Cup. Ranjit Fernando, with the classy left-hander David Heyn and the elegant Anura Tennekoon, had played against Clive Lloyd's visiting World Cup champions in late 1975 (the Windies were bowled out for 119), and had been in the side that had done well against Tony Greig's visiting England in 1977. A strong Pakistan team that boasted all of its mid-1970s stars had also been beaten in Sri Lanka, as had the West Indies in 1979. These various memorable performances against touring sides were all fuel for 'stories around the campfire', and until we became a proper Test nation these games were accorded a grand status in our cricketing annals. These had all been games in which participants had fought tooth and nail, eager to show Sri Lankan capabilities. Back then, when foreign teams seemed so elite and glamorous, every good performance in these 'mini-Tests' and one-dayers was seen as bringing Sri Lanka closer to Test status. Today, it would be like Kenya or Bangladesh taking on and beating a top Test nation.

But try as he might, Ranjit Fernando couldn't have prepared me for the demands posed by eleven combative opponents in a Test match when people are playing for so much more than a love of the game and/or oneself. No one could have. For the simple reason that no one in Sri Lanka had ever played Test cricket before 1982. The whole structure of Sri Lankan domestic cricket with its amateur two/three/four-day games went against building up the levels of concentration and application necessary to play the five-day game. Winning and losing meant very little when easy wins were always just around the corner. It was impossible to develop mental muscles. Games were invariably decided by individual performances, not sustained, opposition-denying team effort. Anyone who played cricket in Sri Lanka could become a star at some point or another for at least 15 minutes, but never over 15 sessions.

By the time I came into the national side in 1984, I had the advantage of perceptive people like Sidath Wettimuny, Duleep Mendis and Roy Dias to help me and all the other juniors understand just how important it was to play well for hours and hours on end, and not think that one session's good work would be enough to decide the outcome of a cricket match. Maybe we were the equal of some of the other Test-playing nations when it came to talent, we were certainly way behind them when it came to understanding what five-day cricket meant. Our inaugural Test Match against England in March 1982 was the perfect example of this. A few days before the Test, Sri Lanka had won and lost one each of two very closely contested one-dayers against England, and the momentum of playing in front of passionate home crowds for the first time in a Test Match gave Sri Lanka the measure of England for three-and-a-half days. But then, against the nagging, probing bowling of Underwood and Emburey we took our foot off the gas, and from a position of 167 for 3, lost our last 7 wickets for just eight runs. As a 16-year-old it was the biggest loss I had yet experienced, and I hadn't even been playing. But I was a fan, my heroes had been out there on the field, and my near contemporary Arjuna Ranatunga (still a schoolboy at Ananda College), had scored a splendid half-century in the first innings. If we had been able to set a target of only a hundred runs more we could have in all likelihood forced the victory. Against mighty England, founders of the game. In our first ever Test.

It must have been hard for all those who learnt their cricket in the non-first-class era to adjust to the demands of high-stakes first-class international cricket. I for one, have had to reinvent my game and my attitude to batting. I play fewer shots nowadays, but I score more runs. It was good that my childhood cavaliering didn't result in any substantial innings – if they had, I fear I would never have amounted to much. By failing so often I learnt that I needed to improve and made adjustments every time. If I had been successful then, I wouldn't have bothered to tighten up my defence or broaden my range of strokes. Nor would I have learned to use my head. Short-term success would have meant long-term failure. I wouldn't be playing for Sri Lanka today and would now probably be an import-export trader of some kind. Happy, but not fulfilled.

Even if I had never made it to the top, representing Sri Lanka abroad at junior level was a terrific thrill. In those days everything was an adventure: the flying, the hotels (even if there were seven of us to a room), the chance to fill your blank passport with some visa stamps, the chance to show people you didn't know that you were just as good as them, the chance to try out new flavours of ice-cream. I really cherish the experience when I was 15 of going on an U-19 tour of England in 1981. It was a glorious English summer, it was the summer of Botham's Ashes. Whenever we could we would watch the cricket on television and the things that Botham and England did were simply amazing. When we played, all the English would be talking about the Test Matches. I've been to England several times now, and in the people at the cricket grounds, I can see the differences in their attitude when the England cricket team are doing well compared to when they are doing badly. Ian Botham must have inspired a huge batch of youngsters to take up cricket that year. It is the same in Sri Lanka, only more so. We have less options for entertainment than countries like England or Australia, song and dance and weddings and social entertaining notwithstanding, and thus cricket, the national game, takes up a bigger part of people's lives. The Sri Lankan team doing well is a big boost to the national psyche. And with the deep interest comes deep scrutiny.

I scored the first 100 of that tour of England against a Royal Navy XI. Arjuna was on that tour, Rumesh Ratnayake and Graeme Labrooy too, along with Ashley de Silva who got credited with my hundred by the papers back home as he was the more established 'A. de Silva' in the team and thus more likely to have scored a ton. Even my father believed it to be Ashley's hundred. From that time on, I've become known to scorers as P.A. de Silva – Pinadduwage Aravinda. As with the Khans of Pakistan, no Sri Lankan representative team has ever been short of a 'de Silva' or two. Irrespective of the cricket we watched and played however, for all of us the highlight of the trip was our pilgrimage to Lillywhites sporting goods store to buy some cricket gear. The whole squad, 21 of us, were dying to go, and if we'd had anything more than pocket-money we'd have denuded Lillywhites of every cricket item in our size. We gasped in amazement at the sight of not just a range of bats by one manufacturer, but a range of manufacturers. Each bat promised untold pleasures, each bat stood there on the shelves pregnant with the runs that it would release in the right hands. The tour manager bought one bat with the money made available by the Schools Cricket Association. It was a special bat, symbolic of our trip to England. Just picking it up was a thrill.

It had been useful certainly to play in England and find conditions we weren't used to like velvet outfields, smooth and plush like a snooker cushion. And these were schools grounds mostly! The pitches were usefully slower than we were used to back home too. We already knew that Sri Lanka would be playing a Test in England in 1984 and would be sending a team to the 1983 World Cup in England. I had no real ambitions to be part of those sides, I just thought that if I kept on playing well, then maybe I'd be in with a chance some time in the not too distant future. It was Arjuna who rose head and shoulders above all of us and six months later became a Test cricketer at 18, in our inaugural Test. There was a fire in Arjuna, an almost grim determination, as though every practice session, every shot, catch and delivery was a tiny step towards his goal of getting into the national team. He was a leader amongst us because he knew better than any of us how to manage his talent. He was always thinking ahead. Once he turned his cricket brain on, he left it on all the time. He wasn't the very best bowler we had nor even the very best batsman, but he was the best thinker we had, the one who kept telling himself he was worthy to play for Sri Lanka in Tests not perhaps sometime in the future, but soon, very soon. He saw everything in front of him, and nothing behind, his eyes firmly fixed on a future he already seemed to be hurtling toward at maximum speed. The minute I heard that Arjuna had been picked for Sri Lanka, I realised just how much better I yet needed to be. It was a wake-up call I needed to hear.

I was so close to and yet so far from the national team. All I wanted to do now was play for Sri Lanka and once I got into the side, my aim was to be the best I could be in every possible game. I was in that unpredictable category 'promising'. There were some very talented young cricketers around that was for sure: Ranjan Madugalle, Anura Ranasinghe and Arjuna were impressing greatly. Personally, at seventeen I was beginning to realise that batting wasn't just a case of dismissing well-pitched-up balls for four. Within my own school, I would look in awe at such players as my last first XI captain Channa Wijemanne and the supremely talented K. Siriparam. Had Channa and Siriparam waited or been able to wait just that little bit longer, they would have definitely graced the international scene. But with there being very little money in the game, many young men on the fringes of the national team just couldn't sit and hope to be selected and sacrifice an opportunity for a job and career in civilian life. Well into our entry into the Test arena, cricket was still run on largely amateur lines and was seen as an adjunct to one's occupation, not as an alternative. I had no real thoughts of a career but I didn't ever want to reach a certain point and then find I could go no further. If I didn't make it, I really didn't know what I would do with my life. In conversations with the English schoolboys and collegians, and the young RAF and Army cricketers we had played against on our 1981 U-19 tour of England, we knew that if they never made it as first-class cricketers in England they would have a wide variety of interesting jobs to apply for. I and my team-mates had very little in comparison. In Sri Lanka you either go into the family business if there is one, or you get a respectable job, or you start a business of your own, or you go abroad. My father was a salaried professional, I didn't think I was cut out for vocational further education, I had no capital with which to start a business about which I had no idea, and I loved Sri Lanka too much to ever think of leaving to study or work abroad. I had to be a cricketer, and see how far I could go on my adventure. I kept remembering what one of my uncles at the Airport Club once said, 'your worst day on the field is better than your best day at work'.

Two words why Arjuna got the nod for the Inaugural Test when any one of a half-dozen others didn't – mental toughness. He played like a veteran when he was 18 while the rest of his age-group played like Vietnam veterans. Even when I myself graduated to full representative honours, I was for many, many years the 'baby' of the side. Not much was expected of me, except to keep on playing like the assumed talented prodigy I was. I had ways of scoring that I'm glad to say that no one else in the team had. I also had ways of getting out that no one else had. My failures and successes were all held in the same regard as if I were a coltish racehorse. If I came off, well to the good. If I didn't, well that was in the nature of the beast. I had always been the 'baby' of just about every side I had played for, and I revelled in the attention it had brought me and the freedom it gave me to play in the way that was most comfortable i.e. self-indulgent. Perceived as a youngster and thus constantly in a state of development, I could blithely side-step the dreadful question that instantly hangs over everyone once they become adults: 'Is that all there is?' While I was the equal of almost all the adults I had met when it came to exercising my skill, I was still someone who lived and thought as a child, and had the emotional maturity of my calendar years. I was distinguished by my daring and sometimes injudicious strokeplay, by my sparkling attacks; Arjuna had gained a reputation for his staunch defence and opportune counter-attacks. His temperament was often compared to that of a mature batsman. He became the role-model for many an aspirant Sri Lankan cricketer.

A sensibly scheduled series of U–19, and U–21, U–23 or even A–Team level international exposure does wonders in developing prospective players for the highest honours. Playing cricket abroad for any length of time in the formative years, you can come back as a different person altogether. It can make you or break you. This kind of exposure shows players and selectors whether individuals have the necessary fighting qualities at international level and are up to the demands of giving their all day in day out. Doing well here definitely translates into the national side, and it has been the Sri Lankan Board's virtue that it has always seen fit to schedule matches and tours for all those with a chance of making it to the very top. Some youngsters make exciting debuts, but only time evaluates a career. I know that on the subcontinent the thinking goes that 'if they're good enough, they're old enough', but I am convinced that time is never wasted on a journey well travelled. Character outshines talent. Only the finished article, one without any technical or temperamental flaws, should be elevated to top honours. To do anything else can destroy the player and devalue the opportunity. It is far better to bring 'promising' talents into the fold, invite them to participate in national team practices and observe them as much as possible under hothouse conditions. A player can really benefit from this kind of long-term grooming in the levels just below Test cricket. This has been the Sri Lankan way since the start of our international contests, and it is a process that has really helped us to achieve our present success.

Without a doubt, one of the most promising young batsman in Sri Lanka in the early 1980s was Marlon Vonhagt. Whatever capabilities I had he could match, and better. And it was he who got into a representative side against the touring Zimbabweans (still not full ICC members in those days) in December 1983, ahead of me. Apparently he was next in line for full national service. We youngsters faced our toughest examination early in 1984 when an U–19 side went on a tour of Australia for three 'Youth Tests' and three one-dayers. It was a pretty tough test of our abilities because having been brought up on pitches of some docility against bowlers of relative tameness, we knew that we'd have to be at our very best in order to succeed. It was a tour that was going to separate the men from the boys. The Australian U–19 line-up included the Waugh brothers, Craig McDermott and Mark Taylor, all of whom were to feature prominently in the series.

I captained and had a good team; I knew who was good simply by having played with and against those in my age-group for so many years in domestic competition. Roshan Mahanama and Asanka Gurusinha practically picked themselves such was their talent, but Marlon Vonhagt's name was the first on the list. Sri Lanka were going to be playing in the World Series Cricket triangular in Australia the following year, and this was Marlon's opportunity to get some useful experience of the conditions. He had the strokes, the 'eye' and the reflexes, and he was not without guts. What Marlon lacked, however, was what is vitally needed to succeed, and what ultimately separates the men from the boys – the ability to play fast bowling. The Aussies had heard he was our top player and thus targeted him with plenty of short-pitched deliveries. As good a player as he was, he couldn't cope with failure, or things going against him. For the first time in his life he'd discovered he was fallible. Marlon lacked the mental toughness needed to survive as an opening batsman, and couldn't understand quickly enough that against good hostile fast-bowling he couldn't be expected to dominate proceedings and would thus have to redevelop his game and attitude. He put together some good scores towards the end of the tour, including a century on the last day of our Test at Melbourne, but years of having it easy had irreparably dulled his appetite for ruthless self-examination. The ability to face up to certain painful truths is just as significant as facing up to top-class fast bowling in determining the arc of a batsman's career. If you don't know your faults you can't improve them. In our work there is a lot of failure. You have to be a strong person mentally to keep working hard and to continue getting better.

It was a good effort by us to come back after a pretty comprehensive defeat in the first Youth Test at the Gabba where Craig McDermott had run through us. I was out to him twice, caught in the gully on both occasions. We drew the next two Tests and the tour ended on a high note with us winning the last of the three one-dayers in the last over with one wicket to spare. The lesson of this tour was that Australia had the bowling and we didn't. We only had a couple of spinners with any pretensions to trouble the batsmen. Priyalal Rodrigo showed himself to be a good all-rounder, but none of the bowlers ever made it into the national side in the years to come. We used to bowl defensively because that was the only way we could get the Australians out. As soon as new batsmen came to the crease, we would attack, but invariably the batsmen settled down and played themselves in before starting to milk the bowling. It became a matter of us chasing big scores all the time. But after the first Test we adapted quite well to the circumstances, putting in a lot of hard work, and the results showed.

It was a thrill for all of us, Australian and Lankan alike, to play in the legendary Test grounds of Brisbane, Adelaide and Melbourne. The crowds were very small but one person did come to see us at Adelaide: Sir Donald Bradman. Introduced to this seventy-five year old man with the gimlet eyes and firmest of handshakes, few of us teenagers could imagine ever scoring a hundred 100s or averaging 99.94 in Tests. But I'm sure that many resolved to see how far they could go down that road. As Roshan in his wisdom put it, 'to average 100 you only have to score 200 whenever you make a 0'. I haven't made too many 200s. But the most amazing thing I learned about Sir Donald was that he hit only 45 sixes in the whole of his career: 41 of them after passing 100, only four before reaching three figures. The differences between us!

Some say that cricket at the highest level is all about probing weaknesses. In that case, I've never wanted anyone to feel I have a weakness, hence for a long time I adopted the guise of attacking bluster, putting the onus on the bowler to discover his own weaknesses. The stakes are very high in cricket. Sometimes when you beat your opponent, you destroy his ego for a while at least; for a time you make him lose confidence in himself as a person. My policy of attack had my opponents on the back foot and won me many victories. I thought I was smart but ultimately I wasn't smart enough, like the master-criminals who get caught right at the end of the Bond movies. There have probably been many batsmen over the years who hit better than Bradman, but he thought hitting better than any of them.

Ranjit Fernando was the assistant manager on this tour and he was very supportive. He knew just what little things in practice would magnify into big things in performance, and he really helped us improve our games. He was also a very strict disciplinarian. He would always emphasise the fact that we were ambassadors for the Sri Lankan game and that our conduct would reflect on our schools, our families and our cricketing culture. We had standards to uphold. Doing the best for ourselves meant doing the best for Sri Lanka. As captain I had to set a particularly good example. Which was like asking a dyslexic to mind his p's and q's. While a few of us had already been on trips to England and India, Australia was the furthest away from home, figuratively, culturally and spiritually that any of us had ever been. As U-19 cricketers we felt we were ready to experience anything this free-wheeling country had to offer. There was a joyful carelessness about us that tour, an intimate, comforting, insular world created by a clan of young bucks. Plenty of male bonding goes on during a long tour; and while it's always true that a winning tour is a happy tour, sometimes being in a team that's having to fight hard to be competitive can do wonders for team spirit. We all pulled together on that tour, and it remains one of my happiest touring experiences.

Early on in our trip, pulling up at a suburban hotel in Adelaide one evening, we got off our coach to find a party in full swing in our hotel's lobby. Very attractive ladies including the first blondes and redheads that many of us had ever seen close-up were in prominent view. And there was music and dancing. And there was beer on tap. And there we were, young buck cricketers in our dashing tour blazers and incredibly well-tended hairstyles, looking to taste something of Australia's delights. And with the hospitality that is so typical of Australians we were all invited to come and join the fun after we'd checked in. To this day, I will deny being the ring-leader, but I must admit to conspicuously drawing Mr Fernando's attention to the fact that after our long bus-ride we would all be in bed well before the 9 p.m. curfew. Just after we'd gone out for a little stroll to stretch our legs of course. And so it was, after showers/hair combing/after-shave dousing, everyone gathered in my room to formulate a plan of action for the evening. Should we all go down to the party together? Or should we slip out one by one in order not to attract attention? We decided on the former (Country Before Self), thinking there'd be safety in numbers. Who knew what would happen once we'd started flirting with these Australian ladies? We might have gotten hideously drunk and woken up the next morning somewhere in the middle of the outback to find ourselves married to someone we didn't know, who had three children from a former marriage and wasn't anything like as pretty in real life as she was in the red-light of a hotel bar. Or so Asanka reckoned.

However, before we went downstairs we decided to watch the last-innings of an Australia vs West-Indies day-night World Series match on television. Even with the exciting cricket broadcast, our sleepiness after a long journey won over us and we gradually nodded off one by one in front of the television. Meanwhile Mr Fernando, somehow having got wind of our plan to connube with the wedding party, was waiting for us down in the hotel lobby from well before 9 o'clock. Come 9 p.m. and with us not showing up either through the front doors of the hotel, or amongst the wedding-guests, he became very concerned. Angry too. At 9.30 he started looking for us in our rooms. Which were empty. Except for mine. Where he found, with beds, pillows, blankets and towels all in disarray, his team all crammed together shoulder to shoulder, dozing in front of the television. All dressed up and having gone nowhere. I would have gone to the party but Roshan had his head in my lap and I didn't want to wake him. We were U-19 cricketers, young men but children still. Only a few of us had ever been ten miles outside Colombo let alone ten thousand miles outside Sri Lanka. The roof over our heads when we fell asleep had always been that of our parents. None of us really had a clue what to do socially with real-life grown up women-in-the-flesh and given the choice between going to a party and doing anything cricket related, in spite of all our yearning for the wild life, we'd choose cricket every time. Few of us were sure of our places in the team let alone in society.

CHAPTER FOUR

While the U-19 team had been away in Australia, places had opened up in the national side. From thinking I was a season or two away from national team selection, following the conclusion of a home Test series against New Zealand in March 1984, I was selected for the one-days against them.

At this stage, after the Tests against England, Australia and New Zealand at home, and following tours of Pakistan and India, Sri Lanka were known for their dashing batsmen, big-hearted bowlers and suicidal run-out tendencies. Roy Dias and Duleep Mendis stood out from the pack for their big shots, bold batting and regular heavy scoring. Individually talented all the team were, they just lacked exposure to the most testing of standards and an appreciation of just what international cricket meant. The learning curve really was pretty steep, as I discovered when I came into the team. Roy, Duleep and Sidath Wettimuny were already at the top of the slope, others such as Ranjan Madugalle, Asantha de Mel, Rumesh Ratnayake, Ravi Ratneyeke and Arjuna Ranatunga were climbing it quicker than others. Their pride and desire to succeed and their need to prove that Sri Lankans were worthy of a place at the international table shone through in their performances.

What made New Zealand match-winners in those days was Richard Hadlee. In the three-Test series in Sri Lanka, he took 23 wickets at an average of 10 runs each. He had destroyed Sri Lanka in the first and third Tests. Sri Lanka would however, in all probability, have won the second Test had it not been for Martin Crowe's and John Wright's great stonewalling efforts on the last day. Crowe's and Wright's rearguard action was a terrific eye-opener to us as a Test-playing nation – apparently, coming from behind and grinding-out draws could be just as satisfying as a victory. Those days going into Test matches we'd hope for victory but would end up losing just about every one of them. After eight Tests and a dozen or so one-days in two and a bit years we had become familiar with two kinds of results: losses for ourselves and wins for our opponents. We just let things happen to us instead of making things happen. Against New Zealand, it became apparent that when it came to keeping out a bowler of Hadlee's class when conditions were in his favour, for anything more than a few overs at a time, was a task beyond Sri Lankan batsmen. Sidath Wettimuny did it best of all though, having once carried his bat in a Test at Christchurch. He alone in Sri Lanka knew that an opening batsman's responsibilities are measured in hours and not just in mere runs. As an opener, Sidath's natural tendency wasn't to play with the freedom that batsmen down the order allowed themselves, and his judgement against the moving ball was pretty sound.

I made my international debut in the second limited-overs game at Moratuwa. Prior to my baptism of fire against Hadlee, Sidath had a few words of advice: 'that ball outside off-stump and moving away: leave it alone'. I wouldn't say I was cocky, but on the back of some good scores in the domestic club games, I felt confident in myself and my game. Most importantly, I didn't feel traumatised by Hadlee because I hadn't yet faced him and I had yet to meet the bowler who could beat me for pace, bounce and movement.

But deep down I had a fear of failing, of finding out that my upwardly mobile adventure as a cricketer was going to come to an end. I had never set myself goals in my life, first because I always felt I was progressing in my cricket and manhood, and secondly because I didn't ever want to set myself a marker by which to be judged. It was all internal for me. I never wrote anything down, never said anything out loud. I just concentrated on the next step. If you don't set yourself goals, you certainly reduce your chances of advancement, but you also don't ever risk failure because a particular standard hasn't been reached. I knew that my debut would either prove to myself that I really was the good cricketer that I thought I was, or it would reveal that there was nothing more to my game than an ability to hit teenagers, amateurs and local bowlers around the park. Against the New Zealanders I was going to play top-class adult bowling for the first time in my life and find out whether in the company of men I played like the eighteen-year old I was, or the man I wanted to be.

In Moratuwa, batting at No. 6, I joined Arjuna at the crease. He had been in for some time and was playing pretty well. Hadlee came back on. The first couple of balls from him were regulation leg-cutters pitching on a length outside off-stump, which I saw pretty early and left well alone. The next was pitched just a little further up and I was on top of it, hitting it away for 4. Mr W.A.N. Silva would have been proud of that one. Hadlee wasn't invincible after all. The next ball had me swishing Moratuwa's humid air looking for the scarlet pimpernel that was Hadlee's leg-cutter. The ball pitched on a length on leg-stump, I opened up my stance slightly to push the ball through the on-side, and then it just disappeared on me. Next time I saw it, the ball was in the keeper's gloves in front of first slip. From beneath his moustache, and over his huge boots, came Hadlee's comment, 'Is it easy now ?' It sure wasn't. Following some more runs the next over, I was facing Hadlee again. Expecting more of the ones that moved away, I got one that cut back in and was comprehensively bowled. Arjuna played a gutsy knock; having been hit on the mouth early in his innings he had retired hurt, took some stitches in the lip, and then came back to make an unbeaten 50. Defending 157 off 40 overs wasn't going to be easy, but everyone bowled really well, and particularly good bowling by fellow débutant (and Lankan hockey international), all-rounder Uvais Karnain took us to victory by 41 runs. It felt good to have made a contribution by catching the dangerous Hadlee and Ian Smith off Arjuna and Somachandra de Silva respectively. It was the first international match Sri Lanka had won in nine months.

The very next day we played another one-day international against New Zealand. Chasing 201, we were all out for a pathetic score. I didn't help the cause by running myself out early on in a mix-up with Sidath. I recognised that this was a game we lost purely because we played badly not because the other team had overwhelmed us with their talent. It was a pattern we would repeat many times in the years to come. We were such a mixture of flourishing fulfilment and hapless mediocrity. It seemed there was no middle way for us. Our collective form was as temperamental as a monsoon wind and none of us had the application needed to weather storms. The last match against New Zealand completed, we flew off to Sharjah for the first ever Asia Cup, opening with a match against Pakistan.

Sharjah was initially developed as a cricket venue for the sole purpose of staging as many one-day matches as possible between India and Pakistan, Sharjah being practically a mutual second home site for them. Anybody else, especially in the first years tended to be invited just to make up the numbers. Obviously, the first ever Asia Cup tournament was supposed to be a showdown between India and Pakistan. So our game against Pakistan went some way in upsetting the perceived order of things. Winning the toss and putting Pakistan in, we held them to a total of 187 in spite of all their batting superstars. I went in to bat in the middle of an Abdul Qadir spell when, after a good start by us, he was just starting to turn the game back Pakistan's way. I had always considered Duleep Mendis as a master of spin-bowling, and was looking forward to watching his battle with Qadir, then the world's best leg-spin bowler. So it was with some astonishment that I came in to bat at the fall of Duleep Mendis' wicket, Qadir having bowled Duleep with a googly (one of the three varieties allegedly at his disposal!). Duleep had come down the wicket, looking to hit with the anticipated spin of the leg-break through the covers, and was simply beaten all ends up by the one that turned the other the other way. Bowled middle-stump. If it was any consolation to Duleep, the wicket-keeper had also moved to the offside thinking that

Qadir was bowling a leggie. Pakistan were right back in the game. But at the other end, Roy Dias continued to play brilliantly, and I managed to stick with him to the end. We won by five wickets, and had beaten the mighty Pakistan in their own backyard. Three one-day internationals in two different countries within a week, with two victories. I'd faced up to the world's best seam-bowler, Hadlee, and the world's best spin-bowler, Abdul Qadir, and not done too badly. The new boy is never expected to be a match-winner, so whatever he achieves is a bonus. I felt I'd contributed just enough to worthily join in the celebrations. And I had found out that I was just about able to play it. Life as an international cricketer felt great.

Hadlee and Qadir weren't as overtly fearsome as the West Indies pacemen of that time, but in their own way they were just as hostile. Qadir was a spinner with a fast bowler's temperament, always looking for the ball that sliced the batsman in half. Hadlee was always at you and never, and I mean never, bowled a loose ball and always seemed to have a plan of attack. A series of off-cutters could be followed by one that held its own or moved away, doing just enough to get the edge. Such was Hadlee's control of length, he had your front-foot on a string. He would draw you forward, little by little, lulling you into thinking you had the measure of him before forcing you back, off-balance, with one that jagged in from short of a length. If ever you thought you had the measure of his fast-medium pace, he'd remind you of what he held in reserve by letting go of a fast one. Batsmen could go out to face him with all their faculties raised to the highest possible level, confident that their reflexes, footwork and experience should be able to overcome any moving ball, and simply find that against Hadlee, their defences were made of wet cardboard. Hadlee's bowling at its best, was head and shoulders above anyone else's. There was a logic and plan to every ball that he bowled. The ball pitching on the stumps and moving both ways will unsettle any batsman and Hadlee bowled more of those balls than anyone else in the 1980s. He was the best seam-bowler in the world for a very long time.

Abdul Qadir was a magician. He had a magician's goatee beard, incredible powers of deception and a great sense of showmanship. He could cast his spell and be simply irresistible. Playing leg-spin isn't difficult. If you concentrate totally and look closely at which way the seam is rotating in flight, if you get to the pitch of every delivery keeping your weight balanced and your head over the ball and if you play as late and as safely as possible, then not even the very best spin–bowling can cause too much problems. If . . . At that time, rumour on the circuit had it that amidst his leg-breaks of varying magnitude, Qadir had three kinds of googly, and a couple of top-spinners. There are always signs which reveal the variation coming towards you, before your eyes have picked up the spin of the ball in flight. You could for example, pick Abdul's googly by seeing the 'double-waggleflip' of his wrist just after he released the ball, showing that it wasn't the standard leg-break. But even if you pick the variation, you have to play it. And picking Qadir was no guarantee of success. Committing yourself to a stroke against him even a moment too soon was laced with danger. Along with spin and bounce, he had flight and dip. The only way to play him was to play him off the pitch. Paddle him, pull him, cut him at every opportunity, play him as late as possible; get over the top of every drive and forward stroke. When conditions were to his liking and he had that extra bounce in his step, he really made life very difficult for batsmen. Being a left-hander against him, however, was a definite advantage. For some reason he would prefer going round the wicket to them, and was thus always more easily swept and paddled for runs. Little things made him happy, little things also upset him. Anytime his rhythm and peace of mind were upset, he was half the bowler. When he felt in the groove, he could be diabolically difficult to play against. Abdul Qadir apparently had eight different kinds of delivery, all of which he might try to bowl during a six-ball over. Sometimes I think he even bamboozled himself with his variations, but he was always a danger.

We didn't win that first Asia Cup, losing to India by a big margin, but we came home feeling reasonably satisfied with ourselves. We had definitely improved over the past two years. Obviously we lacked out-and-out match-winning bowlers and our fielding really let us down on a number of occasions, but we were a dangerous batting-side particularly when chasing in a limited-overs match. And we had shown that we were capable of winning under pressure. Our batting rested on the shoulders of Sidath Wettimuny, Roy Dias, Duleep Mendis and Arjuna Ranatunga and we had a pretty competent attack of seam-bowlers Asantha de Mel, Ravi Ratneyeke and Rumesh Ratnayake and a wily leg-spinner D.S. (Somachandra) de Silva. Stalwarts of the side, and losing many more matches than they won, they had yet built up a confidence in their abilities that depended not so much on an inflated sense of their worth rather than on the knowledge that the mighty Test cricketers of the rest of the world weren't totally invincible. What we did not do then, and it took several more years for us to do, was get the job done when we weren't really playing our best: grinding out runs, plugging away at batsmen, keeping things tight in the field. What every professional cricketer learns to do in order to get by.

We thought we had to be at our best all the time when we played internationals, because we assumed all the other teams would be excellent, these teams peopled with living legends of the game. But that wasn't true. Teams that we had the beating of, would beat us half the time purely because they knew how to punish our mistakes. They held their catches. We didn't. They swooped on every run-out chance. We didn't. They would wait for the loose ball, confident in the knowledge that it would arrive. We wouldn't. They had developed techniques to counter the moving ball on seaming wickets. We hadn't. They paid the proper kind of attention to physical fitness. We didn't. Our opponents had squad-depth, street-smarts, and an overwhelming belief in their right to beat Sri Lanka. We were just happy not to get unnecessarily humiliated. What we did have was pride. Pride and a sense that we were Sri Lanka's first representatives in international cricket and that our performance really mattered to our countrymen. After years of reading about other countries' Test matches, Sri Lankans were starting to read about their own cricketers on the international stage and were really investing themselves in the performances of the team. We didn't expect to set the world on fire in those early years but neither did we want to appear to be hapless whipping-boys for the established countries.

Our tour of England that summer of 1984 was a big boost to our confidence. We did pretty well in all the county games, our batsmen and bowlers all running into good form prior to the Test at Lord's in late August. I played in every first-class match until I fell ill for a period. Marlon Vonhagt was one of our touring party too. It had been a hot, dry summer and the West Indies in their five-Test demolition of England that summer had really enjoyed the bouncy wickets. As we also did in our tour of the counties. Against us, England came into their sixth Test of that summer obviously expecting a much easier time than they'd had against Marshall, Holding, Garner, Lloyd, Richards, Greenidge, Haynes, Gomes and the rest. If there was a World XI in those days, the West Indies would have taken up the majority of places. We had seen the West Indies steamrollering of England's best on television, in the off-duty hours of our warm-up matches, and were thrilled and chastened at the same time by such a spectacle of sheer cricketing ability. The English players who had been only twenty-two yards away from such awesome power-cricket looked shell-shocked. Batsmen were regularly hit about the body, tail-enders were bounced mercilessly, and every English bowler was repeatedly rifled to the boundary, as it appeared from watching the BBC highlights. It was an England who were expecting a soul-salving victory against the cricketers of Sri Lanka, whom we encountered at Lord's in our only Test that summer.

Before our tour had started, it would have been a toss-up between Marlon and myself as to who would get the nod for Lord's. We had both shown good form in the warm-up matches but I had put together a better run of scores, so it was Marlon who became twelfth man, and I was selected for my debut Test. Short of wanting it to have happened in front of my folks back home in Colombo, I can't think of a better place for it to have happened than at Lord's. In fact, it was a dream Test for all of us. David Gower won the toss and put us into bat on a muggy morning, obviously expecting the ball to move around in the conditions. We did lose two early wickets, Amal Silva and Ranjan Madugalle. But Sidath easily handled everything that the English seamers Botham, Agnew, Allott, and Ellison threw at him and only the off-spinner Pocock was able to restrict his scoring through the off-side. Watchful, head over the ball, with a crouching stance at the wicket, he played some glorious cover-drives. As the day progressed his reach outside the off-stump lengthened and lengthened until he was practically flat-batting wide half-volleys to the boundary. This from a batsman who would keep telling me of the importance of not playing at wide ones outside the off-stump ! He even outscored the normally free-scoring Roy Dias in their partnership. We ended the first day with only three wickets down. Sidath and Arjuna rested overnight on a century and half-century, respectively.

Overnight in those situations, the remaining batsmen do think of the importance of not letting a good position slip away, and yet, by subconsciously relaxing in a position of strength, often find themselves getting out quickly the next day. But the next day went even better for us. The crowd had grown by several thousand Sri Lankans who had come to cheer us on, and they were not disappointed. Rain showers disrupted play all day but Arjuna and Sidath batted on serenely, and it looked like Arjuna too would score his first Test century, until a quicker ball from Agnew clipped the top of his off-stump. Which brought Duleep in to bat on his thirty-second birthday, and playing in all probability for the first and last time at Lord's. None of us could be sure of ever having the chance to play at Lord's again, certainly Duleep didn't expect to be playing cricket by the time of our next Lord's Test in 1988. He very much wanted to make this a memorable occasion for Sri Lanka and himself. And he did.

Duleep simply flayed the English bowling to score a hundred in a little over two hours, reaching his hundred just before the close of play. Sidath too, finished the day just a few runs short of his double-hundred having carried his bat for the second consecutive day. It may have been a difficult day for the batsmen on the pitch what with having to stop and start their innings several times, for me who was padded up ready to go in at the fall of Duleep's wicket for my first ever Test innings it was incredibly frustrating. I've never been a great one for sitting out on dressing-room balconies watching play, much preferring to rest my eyes and relax my mind, but I'd been padded up for a day and a half which was the longest time I'd ever had my pads on in my life. With all the best intentions for the side and the batsmen ahead of me, I couldn't wait to bat. And to have to wait until the third day, with a declaration imminent and the two overnight batsmen in such commanding form, I was seriously thinking that I might not get a chance to play an innings at Lord's after all. Now that I'd somehow found myself making my debut in a Lord's Test, I just wanted to go out there and play a few shots, and perform on the biggest stage in cricket.

Rain held things up a little bit on the third day, but soon after play started Sidath fell, caught behind for a great 190. Not quite the highest score made at Lord's, but the longest innings ever played there. It was a great shame he didn't make it to 200 for what would have been Sri Lanka's first double-hundred in Test cricket. His departure was my cue. I've never been a nervous starter, and have always been pretty calm at the start of an innings but as I walked down all those pavilion steps on to the pitch, I was wound up like a bomb waiting to explode with what I hoped would be some quick runs coming from my bat. I had reached Test level playing my natural attacking game and I saw no reason to change my style once the stakes became higher. If I have any authority at the wicket, its because I'm very relaxed. I'm comfortable. It's where I want to be. At that time, my attitude was to do what I wanted to do. People could either take it or leave it. Needless to say, it was a comforting thrill to have Duleep at the other end as an affirmation of how productive attacking the English bowling could be.

A couple of good-length deliveries from Paul Allott were met with a straight bat, until he put one in short and wide of off-stump and I was off the mark with a four to the Tavern boundary. Hit clean and hard, it may have been the best-timed shot I had played all summer. It certainly felt like it. We were looking for quick runs before a declaration, and it felt good to have made a contribution. I had grand visions of maybe scoring a 20 or 30. The English had Pocock on from the pavilion end, and he alone had been able to restrict Duleep's scoring the previous day's play. Just occasionally he would have Duleep playing a false stroke. And so it proved again. Launching himself violently at one that was tossed up by Pocock, Duleep got a leading edge and was caught in the covers for 111. As with Sidath, the crowd rose to its feet and cheered him off. I managed a few more boundaries before I too was caught behind, glancing down the leg-side, and soon after we declared at 491 for 7. The plan was to get a couple of early wickets, put the English under pressure and enforce the follow-on leaving us around a day or so to bowl them out on the last day.

It didn't go to plan but it just may have done. England ended the third day with two wickets down, David Gower and Chris Broad at the crease. We kept plugging away the following day. Gower finessed a quick fifty until he fell to a terrific catch by Amal Silva the wicketkeeper. Broad stuck in and ground out a painstaking 89; it took a sharp ball from Asantha de Mel to finally pry him out. Botham went quickly to a good catch by Marlon who was on as sub in place of me and at 218 for 5, having lost three quick wickets and the follow-on saving target of 292 some way away, England must have been worried. Allan Lamb who had already scored three centuries that summer in Tests against the West Indies (two more than all the rest of England's batsmen), remained the danger-man however. We played against him several more times after that and he was always dangerous but I guess that back then in 1984 Allan Lamb was at his peak as a batsman. Actually, from where I fielded at cover, there would always appear to be a big gap between his bat and his pad which makes his batting record all the more remarkable. It was obvious he had learned his game in different conditions to those of the other English batsmen, for he was always quick to rock back on to the back foot, which is not typical of batsmen in England. Allan Lamb's top hand was obviously an irrelevance, such was his manner of striking the ball, and he wasn't too sure of himself against spinners. He enjoyed fast bowling, that was for sure. But his strengths far outweighed his weaknesses and he made a ton of runs in all sorts of conditions through the years. Most important, he played with confidence when the odds were stacked against him. That Test at Lord's, after England were 218 for 5, Lamb was dropped early on. He went on to make a hundred, and the follow-on was comfortably saved by England.

England were all out to the last ball of the fourth day for a total of 370, giving us a big lead and the freedom to bat any way we liked on the last day. There was just the thought that a blazing first session by us could lead to a declaration to put the English under pressure and have them lose wickets in a run chase but in our hearts we knew that we just didn't have the attack to bowl England out twice, the second time in less than a day. As it was, following the loss of some quick wickets, Duleep came to the wicket wanting to show everyone that our first innings performance was not a fluke. This he duly did. Duleep had actually sent me in ahead of him at No. 6 to get some more experience of Test Match conditions. I lasted about an over before edging Pat Pocock to the keeper. Off-spinners had arm-balls, I realised, ones that were particularly useful when they held their own up the slope on the Lord's pitch. Notwithstanding the acute discomfort of the split webbing on my right hand as a result of dropping a chance off a sliced drive by Chris Broad, I had missed a valuable opportunity to show myself and everybody watching that I undeniably deserved my place in the team.

Botham, who had taken the wickets of Roy Dias and Arjuna in quick succession, then fed Duleep a bouncer. Which Duleep hooked over the man three-quarters of the way in from the boundary at square-leg, for six. Botham bounced Duleep again with this time the square-leg fielder, Chris Broad, on the boundary line. Duleep had seen the trap being sprung but couldn't resist hitting the next bouncer from Botham in exactly the same place, right in line with the square-leg fielder. And ten feet above that fielder's head. Another six. Botham bowled another bouncer, a little faster this time. Another hook. Another six. Duleep was on a roll, looking for his second hundred of the match. Whether it was Duleep's fearsome presence at the crease or the fact that the pitch was unresponsive to his medium-pace, or even because he was injured, soon after these bouncers Botham started bowling off-spin. Duleep was scoring in his second innings even quicker than in his first, and was all set for another landmark century until he miscued a Botham roller to midwicket, going for the big hit to bring up his hundred; out for 94. At the other end, Amal Silva the wicket-keeper-opener scored his maiden first-class century just before the close of play. A nice moment for him and it went some way in relieving him of his sorrow at dropping Lamb in the first-innings. Good performances at places like Lord's, Eden Gardens and the MCG really put you on the map in terms of world-wide cricket awareness, as an individual and as a team. Sri Lanka's showing in our first visit to Lord's really established us in the public eye as wholehearted performers, flamboyant batsmen and fine ambassadors for the game back home. The full range of our abilities had been on display. Sidath with his marathon innings had shown that Sri Lankan batsmen had stamina and concentration and Duleep had shown the kind of explosive strokeplay that makes Sri Lankan cricket so popular. In between these two the talents of Arjuna, Amal Silva and Roy Dias had shown that we were a team of considerable batting ability. Somachandra de Silva's leg-spin bowling, in this his last Test at the age of forty-two, had displayed considerable guile and Asantha de Mel, Vinodhan John and Ravi Ratneyeke had bowled better than the English seamers. We had done our job as Sri Lanka's premier cricketers and we took deep satisfaction from that.

CHAPTER FIVE

Sri Lankan cricket had risen to this level thanks largely to the performances of our senior players. For some great cricketers, from whose performances Sri Lankan cricket gained a distinct identity in the 1970s, the elevation to full international status came a little too late. Batsmen such as Anura Tennekoon, David Heyn, Michael Tissera and Ranjit Fernando and bowlers like Somachandra de Silva, Ajith de Silva and Lalith Kaluperama would have all have performed admirably on the full international stage as young men. For Roy Dias and Duleep Mendis however, juniors in those teams of the 1970s, the call to arms in Test cricket came just at the time they were on the cusp of their best form and Sri Lanka was very lucky to have them in those difficult first years of international exposure. To many it was they who epitomised Sri Lankan cricket.

Duleep Mendis strode across Sri Lanka like a colossus. He was my hero, pure and simple. Short and stocky, he impressed upon onlookers a sheer physical presence that promised a ton of runs every time he came to the wicket. He lived and died by the sword; not for him the push into the covers or the nudge into the leg-side for a single (unless he was looking to keep the strike). In domestic cricket, opposition captains would set nothing but the stiffest of targets for Duleep and his Sinhalese Sporting Club (SSC) team-mates to chase on the last day of a club match. The bigger the target, the better he played. When he was a young man and I was a boy, the newspapers would be filled with his performances. His score was always the first and only one I looked to when I grabbed the newspaper off my father in the morning. If he'd done well, I felt that all was right with the world and that the coming day would go well for me too. I don't think I ever saw, or read of, him being bowled. Allied to pure physical strength of arm, body and thigh, Duleep had a daintiness of footwork and speed of hand that could make a mockery of anything less than the very best bowling. He gave the impression of ruggedness of stroke but that was only because he despatched the ball in so many different directions with such violence that he looked like he was clearing a forest whenever he spent time at the crease. His backlift was imperious, rising like a palm tree at the top of his backswing, before falling like a mother's slap on the ball. His style wasn't merely to 'time' balls to the boundary, he smote and smashed them – with perfect timing. He was embarrassed whenever he hit small sixes. He had a simple philosophy: if in doubt, hit out. Indeed it was this attitude that led to him famously getting knocked out cold by Jeff Thomson in the 1975 World Cup in England.

Back then Jeff Thomson was rated the fastest bowler in the world, a hurler of 90mph thunderbolts. With Dennis Lillee he had shell-shocked the English in the 1974–75 Australian season, ripping through batsmen's defences with a mixture of devastatingly angled throat-balls, rib-ticklers and stump smashers. In that 1975 World Cup match against Sri Lanka Jeff Thomson struck four batsmen, sending two to hospital. Ranjit Fernando and Sunil Wettimuny (Sidath's elder brother and later an author of *Cricket – The Noble Art*), had gotten Sri Lanka off to a good start chasing a big Australian score. Duleep and Sunil continued to score pretty freely until Thomson was brought back on by Ian Chappell for his second spell, in order to break the partnership. Sunil Wettimuny was immediately the footsore victim of a Jeff Thomson yorker, beaten for pace. And still no sign of the famed Thomson bouncer; the bouncer that jagged in from wide of the crease, looking for the edge of the bat, the tip of the cap, the end of the batsman's chin. With sheer explosive hostility this ball was meant to destroy a batsman's composure, and make him question his appetite for the contest. Short-pitched bowling you either duck or hook, there's not much point in trying to control a sharply rising ball with a straight bat from above your chin. You can jump up in trying to get hands above the ball at point of contact, but you have to be supremely talented in order to succeed at this. Gooch, Atherton, Steve Waugh, and before them Gundappa Vishwanath are the only ones whom I can point to who have made a success of this high-risk technique.

I don't think many hooked Jeff Thomson in his prime. But Duleep was game. Like any other Sri Lankan batsman coached rigorously by followers of the MCC coaching book, when faced with a ball rising sharply off a length, Duleep moved right into line with Thomson's first short-pitched delivery. Thomson being, in Duleep's oft-repeated words, 'quite a few yards faster than anything I'd ever faced . . . I shaped to hook one delivery, but the ball grew big on me before I'd even brought up my hands, and before I had time to duck, I was hit by the ball'. He woke up half an hour later. Mere correctness of technique was inadequate in the modern arena of speed-cricket as batsmen were coming to realise. But the news hadn't yet reached Sri Lanka. And no one in those days was wearing helmets. All that Duleep had on to protect him were his pads, his gloves, his box, his bat, his Sri Lankan cap, and a couple of balled-up handkerchiefs on thigh-pad duty in his hip pocket. It must have been some kind of miracle that allowed Duleep to escape with nothing more than concussion and a monster headache. Jeff Thomson and Duleep laugh about it now of course, but it must have been a genuinely scary time for all those at the ground.

Duleep's international career carried on from his club cricket. He was presented with fewer balls to hit to the boundary, so it took him a little longer to post a score, but he nevertheless looked to take full advantage of anything loose. His hallmark was hitting the ball over the top. When he was feeling at the top of his game, bowlers were simply deliverers of balls which would allow him to score runs, his reason for being on the pitch. Allied to his vast talent and force of personality was also an ability to read the game, which made him a good captain for Sri Lanka once he came to the helm. He was an elder brother to those like Sidath and Roy, a father figure to the rest of us. His was a giving heart, one that simply asked those who represented Sri Lanka to do the very best for themselves and their country. Playing a Test in Dunedin or in Faisalabad may mean that very few are actually watching, but he knew that whenever a Sri Lankan cricketer stepped on to the field in those days he was playing for Sri Lanka's right to belong at the highest levels of world cricket. His bristling, confident presence at the crease against anything less than the very best bowling would always do a great deal to bolster the confidence of his batting partners. In those first years of Sri Lanka's international cricket, it wouldn't be unusual for the whole team to feel like débutantes, so very much was new to them – the big grounds, the travel, the itineraries, the intensity of combat with seasoned veterans – but Duleep and Roy always took things in their stride.

The example of Duleep Mendis may have dominated most of my waking moments when I was younger, but it was Roy Dias whom I dreamed of. He was a beautiful batsman, the best Sri Lankan batsman I have ever seen. He had so much grace, so much style, he was so economical of effort. When you looked at Roy Dias, you said to yourself: 'take a lesson'. If he had come into top-level international cricket as a young man, rather than as a man on the brink of 30, he would have really embedded himself in the world's consciousness as a brilliant batsman. I can remember very clearly the first time I saw Roy bat. I was twelve years old, still of an age to have my cheeks tweaked between the fingers and thumbs of my father's friends, as we all took our seats at the SSC ground for an international game. What with playing my own games of cricket and concentrating on watching Duleep Mendis' play, I had never yet seen Roy play a major innings. Seeing him that day put all the bowlers to the sword, I realised just what a great player looks like. It was the first time I'd been anywhere near to stylistic perfection and I was dumbstruck with admiration.

If Duleep at his best was all swagger and bravado at the crease, Roy was all sleekness and poise. As cricketing musketeers, Roy was Aramis to Duleep's Athos. Duleep gave the impression that he hit boundaries because he didn't see the point in running between the wickets in tropical climes; Roy gave the impression that he hit boundaries because there was nothing else that he could have done with the ball other than let his bat send it to the boundary. His innings that day and so many times since was like a brilliant net practice. Fielders had absolutely no influence on proceedings. Predominantly a front-foot player, Roy batted like a top tennis-player who off the forehand can make winners from anywhere. No length troubled him, no line was immune from dynamic deflection. Most significantly, he rarely wasted a good stroke by hitting it straight to a fielder. Driving on the up was his trademark. Like Sunil Gavaskar, he could 'lean on them', and they went. And there always was the smile that lifted the corners of his moustache. Like a cat who kept getting the cream, Roy had so very many opportunities to be pleased with himself. The whipped on-drive, the caress through the covers, the finest of glides behind either side of the wicket, the dancer's shimmy down the wicket to meet a ball. The most resonant and impervious of forward-defensives. All his strokes brought pleasure to the onlookers and himself. Front-foot cricket as it would be played in heaven was on display. And he was a great fielder in the covers, repeatedly pulling off stops and catches that were beyond the abilities of the rest of his team-mates. Roy's smiles were simply the symptom of a man responding to the beauty that he had been privileged to uncover.

If Roy could be said to have one limitation, it was that he didn't play shots off the back-foot. Bowlers would just waste their energy in bowling short at him because he either left these deliveries alone (and he had one of the best 'leaves' in the game), or he'd find the most effortless way to stun the upstarts down. He had patience and patience is a premium virtue in Test cricket. He wouldn't fret when faced with a steady diet of short-of-a-length bowling because he knew that 'no one can bowl short for ever'. Bowlers hate nothing more than an assured batsman and the thought that they can't get a rise out of him. As soon as they'd pitch it up Roy would pounce. For years he taught opposition bowlers a thing or two about Sri Lankan batting. He was hardly ever dismissed as the result of a defensive stroke. No Sri Lankan bowler could cope with him in domestic cricket, and he thought that something close to that would be the case once he started regular international cricket. For sure he scored heavily against Imran, Qadir, the West Indian quicks, the Aussies, and Kapil Dev in Tests and one-dayers, the wonder was that he wasn't able to do it all the time. His self assurance never wavered. He always backed himself to do well. It is hard enough to shine as a batsman in world cricket, it is even harder when you're in a team that struggles to win matches. When it was genuinely important that Roy perform, he almost always had the ability to come through with the crucial innings for the team. But as with the rest of the side who had established themselves in domestic cricket, he quickly found that he had to adjust his style to deal with the greater abilities of international bowlers. Being seen as the team's premier batsman it was he who set the batting standards for the rest of the team. If he would have been unable to handle any particular bowler, then it was unlikely that the rest of us would have been able to cope and seeing him struggle, the rest of us in the pavilion would be defeated before we even walked out to bat.

Looking at Roy taught me that there was a right way and a wrong way to do things at the crease; he seemed to do everything right as if by instinct. His feet were always in the right place, his body always perfectly balanced, his hands were always in the right position. It was so inspiring to be in the presence of a batsman who was so good and who also took so much pleasure from what he did. He loved to bat. It was what he lived for. He respected the game so much, he knew how technical it was, how difficult it could be. He alone of all our batsmen in those early 1980s had worked out a way to translate the Sri Lankan penchant for exotic strokeplay against domestic-standard bowlers, into free-scoring orthodox runs against world-class bowling. Sri Lankan wickets in those days were pretty batsman-friendly: even-paced, flat and rolled to within an inch of their lives. These surfaces encouraged front-foot strokeplay. Bowlers soon learnt to pitch the ball up and aim to hit the stumps if they were hoping to succeed, for anything short and wide would just sit up and beg to be despatched. But on the international stage it was a different ball-game. Bowlers aimed to keep the ball on, or just short of, a good length, looking for that rising ball to take the outside-edge or force the involuntary fend-off to the close-catchers, and always looking, especially in one-day cricket, to cramp the batsman's freedom of stroke. If Roy was to prosper as a batsman outside Sri Lanka, he knew he would have to find a way of making his style succeed against the most restrictive of bowling.

Yorkers are the hardest to hit for runs and are loaded with wicket-taking potential, but they are a weapon bowlers are loath to overuse: bowl too many and the batsmen can recognise their approach and play them with time to spare. And there is a fine line either side of a yorker between a half-volley and a full-toss. So bowlers looking to tie down a batsman prefer to bowl just short of a length on a line on, or just-outside, off-stump as their stock-ball. Bowlers feel they can deliver this type of delivery with a greater margin of error for themselves. With the ball rising so close to the batsman's body the arms cannot be swung in a wide enough arc to generate power, the batsman is tucked up, his range of attacking options reduced. Any attempts to pull or cut can easily lead to splicing or top-edging the ball and driving on the up is pregnant with the potential to mistime the ball into mid-off's or cover point's hands. (All the above is true for all batsmen apart from Sachin Tendulkar. His back-foot driving is peerless). Whereas Duleep took on the world's best bowlers' short-of-a-length deliveries with a cross-bat, Roy's bat didn't deviate from the perpendicular unless it was absolutely necessary. Being predominantly a front-foot player, Roy dealt with the short ball with balance and the most judicious of 'leaves'. The method that Sunil Gavaskar made famous in the 1970s of going back and across the stumps when playing fast bowling had to be modified by someone like Roy, because 1) he liked to attack more than he liked to defend, and 2) he couldn't bat at both ends. And if he wasn't scoring runs then for sure not many others in the team would be able to. His defending solidly while all else was collapsing around him would have been of no use at all to the team. The onus was always on Roy to be the top-scoring batsman. He had to play more shots than anyone else in the team and he had to play as long an innings as possible. It was a huge responsibility to have to carry.

So Roy was the first Sri Lankan to play 'like a West Indian': driving on the up whenever possible, with the proviso that it was done in the most elegant and controlled manner he could manage. Not for him the 'pissing-dog shot' whereby, in flinging his bat at the rising ball, the batsman raises a leg in order to counterbalance himself. Roy's was the batting of straight-lines and classicism. He always played the ball back from whence it came. You learn once you've played the game for a little while, how easy it is to hit the ball inadvertently into the air. Factor in fast hostile bowling and the possibilities of playing an uncontrolled shot increase exponentially. But Roy showed every Sri Lankan batsman that there was nothing to fear. Predominantly a front-foot player, controlling the ball was really quite easy with his style. As he said in explanation when I asked him how he did what he did, 'the secret to driving on the up is to keep the head and weight forward in front of the body. That way you keep the ball on the ground and send it where you want it to go.' He took hundreds off Imran and Hadlee when they were at their peak, when all but a few batsmen in the world found Imran and Hadlee too much for them.

A batsman has to make up his mind about his intentions towards a delivery in the split-seconds after it leaves the bowler's hand; it's all based on conditioned responses: the responses of hands, feet and body grooved through years of play. These are what buy one the time to react decisively to the bowler's attacks. More than reflexes and athleticism, these responses are what govern cricketing success. Roy was never in a rush to meet the ball, because he knew the ball would be coming to him, all he had to do was wait and aim to drive the ball at the most optimum time, just when it was almost under the 'line' that stretched from his chin to the ground. That meant perfect timing. The principle was the same for all kinds of bowling, fast, medium and slow. He kept his blinding hand speed to himself until the last possible moment, when with clinical precision he would punch the ball away from him. As Roy would say, 'the quicker I am, the longer I can wait. The longer I can wait, the less likely I am to get fooled.' His bat was light enough to allow him to bring it down from his backswing quickly, and his hands rarely strayed more than a foot away from his body, keeping his response time as short as possible. Compact, precise, clinical. And always there was this perfect balance. He played like a king. It is almost always true that a front-foot player is severely handicapped by pace and bounce at the highest level, but Roy overcame any potential problems very easily. He chose the balls he wanted to hit in the knowledge that no bowler could bowl short for ever. As soon as he had the chance to play a shot, he took it. If the ball was swinging away, he'd glide with the swing, ride with it, not attempting to touch the ball unless he had to. Sideways on. Always sideways on. When the ball was right, he put it in the gaps rather than blasted it. When the force was with him, he could make bowlers his droids.

If you look at Duleep's and Roy's international records, you can see a healthy aggregate of runs, several centuries and half-centuries, decent averages. So you may wonder why with all their talent, they didn't score even more runs and centuries and post even better averages. Their figures in the twenty or so Tests and thirty or so one-day internationals they played together don't do them justice because they came to the game late, as 'old' rookies, when they had to combat inexperience and age as well as their opponents. Time was not on their side nor were the rest of the team able to support them that often. It's so much harder to do well when others are struggling around you. But Duleep and Roy had the real cricketer's indifference to statistics. We all knew that their contribution to Sri Lankan cricket was more than runs; their gift was leadership, and an embracing pride, a living demonstration of what determination and guts could do for you out in the middle. They had style, weight and confidence: they were people who lived life with authority. Duleep and Roy were dynamic and exemplary figures; they didn't need 'personality' because they had character. They had presence and bearing, plus dignity, voice, dress and looks. Their stature and performance gave all us Sri Lankan cricketers self-respect and the respect of others.

Batting at the highest level takes so much out of you as an individual, that it is almost impossible to bat for everyone else as well. Sidath's and the other top-order batsmen's efforts notwithstanding, it was pretty rare for Roy and Duleep batting at No. 3 and No. 4 or No. 4 and No. 5, not to have to come in and find the ball still hard, the seam still prominent, the shine still glinting and the bowlers all too fresh. Too many times they were put in the position of having to score runs quickly to compensate for the weaknesses of batsmen at the other end. Roy in particular was a master of farming the strike in order to protect his batting partners whenever necessary. Both never ever played for a 'not out', and would rather go down all guns blazing than wait grimly for the inevitable closure. It was unfortunate that they didn't more often enjoy substantial partnerships together because when they were both on fire they were fabulous to watch. Whenever Duleep or Roy were batting together the whole team would be out on the players' balcony not wanting to miss a chance of seeing them in action.

Had they come to Test cricket as young men, had they not had to devote themselves as soon as a series was over to their business careers, had they laid the foundations for peak physical fitness as young men in their twenties, then Duleep and Roy could have played on for more years than they did. They only played twenty or so Tests together, and their last Test together was against New Zealand in Sri Lanka's only Test of 1987, the first of a scheduled three-Test series that had to be abandoned because of a Colombo bomb blast that signalled a wave of political unrest in Sri Lanka. Roy and Duleep had so many runs in them which they were never given a chance to score. Their fault was to be cricketers of a late-emerging nation, but at least they had shown the world what they were capable of in the brief time they had to flourish.

CHAPTER SIX

Duleep's and Roy's most useful advice to me when I first came into the team was what a young player needs to hear most of all: they told me I must play to my strengths. Which were at that time, an ability to hit the short ball very hard and an itch to take the attack to the bowlers. In addition, Sidath Wettimuny helped me greatly with developing my temperament and technique. My most persistent and irresistible dream was the dream of being good. Notwithstanding a few decent scores in one-day internationals and in the county games on the tour of England, I still wasn't completely sure that I had 'the right stuff'. Only greater exposure would reveal my true capabilities. Sri Lanka were scheduled for a long tour of Australia at the start of 1985 to play in the World Series Cup against Australia and the West Indies, and then stay on in Australia for a mini-world cup with all the Test-playing nations. Thus within a year of my international debut it was quite possible that I would play against all the world's top bowlers and batsmen! I would learn a great deal just by watching, I would get better just by playing. Sri Lanka had come far and were going even further, and I was glad to be going along with them.

To me in the full flush of youth, all this was a challenge. To some of the others, understandably so, the prospect of facing the West Indian pace battery on bouncy Australian pitches was a very worrying thing. We had seen for ourselves during our tour of England the way the West Indies played the game: HARD. With no quarter given. The ball was there to be hit as were the opposing batsmen if they kept getting in the way. Not even tailenders were safe. Before we left for Australia the talk in our camp was not of how many runs we'd score and wickets we'd take, but of how many of us would come back with injuries and what bones we'd break. Fear was a big weapon in the West Indian armoury. To prepare us for the ordeal, the Board brought in bowling-machines which we'd crank up to maximum velocity to deliver short-pitched balls. The difference between the fastest delivery from a machine and the fastest delivery from a bowler? You can set the machine to deliver the balls you'd like and therefore condition yourself to receive a certain type of delivery. Bowlers tend not to be so helpful. We'd coped with the bowling-machine much better than we expected however, and that gave us a lot of confidence. Still, little could prepare a Sri Lankan batsman who had hitherto played the game as best as he could against the medium-pacers of the world for the real sensation of facing Holding, Garner, Marshall, Walsh and Davis on a fast track when length balls fly past the shoulders of bat and body, when the slightest miscalculation can lead to serious injury. The one time Sri Lanka had played prime fast bowling, that of Imran Khan in a 1982 Test, he had taken 14 wickets. Nothing can really prepare you for facing something you have never encountered before. You have to rely on natural ability and the will to prevail.

Always hospitable, and eager to have Sri Lanka play as much top-class cricket as possible, the Sri Lankan President in November 1984 invited the England team that had temporarily suspended their tour of India following the assassination of Mrs. Gandhi, to play some fixtures in Sri Lanka while the situation in India eased. So it was against an England XI that I actually made my maiden first-class century. Which is actually a little surprising when domestic cricket in Sri Lanka had been accorded first-class status for almost three years, but it just goes to show that back then I wasn't paying too much attention to crease occupation. I was batting lower middle-order when I played and thus not getting many chances to build innings and I just wasn't taking 'figures' seriously.

In those days, when international fixtures were less common, a visit by England was a big event in Sri Lankan cricket and there was much local interest in our game. Apart from my quickfire century the Board President's XI match against England was memorable for one other reason too. I was hit on the side of the head, second ball, by the fast-medium seamer Neil Foster. The ball flew up off a length and was impossible to avoid, hitting me on the cheekguard section of my helmet. I had come in to bat a little before lunch, and though conscious of a big bruise forming almost immediately on my cheekbone, I felt that I could go on to lunch at least. During the interval a golf-ball lump of flesh arose below my left eye. My father came into the dressing-room and with his immense concern for my well-being and drawing upon all his years of medical experience (i.e. none), pushed away the ice-pack I was holding to my face, briskly looked at the lump and said that I could always go to the doctor after the game but that I should play on in a prestigious fixture like this. And if I couldn't handle this attack, I certainly wouldn't be able to survive for too long at the top level. Resuming after lunch, with my left eye half-shut and my helmet painfully pressing very tight against my face, I think the English bowlers then tried too hard to exploit what they thought must have been a weakness of mine to short-pitched bowling and gave me plenty of opportunities to cut and hook. Marlon Vonhagt enjoyed himself too, and we both reached 50. In pain, I concentrated perhaps a little bit more than usual on sighting the ball and watching it on to the bat. My second 50 came very quickly. I actually found that I enjoyed gutsing it out, playing at my best when circumstances were against me, and this new level of performance was more significant to me than scoring a century. You could call it my first grown-up act.

Our 1984–85 tour of Australia was scheduled to be a long one: over twenty fixtures spread over three months although only one of them wasn't a one-day game. In between the World Series Cup games some of our fixtures were played in places where I'm sure the local Australians hadn't seen any Sri Lankans before, and we drew crowds for our curiosity value if nothing else. In these smaller venues there'd be the heartening sight of a few Sri Lankan expatriates who'd made the journey from the bigger towns in order to see us up close. Too often they saw us perform a little disappointingly but in the first weeks of the tour at least, until injuries and the cycle of defeats against players of greater resource and experience had dampened the enthusiasm of the side, Sri Lanka's cricketers gave their supporters and neutrals plenty to cheer about. Our first WSC game against Australia in Sydney was actually Sri Lanka's first day-night match, and as much as battle-hardened combat veterans like us should have been unfazed by occasions like this it was actually a considerable thrill for a kid like me from a Colombo suburb to step out after the innings-interval on to floodlit turf that spread out like lush dark-green velvet and play underneath the most amazingly phosphorescent sky I had ever seen. It felt as if I were playing inside a diamond. Showtime! The team pulled out a good performance too, with Australia winning by 6 wickets only after a hard struggle.

Two days later, we were in Tasmania playing the West Indies. Undoubtedly by far the best team in world cricket at the time they had convincingly beaten Australia home and away, either side of their demolition of England. We told ourselves that India had beaten the West Indies in the 1983 World Cup, so a team of medium-pacers and slow bowlers had a chance against them, and the West Indies were not quite so formidable in one-dayers as they were in Tests. But really we were just kidding. In those days Sri Lanka would just step out on to the field and hope for the best. There was no real game plan apart from bowling line and length and not losing early wickets. One-day cricket was still a learning process for all of us. At that time we always felt that chasing a target was the easiest thing to do: whenever we batted first we felt that games would slip away because we didn't have a containing attack. The West Indies pace attack was undeniably formidable and was indeed a disturbing prospect to some of our batsmen, but their full range of menace was reduced by a slow and low Hobart wicket, and the West Indies part-time spinners Viv Richards and Larry Gomes did plenty of bowling. By the time I came in to bat, following good knocks from

Duleep and Roy, the spinners were on from both ends. The first ball I faced was from my all-time international batting hero Viv Richards and he craftily soon had me caught close in, playing too early at one that 'stopped'.

Two games and two losses against teams who were playing within themselves. We played the West Indies again a week later and were absolutely taken apart by Viv and Clive Lloyd. We dropped catches, missed run-outs, lost concentration at crucial times and were generally well below par. The only good thing about our performance was Roy's stylish and well-composed 80. The rest of the batsmen's fears were allayed somewhat, by finding themselves able to get bat – or at least the outside edge – onto the West Indian pacemen's deliveries.

The West Indies bowled with variety and control and made us play at almost everything. Every once in a while they'd really bend their back and send down a short, sharply-rising ball to rattle the batsmen. Happy hookers in normal circumstances, we'd end up looking to deflect runs off them rather than even think about going for the hook. Marshall in particular was just too fast, his right-arm a blur of speed as it released the ball. Ironically, it wasn't just the deliveries that we fended off our faces to which we'd succumb, we fell to sucker deliveries too – long-hops and full-tosses. Tied down by accurate fast bowling which had us pinned to the crease, we'd actually often perish to attacking shots attempted whenever a batsman, just that fraction too late, sensed an opportunity to break free from the stifling binds of off-and-middle stump accuracy. We'd sometimes get out to the most hapless of strokes which made us look even more like a novice side. It was all just so embarrassing! Moreover, you could always sense that apart from their extra efforts against Duleep and Roy, the West Indian bowlers were each keeping a little back when bowling to us. Michael Holding in particular was a master of deception, he could disguise the pace between his fast and slower deliveries while using the same action, just like Richard Hadlee could.

But just being near the West Indies, watching them practise and then seeing them in matches do the occasional phenomenal thing (even at our expense) was a thrill. All eyes would be on Viv. Viv had the physique that I could only dream of, with shoulders that looked twice as broad as his waist. Beneath his alternating airs of swagger and poise was, you sensed, something very strong, powerful and rooted. He had the ability to dominate in the middle through the sheer power of his presence. I was a teenage fan of Viv's, like so many around the world, and yet I was also one of his opponents so I didn't want to appear too gushy or appear to be in awe of the great man. But whatever he did, I'd always be watching. I would see him take net practice against the young West Indian and local quicks and I'd see how he prided himself on never playing a false shot.

He'd laugh with the net bowlers, tell them to bowl faster and straighter and with more hostility, challenge them to bowl bouncers at his unhelmeted head and, even as the balls flew faster and faster, he'd always have time to play them just as he wished. A baby could have been behind his stumps, and it would have been safe from getting hurt. Naturally, I tried to adopt some of his characteristics to my game. I think it was the seventh or eighth time that I failed to connect properly with the intended Vivian Richards trademark whip-through-midwicket of a ball on off-stump, that I gave up trying to play the great man's shots. Sanath Jayasuriya might be able to, but I'm not. Still, the attitude that every fibre of Viv's being projected, that he was better than anything anyone could bowl at him, I've tried to hold to as well. You need to. It adds runs to your game.

In our next World Series match, against Australia at the MCG in front of a large crowd with a big Sri Lankan contingent, we were much better than we had been against the West Indies. Rumesh Ratnayake and our leg-spinner Somachandra de Silva in particular, bowled excellently as we restricted Australia to 225 off their 50 overs. In reply, we made a good start for once and were always in touch with the required run-rate. Duleep and Roy enjoyed a typically aggressive partnership which ended on Duleep's being caught in the deep. Roy thrived on pace bowling and Australian wickets where the ball came on to his bat suited his strokeplay. When I came in to bat following Duleep's dismissal, another 70 or so runs were needed at a run a ball. Roy was nearing his 50, calmly hitting through the infield, finding the gaps without any difficulty. He was well set for the final acceleration down the home stretch. At which point I promptly ran Roy out, looking to get off the mark with a shot that I thought was worth two runs and which proved to be worth less. Roy was man enough not to pay my apologies any attention. As he left the middle, he just said to me that we could still win. Uvais Karnain was next man in, and he made a quick 16 until he was bowled by Lawson at just the crucial time that can really set back the momentum of a chasing side and which gives the defending side a good chance to get their hands a firmer grasp on victory. Rumesh came in next, with the target 31 runs off the last 30 balls. Lawson pitched one up, and I was delighted to hit it straight back over his head into the crowd. It was still anybody's game but my running out Roy when he was batting so well made me that much more determined to see us through to the win. Rumesh was the ideal batting partner in this situation because not only was he lightning fast between the wickets, he was possessed of strokes to which no orthodox field could be set. Plus he was never overawed by any situation. Here, in front of the biggest crowd of our lives, with the Australians fired up and scrambling desperately not to lose and us so near to and yet so far from our first win in Australia, Rumesh came to the wicket grinning. His confidence was infectious. In the middle of all the sound and fury, the whole game suddenly became about just what we two could do, and we were looking to win.

Geoff Lawson and Craig McDermott, Australia's two front-line bowlers, gave it their all but Rumesh and I kept going until only 4 runs were needed off the last over, to be bowled by McDermott. Rumesh scrambled a single off the first ball, putting me on strike. Three runs wanted, five balls left. I saw some wide-open spaces behind the bowler. In those days the theory and science of bowling yorkers and slow balls at the death hadn't yet been fully developed so I expected McDermott to aim to tuck me up with a ball short-of-a-length on off-stump. I decided I would come down the wicket to McDermott's next ball to give myself the momentum and leverage to either flat-bat the ball back behind him, or at least give me some scope to swing my arms. McDermott's next ball was short and, having come down the wicket, I swung at the ball and connected with a top-edge. I had no idea where the ball went, but looking at McDermott in his follow through, I sensed that the ball flew somewhere behind my left shoulder towards fine leg. The umpire signalled a six.

The reason you play is for matches like that, the feeling coming off the pitch knowing you won because you didn't give up. We'd won our first match in the World Series Cup. What's more, having beaten Australia, we were in with a chance of reaching the finals against the West Indies as Australia themselves had won only one game in the tournament while having already played one game more than us. The whole team had come out of the MCG match with a boost and we really felt that even though the West Indies were considerably stronger than us, that against Australia we had a chance, because they too were only able to lose to the West Indies. Round-robin tournament success when you play a clutch of games in quick succession is so much about momentum: a winning team tends to keep finding ways of winning. But one defeat can totally disrupt a team's confidence and performance. Our next game against Australia was a crunch game. Win this and we'd be well on course for the finals at the expense of Australia and really put ourselves on the map. Batting first, we made an unfortunate start. Amal Silva was narrowly run-out by Dean Jones and Ranjan Madugalle thin-edged a hook to the wicket-keeper. Sidath and Roy steadied the innings until they too fell in quick succession. I joined Duleep at the wicket with the score at 55 for 4, very much aware of the need to make a contribution. Duleep and I were both able make 80s, and we finished with 240 off 50 overs, a total that would challenge Australia. In the event, after a poor start of their own, Kepler Wessels, Allan Border and Dean Jones between them set the foundations for an Australian victory by just 3 wickets.

So near and yet so far. The wheels fell off our campaign following this defeat and our remaining World Series performances were marred by team injuries, fatigue, loss of confidence and an inability to raise our game when all around us were raising theirs. Our win against Australia just provoked everyone else to play better against us. In those days you couldn't get two more competitive teams than Australia and the West Indies, but by the time of the last World Series qualifiers, we were so unthreatening that the Australians stopped bothering to sledge us. My tour ended soon after our last World Series game in Perth when the shooting pains in my leg were diagnosed as a stress fracture of the shin. In those days my physical fitness routine was pretty limited in comparison to now. My mainstay was running, doing laps of all the grounds we played at, which I'd do till I was exhausted and dripping with sweat, or until it was time to take the bus back to the team hotel. I figured that not being tired while batting would mean fewer tired shots, less tired footwork and greater powers of concentration. My innings would therefore have more chance to last longer. But apparently the pounding on the hard-baked grounds of Australia had done my legs more harm than good, and I retired from the tour on crutches. I felt it was the end of the world. Nowadays, the Sri Lankan team take fitness matters and physical conditioning, indeed all matters of performance on the field, very seriously. But back then practising, maintaining form and fitness were the players' responsibilities, and frankly we had less idea of how to manage ourselves off the pitch than we had of managing ourselves on the pitch. As our results back then showed. Our bowlers would always be getting injured with niggling strains and injuries purely because no one had taught them the proper ways of warming up and cooling down, and prepared them for the sheer physical strain of bowling 50 overs in a Test match. All our fast bowlers were forced to retire before their time because of chronic injuries. On tour, I would often share rooms with Rumesh, and it was not unusual to hear him complain through the night of a sore shoulder which felt 'like it had been punched fifty times'. Yet he'd still persevere until the next game. He wanted to play for Sri Lanka very much, and the team needed him to. He was our wicket-taking warhorse.

Often new players would come into the Sri Lankan side without even having proper kit. Any English county side had equipment, facilities, stadia, dressing rooms, practice areas, medical support far better than ours. In fact it wasn't until the 1990s, when the whole system of management/coaching/physiotherapy received the investment of year-round staffing that a Sri Lankan cricketer could consider himself a professional athlete. And yet Sir Garry Sobers, one of Sri Lanka's first coaches once we'd starting playing Tests, would always remind us that the world-beating talents of the West Indians were developed in pretty basic conditions back in the players' home islands and that we should not feel disadvantaged. It was asking a lot of people like Sir Garry and all our other early coaches to be the brains behind everything, and to be aware of the needs of the modern-day cricketer. For all their good intentions and the honest efforts of our administrators, the sheer pace, scale and scope of the cricket world we'd come into in 1982 was beyond the reckoning of all those who'd played their cricket in the past. It is no coincidence that the sustained upturn in Sri Lanka's performances as a team, the fruits of which we are still enjoying today, started on the 1994–95 tour of Zimbabwe where Ranjit Fernando (who holds a full coaching qualification gained in England), and Dr. Dan Kiesel were employed as coach and physio respectively. While the regime has developed even further since, in late 1994 for the first time on important things like training and physical discipline, team-wide no corners were cut. Those three Tests against Zimbabwe were all drawn, which isn't much when you consider that Zimbabwe were the weakest Test nation, but these results came after five consecutive Test defeats of the hugest kind against India and Pakistan, and our one-day form had been pretty diabolical too.

Notwithstanding the example set by me, Arjuna, Sachin Tendulkar and 90 per cent of the Pakistan team as cricketers who have made their Test debuts as teenagers, I think it's best not to expose youngsters too soon to the very top. It's far better to identify young talent and then condition them physically and mentally. Australia seems to be doing it best of all at the moment. The physical stresses of contemporary international cricket with it's densely scheduled one-dayers and Test matches and its need for all-round athleticism play havoc with everyone's fitness and physique. Let alone that of a young fast-bowler whose body doesn't stop developing until his early twenties. You see it happening time and time again, particularly among the young Pakistani pacemen, their hips, backs, shoulders simply give up under the strain of desperately wanting to be like Wasim and Waqar. As do Wasim's and Waqar's under the strain of needing to be 'Wasim and Waqar'. In England too, during my 1995 season at Kent it was startling to hear of all the injuries that my team-mates Alan Igglesden, Martin McCague and Dean Headley had suffered throughout their careers. At various stages of their career they couldn't bowl properly for months and months at a time. To still be bowling fast at 30 was considered a triumph by them. Fast bowling just isn't a natural activity. A young man's body needs to develop in so many ways to ensure he can withstand the stresses and strains that come from torquing one's body with such velocity. And ferocious spinners of the ball like Mushtaq Ahmed and Shane Warne have shown that slow-bowlers' bodies aren't immune to injury either. Ironically, I who had chosen to concentrate on my batting rather than my bowling as a youngster (bowling seemed too much like hard work and batting offered more immediate glories), found myself at the age of 19 with my right leg in plaster as a result of over-running. And I didn't even like running singles that much.

CHAPTER SEVEN

The team stayed on in Australia for a mini-world cup, The Benson and Hedges World Championship of Cricket, a one-day tournament which I was desperately disappointed to miss. It would have meant more exposure to the top of world cricket, it would have meant more opportunities to learn and impress. And doing well in that competition would have solidified my place in the team. Invalided back to Sri Lanka to recuperate, I took up a course of upper-body weight training in order to compensate for the enforced layoff from physical activity and to counteract the pounding of home cooking.

A long-term injury does give you plenty of time for reflection. Off the treadmill of play, practice, travel, play and practice, away from the distractions and indulgences of one's team-mates, you get a chance to think about the things you've experienced. I replayed all my dismissals of course and tried to figure out how I could have done better and I thought about our opponents. Back in Australia, apart from Viv Richards, I had seen up close other greats in their prime: Gordon Greenidge, Desmond Haynes and Allan Border. Though their one-day innings did not reveal all that was remarkable about their game what set them apart from their team-mates was their ability and the composure in the way they approached each game. If they were tied down by good bowling and fine fielding, they wouldn't fret but simply continue to meet the ball with the middle of the bat and if even their conventional scoring avenues dried up, they'd simply wait for the right ball to hit over the top. They knew what they could do. They'd been everywhere, and seen and done everything; even if they hadn't, they knew they could. They were supremely confident. Especially against us! We Sri Lankans on the other hand, because we were new to every occasion and experience and because we were playing 'Test Matches' and 'One-Day Internationals', would go into bat expecting international bowlers to bowl their best wicket-taking deliveries every ball. Subconsciously resigned to losing almost every game we played in, our occasional successes surprised even us. Sidath Wettimuny would keep saying about our opponents, 'they're only human'. But so were we.

Man for man, I'm sure that we too had the ball-playing, hand-eye/limb co-ordination of our more internationally illustrious opponents, what we didn't have was the mental or physical conditioning. We were amateurs who'd come out of our schools, colleges and offices to represent Sri Lanka. We hadn't been exposed to top-class cricket for long. We hadn't developed our strengths in adversity for long enough, so our talents were necessarily limited. We simply hadn't played enough competitive cricket. We always tried wholeheartedly to give our best but in each contest we'd be the underdogs against some more established collection of stars. We were often excused and even pitied our short-comings by our opponents and even by our supporters. Pretty soon it seemed that we acquired a 'Noble Loser Complex'. None of us liked losing, but it is in our nature as a race to smile at most anything, even through the feelings of a defeat. The trick was to turn from good losers, all dignified and deserving of sympathy, into good winners, all charisma, style and deserving of praise. A major weakness back then was a lack of fierce athletic wildness; we almost never effected spectacular run-outs, rarely took great catches, never went hurtling into boundary boards, never blasted out opponents with pace. We were most unintimidating. Even our paceman Rumesh Ratnayake's hitting of John Wright and Larry Gomes in the face, off deliveries that lifted sharply off a length, was explained in John Wright's case by doubts about Rumesh's slinging action and in Larry Gomes's case by a combination of a suspect action and a dodgy pitch. Thus even our hostility wasn't perceived to be genuine. Rumesh's fainting at the sight of all the blood streaming from John Wright's nose didn't do his image as a fast bowler much good either.

But the fishing was great even if we didn't catch anything. It was a thrill for us juniors, and a vindication for the seniors, to be playing Test cricket and we enjoyed the competition even though we weren't always very competitive. And with each game we became just that little bit better. Over the years I've learnt just as much by chatting with other internationals as I've done by playing the game. I would soak up everything I could from conversations with, and observations of, the all-time greats of the game who played the game then. Imran, Border, Lloyd, Gavaskar, Hadlee, Javed, Viv, Haynes, Greenidge, Kapil — I'd listen and absorb and then find a way to work their attitudes and practices to my game. Improvement doesn't happen overnight, but if a player does nothing else but think to himself 'how would the cricketer I admire most handle this situation?' then he will inevitably improve his performance.

Sri Lanka on tour has always been subject to countless invitations from Lankan diplomats and expatriate family and friends to whom we represent a heart-warming connection with the homeland, so our time to mix with our opponents outside of matchdays and official events is always limited. And when we're not playing, practising, or being social ambassadors from back home, we're shopping. But just in a few minutes of chat with someone like Clive Lloyd, who embodied a mastery of the modern game, one would get some useful career-boosting advice. He himself could murder all kinds of bowling. He'd been playing first-class cricket for almost twenty years, and he said as his game had developed, so had the bowlers': it was a never-ending battle for supremacy. So at the start of each season, Clive Lloyd said, he looked for something new to do in order to make himself a better player in the campaign ahead. Later when I captained the team in England during our 1991 tour, Clive Lloyd came into our dressing-room at Lord's during the Test and said something which gave us all great heart. We were always just a little behind England in that match, and went on to lose a Test which we could just as easily have won. Clive Lloyd said that Sri Lanka of 1991 were just like the West Indies in 1975–76 when they went to Australia and lost a six-Test series 5–1with players like Greenidge, Lloyd, Richards and Roberts. And since June 1975 they had actually been the world's first World Cup champions. Like the West Indies were then, he said, Sri Lanka were full of talent but had no mental or physical fitness. 'Calypso cricketers' the apparently happy-go-lucky West Indies were often called, in reference to their perceived lack of appetite for a fight. And yet those self-same West Indians went on to conquer the world. They showed what could be done with a burning hunger to succeed.

It is quite simple. The further you get in this game the harder you have to work to stay there. Nets and drills can be really boring but in order to get better this is what one has to do. There's only one way to improve performance and that is to practice and work on one's weaknesses. In my case, and for too many team-mates, the problem was mental discipline. By this I mean not just the need to occupy the crease for long periods, but the lack of the proper thought process that meant thinking through being beaten by deliveries or being marooned on a stagnant score, to stay focused on making a significant contribution to the cause. Not many of us had the concentration involved in waiting for the bad ball. We'd fidget and fret and self-destruct from the knowledge that we were incapable of lasting for too long out in the middle, so we may as well go down attacking. In my case this attitude was compounded by being told to go out and play my natural game. On debut and for some considerable time after, I was the 'baby' of the side. I was a mercurial talent whom the selectors unleashed just to see what he would accomplish this day that he hadn't yesterday. I gained selection by playing shots, I was in the team to play shots. I could play shots that no one else could or dared to. I was not relied on, I carried no responsibility. And when I failed, as I sometimes did, the failure was seen as inevitable in the nature of things. Even Viv only made a decent score every so often and he saved them for when it mattered, I'd tell myself. I wasn't worried by failure. My out was just a result of mistiming the ball: my talent was undiminished, and I could just as easily score a big one the next game. The games we play with ourselves . . .

It simply wasn't in my nature to admit a weakness. If talent is being able to middle the ball, skill is being able to beat the fielders; I thought I had sufficient talent, skill and self-belief to get by and the selectors apparently had plenty of faith in me. But it isn't enough to have natural talent, not when you're playing against the best in the world. That time away from the team in early 1985, perhaps it was through being isolated, perhaps it was a result of just realising how short a cricketing career could be, perhaps it was just another inevitable step in my maturing process, but I started to really turn in on myself and think about what I had learnt. There had also arisen an unbreachable barrier between myself and my friends back home who hadn't played international cricket. In response to their questions of what it was like to face Holding, Garner, Marshall etc etc, I couldn't satisfactorily explain things to them. I was still trying to work things out for myself. Whenever I went out with them to practice, I felt like a fifth wheel. I knew what I wanted to be: a top-class batsman, a world-class batsman, someone fit to rub shoulders with Richards, Gavaskar, Border, Mendis and Dias; I just didn't know too much about how. I thought about nothing else but cricket. I wanted to be a successful cricketer. Cricket was No. 1 and everything else took a back seat. For sure I didn't want to work in an office and get a proper job. I think that what life is for, if it is for anything, is to find out what you do well, and then do it for your soul's sake, before its too late. I was better at cricket than anything else. Life is richest when body, mind and voice are used to the fullest. I wasn't an ego-maniac by any means, but I had to put myself first in order to have the joy, the pride, the pain and the pleasure of a life fully engaged every day. Anyway, being a cricketer looked like a great way to spend a life: doing what I loved while the rest of the world had to work.

Once the shin-bone had completely healed, I had a chance to test my revitalised commitment to cricket against the touring Pakistan U-23 team. It was a mark of the Board of Control for Cricket in Sri Lanka in those days that all levels of top-class competition were found for Sri Lanka's cricketers. And that particular Pakistani team was pretty strong. Salim Malik, Ramiz Raja and Wasim Akram had already played Tests and one-day internationals, and Ijaz Ahmed and Manzoor Elahi were to go on to full honours also. Salim and Ramiz at this stage were almost the complete article; Salim in particular played with a breathtaking ease. He was neat, quick and correct, and into position for every stroke very early. All that and an itch to take the attack to the bowlers. Wasim came to Sri

Lanka fresh from making a name for himself against New Zealand and Australia down under. Those of the team that had seen him spoke of Wasim's lightning-fast bouncer ripping through top-line batsmen's defences. Apparently one played Wasim with the splice as much as with the middle of the bat. At U-23 level, Pakistan and Sri Lanka were actually two quite evenly-matched teams both packed with batsmen. Arjuna Ranatunga, Roshan Mahanama, Asanka Gurusinha, Hashan Tillekeratne, Roshan Jurangpathy and Sumithra Warnakulasuriya (son of my old coach Mr Charlie Warnakulasuriya) all played major parts through the representative games, one-dayers and 'Tests'. Rain unfortunately played a major part too, but we managed to win the last 'Test' by an innings to take the series. Through the series Pakistan and Sri Lanka saw enough of each other to reinforce our preconceived notions of what the two countries' cricketers would be like. We had big-spinners and above-average batsmen, and Pakistan had middle-order batsmen and fast bowlers capable of turning games on their head. As and when the mood took them.

The Test team's next opponents were India, whom we played in three epic Tests at home in August and September of 1985. India at this time were not renowned for winning Tests, and had even suffered a shock series defeat at the hands of the touring Englishmen the previous winter, but we knew that Sri Lanka would have a tough contest against them. In a side packed with batsmen – Sunil Gavaskar, Dilip Vengsarkar, Mohinder Armanath, Kris Srikkanth, Ravi Shastri, Kapil Dev and Mohammed Azharuddin – India were quite capable of huge totals.

The retreating monsoon weather of the late summer months made for some interesting wickets and in the first Test it was our bowlers who were able to exploit the greenish track at the Tamil Union ground better than the Indians, Kapil Dev notwithstanding. Asantha De Mel, Rumesh Ratnayake and Saliya Ahangama (in his debut Test) all bowled well. Reducing India to 65 for 5, thanks to some fine bowling by the seamers, we then kept things very tight until India recovered, run by run, to 218 all out. Sunil Gavaskar held them together with a patient 50, until he was run out attempting to keep the strike towards the end of their innings. Conditions favoured us during our innings and our middle order of Ranjan Madugalle and Arjuna and Duleep all made sizeable scores, with Ranjan and Arjuna both notching centuries. We took a decent first innings lead and by the end of the fourth day India were four wickets down for a lead of about twenty runs. Rumesh again bowled very well, beating the opener Rajput with one that lifted and then just three balls later, he deceived Sunil with his slower ball: Sunil haplessly spooning a catch into the covers. The bulk of India's batting might yet have to come, but with Sunil's wicket, we knew that we'd forced open the door to victory. There could only be one winner in this Test match and for once, overnight the team-talk was of attack, attack and attack. 'Put the ball in the right place and the Indian batsmen will fall.' On the last day however, two hours of play were lost to rain. On resumption of play Rumesh took three quick wickets and we were right back in it. Azharuddin with three hundreds in his first three Tests, had his run broken here in his fourth but try as we might, we couldn't shift Vengsarkar. His last-wicket stand with Maninder Singh crucially ate up the clock. And every single run they scored just added to the total we'd have to chase when it came to our turn to bat at the end of the day. If we did get to bat. Maninder's stand with Vengsarkar took up 45 minutes for 22 runs until Maninder was finally bowled by Saliya, leaving Dilip on 98 not out. It had been a decisive stand. Our winning target was now 123 in 11 overs. A rate of about two runs a ball.

Because I was still the kid of whom not much was expected, I batted at No. 7 or 8 throughout the series apart from in special circumstances, like the second innings here, where I went in first with Duleep. A whirlwind innings was needed, and whirlwinds were my speciality. I hooked Kapil first ball for a big 6, so we were up with the rate from the start with room to spare. Duleep then hit two blazing cover drives to leave us, at the end of the first over, contemplating a gettable target. And India with seven men on the boundary. But then three quick wickets were lost in the space of eight deliveries and in spite of Arjuna's efforts, the chase was called off with three overs to go with us on 61 for 4. A Test we could have won given just another hour. We'd made all the running from the first ball; we'd batted well, fielded superbly and bowled even better only to be beaten by Sri Lanka's weather. To come so close to our first ever Test victory . . .

All too often in those days we flattered to deceive, a good performance being just a lightning flash that briefly revealed the range of our talents rather than the promise of continued good form. Class is permanent, form is temporary as the saying goes. In this series the Test schedule worked in our favour for just two days after the first Test ended, the second Test began at the Colombo P. Saravanamuttu Oval. The Indians having lost twenty wickets within three days just a few days earlier, would have had very little time to regroup. And our bowlers and batsmen were on a roll. The victory we should have gained at the SSC, we had at the P. Sara.

Duleep won the toss and elected to bat. Opening, Amal Silva batted into the second day for a gritty 111, Ranjan Madugalle made a fine 54, Roy fell just short of a well-deserved century. Duleep made a typically commanding fifty too, until he fell to the golden arm of Mohinder 'Jimmy' Amarnath. I came in six wickets down with the score at 372, with instructions to push it along prior to a declaration later on the second day. So I made a brisk 2. We were all out for 385: a little below expectations, but we had made our runs quickly and at least had the chance to attack India sooner rather than later. And attack we did. India were straightaway 3 down for just 3 runs, Rumesh and Asantha doing the damage. Amal Silva held a beauty low-down to his right to dismiss the opener Rajput, Rumesh beat Dilip Vengsarkar with one that left him, and Azharuddin was caught behind as soon as he came in. But Srikkanth held firm, all guns blazing. He scored the bulk of the Indians' runs, as Amarnath made a slow and watchful start. Srikkanth was watchful too. He'd watch the ball as it left the bowler's hand and he'd watch the ball as it left his bat to go to the boundary. By the time he was out to a miscued cut, India had recovered to 79 and he'd scored three-quarters of the runs. Sunil then came to the wicket and between lunch and tea, with Amarnath and Gavaskar at both ends, and in spite of Duleep attacking with all the bowling combinations and field placings he could muster we were given a masterclass in back-to-the-wall batting. Amarnath and Sunil played each ball exactly on its merits, they took no risks, played no false shots, and kept the scoreboard ticking over.

Apparently this kind of patient, non-bravado innings was quite alien to someone like Jimmy Amarnath. He had a reputation for relishing fast-bowling, standing up to the quicks and playing hooks and cuts whenever invited. I know that Imran really rated him and so did the West Indians after he'd taken them on in the Caribbean a couple of years previously. Before this series against us, Roy Dias, who knew him well, said that Jimmy was an 'all or nothing batsman'. Within a Test series he'd either make a string of brilliant hundreds or fail spectacularly. (I should have asked him the cause for this trend, it might have saved me from initially repeating it.) During this series against us and particularly in the first innings of the Oval Test, Jimmy played with uncharacteristic caution. His stance was a little cramped and very square on, a hooker's stance. But we weren't giving him anything to hook. So he made do with thrusting his front pad down the pitch and working the ball through leg.

Jimmy's ruggedness made a fine contrast in style with Sunil. Dapper, economical of movement, left elbow often rising high above his head, Sunil with the softest of hands, would block the short-pitched ball to let it fall softly to his feet: he was grace and dignity personified. From having been the world's premier opening batsman for so long, Sunil had started to drop down the order for one reason or another, but how he could still punish anything short outside the off-stump and how he could alternately punch and caress the ball through the leg-side! It was an education to watch him. And always the ball was kept on the ground. I saw the way he played the leg-glance and tried for months after to play it just the way he did. I'd stand in front of a mirror, bat in hand, and with mimicry of footwork, flicking wrists and flourishing follow-through, attempt to perform the leg-glance just in the way I'd seen Sunil play it. He had so many ways of playing a ball on leg stump, so many ways of beating the field. We see the great batsmen on-drive square of the wicket to the boundary and think of leg-side deliveries as easy pickings, but in reality it is the relative ease of the leg-side strokes that makes them so fraught with danger for the batsmen. It is so much easier to get the head over the ball on the off-side: it's there in the first place anyway. But the slightest loss of balance on the leg-side, as trunk and shoulders swivel to bring the bat through the leg-side, and the ball can easily go into the air. Try and underplay the stroke, and you can end up missing the ball entirely. So many times Sunil proved that there is no power without control. At the crease he has had the strongest powers of concentration of any batsman I have ever seen. When he was batting you could tell that he wanted to bat for ever, or at least for as long as it took for India not to lose a Test match. You always felt that nothing but a very good ball would get him out.

So it was a great surprise when Sunil was stumped off Arjuna's bowling late on the afternoon of the third day of this Test match. Apparently he'd only ever been stumped once before in all his hundred or so Tests! India were all out for 244 early on the morning of fourth day, giving us a lead of 141. Naturally the plan for our second innings was for quick runs to give us a lead of about 350 to insure us against any thunderous heroics from the all-star Indian bats and to give us sufficient time to bowl India out for a second time. Things went well for us again. I was sent in first wicket down midway through the afternoon session to 'push it along', but ironically took half an hour to get off the mark. My excuse: Roy came into bat soon after too, and I deferred to the senior batsman as he kept pinching the strike. After tea, bolstered by some ginger cake and a few words from the manager, Mr Fuard, I found my touch and went quickly to 75 (my first Test fifty) before Ravi Shastri bowled me with a quicker one as I stepped back to play a cut. Roy was undefeated at the declaration, which came just into the final hour of scheduled play. India's target: 348 in a day and a bit.

India survived intact until close of play, but soon after the start on the final day, Rajput the Indian opener was given out lbw to Asantha de Mel's off-cutter. Two balls later at other end, Srikkanth fell lbw to Rumesh and then Dilip Vengsarkar was caught behind for 0. The win was on! Azhar and Sunil then batted on to lunch and were well into the afternoon session before both were caught behind in quick succession. Then, fielding at short square leg, I managed to hold on to a reflex catch off Rumesh to dismiss Amarnath. Six wickets down. Never allowed to settle, Ravi Shastri didn't find it too easy out there: seven down. Kapil Dev then started being Kapil Dev and made attack his team's defence. The leg-spinner Sivaramakrishnan gave him some support and again with the clock being eaten away, we were starting to think back to India's escape a week earlier. We started becoming a little too anxious. The ball became just a little slippery in the bowler's and fielders' hands. And Kapil swashbucklingly punished anything loose. The bat was a sword in his hands. The speed and number of runs he scored were irrelevant – until we got him out, we wouldn't win. The crowd by now had swelled to large proportions with children coming straight from school and people leaving work early to be present at this imminently epochal moment. Even President Junius Jayawardene cancelled all official appointments and came to watch the play.

The scheduled last twenty overs began, and Rumesh came charging into Kapil. One wicket was all that stood between us and Sri Lanka's first Test victory. A victory against India who lose so few Test matches. A victory against India who had such a long history of Test cricket. One wicket between us and our coming of age as a Test-playing nation. Rumesh's second delivery of this over was just a fraction short of Kapil's driving length. And, it was his slower ball. Kapil picked it up just a fraction too late to check his full-blooded swing. The ball was hit back firmly. Rumesh following through, changing direction to his right, dived full-length to take a terrific catch. We had won. Pandemonium. Fireworks erupted in my soul. The crowd rushed on to the field, horns and hooters started blaring, steel-drums started their calypso beats. We were chaired off the pitch. Even Kapil Dev. Why? Because he was Kapil Dev. The victory would have been less lustrous without him. Back in the dressing room we hugged each other and cried and hugged each other all over again. The dressing-room became awash with beer and soft-drinks. Rumesh didn't let go of the match ball throughout, he must have been holding it ever since Kapil had hit it back to him. Somewhere in his possession there must still be a beer-doused cricket-ball bearing the imprint of a thousand fingers. What a trophy! The room soon became filled with everyone who'd ever represented Sri Lanka – and Ceylon – through the years. The current team was delighted of course, but the veterans were overjoyed. The country was on the map. This 'First Test Victory' meant more to the ex-players and older generation of cricket followers than it did to us. The baila songs of Sri Lanka were never sung more loudly, except maybe, just maybe, after the World Cup win. It felt good to see my father in the thick of the celebrations at the stadium.

Arjuna, Amal Silva, Ranjan Madugalle, Rumesh and I always thought that we would win Test matches as we became older and the team developed winning ways. But for those like Duleep, Sidath, and Roy who had played cricket for so long and had for so many years aspired to play

'Test Cricket', to now be part of a team to win a Test was more than a dream come true. It was a vindication of their cricketing careers. Our first Test victory after four and half years of trying was an epochal moment for the nation. We knew we had a right to belong amongst the elite. Sri Lanka's first Test victory had come in our 14th Test Match. India's had come in their 25th, New Zealand's in their 45th. As an emerging nation, we were ahead of schedule. Following the excesses of victory it was quickly pointed out in the sober light of morning, that winning our first series was very important too. We knew the Indians had been stung, and they'd come back at us good and hard in the last Test of the series. Gavaskar, Vengsarkar, Kapil Dev, Shastri: these are particularly proud men.

The third Test was played up at Kandy on the typically good cricket strip which the beautiful Asgariya ground produces. India won the toss and batted and while they were always threatening to make a big score, with almost all the batsmen getting a good start, they were only able to make 249. Roger Binny came into the Indian side for this Test and though he didn't actually take many wickets, he did a great job for them by keeping things tight, forcing us to take chances against the other Indian bowlers. We didn't do too well and had a second innings deficit of 50 or so. The Indians sensed their chance now, and on the third and fourth days piled on the runs. Ravi Shastri opened in this Test, and although he showed himself capable over the years of scoring runs at any position in the order, I always felt he performed best as an opener. His height and reach and deftness off his hips, combated the standard openers' diet of short-of-a-length bowling very well and once he was set, he could absolutely murder slow bowling. And he liked the extra responsibility. He and Amarnath had a pretty big partnership, Ravi getting out close to his 100 and Jimmy going on to an undefeated century at India's declaration. Given a day and a bit by Kapil Dev to score just under 380 to win the match and/or survive the Indian bowling, we realised that the fate of the series depended on what we did over the next 100 overs.

We lost two quick wickets before the close of play on the fourth day, however, and at the score of 34 for 3 on the final morning, Duleep joined Roy at the crease. If either of them fell quickly, the game was as good as lost. I've written earlier that it was a great shame that Roy and Duleep didn't enjoy a greater number of long partnerships, because in this innings at Kandy they showed just how good they could be together. In almost no time at all they raced to a century partnership during which Duleep first, then Roy very next ball, notched up their 1000 runs in Tests for Sri Lanka. Midway through the afternoon session, such was Duleep and Roy's progress, thoughts of a Lankan win were being entertained. The 200 run partnership came up shortly before tea. Roy reached his hundred, an innings of dash and panache. At this point, as son-of-an-accountant-therefore-arbiter-of-run-rate to whom all dressing-room maths was referred, I reckoned that in order to win we needed a run a minute/four an over for the remainder of the scheduled play.

The story of Sri Lankan cricket would never be complete without a run-out or two and just as the push for victory was really revving up, Roy was run out by Azhar going for a tight single. Arjuna then played on first ball, and Duleep went soon after for 124. Six wickets down, almost an hour and a half to go, and not much batting to come. And we still needed the small matter of a hundred runs to win. I realised I wasn't out there anymore to win the game, but to save it. In situations like those if you show the opposition that your only thought is defence, they go all out for the attack and your job of survival becomes even harder. So I played some shots, a couple of hooks perhaps a little too close to Ravi Shastri's fingertips on the boundary's edge at square leg. Only six runs each time but it got the point across. There was fight left in us. At this rate, a win for Sri Lanka was still possible. Asantha de Mel was at the crease with me and as senior player and prime bowler, he kept telling me that he hadn't bowled his heart and soul out over the past three weeks just so that India could spoil the party at the last minute. If we both stayed in, we'd not only save the Test, we'd win the series. We stayed in. A small not out like this was better than anything else I'd yet done in Tests. It was great to be embraced by Duleep and Roy back in the pavilion.

The series had been a triumph for all of us. Asantha and Rumesh had bowled us to victory, Amal Silva had a blinder behind the stumps, we'd taken some great catches and all the batsmen had made runs. Arjuna coming on with his floaters when Sunil and Amarnath were coasting in the second Test, for Sunil to be stumped, was instrumental in turning the decisive second Test irrevocably our way. And then with our backs to the wall, Duleep and Roy had transformed the third Test from a losing situation into a near victory. Having played our first competitive series where each day had seen an escalation in pressure, we were really starting to understand what Test cricket was about. It wasn't about brief flashes of potential and cameos of brilliance and being content with showing what you could do. It was about results. Winning Tests was about weathering storms, looking to strike home advantages; never going down for the count, hanging in there, soaking up pressure, deflecting opposing thrusts, counter-attacking calmly and methodically whenever possible; playing to a plan, analysing opponents, working out their strengths and weaknesses and acting accordingly. We had learned the best of lessons the best of ways. We had learned by doing.

CHAPTER EIGHT

Our next Tests were away to Pakistan. They were going to present us with a tougher test than India for two reasons: pace and spin/Imran Khan and Abdul Qadir. Abdul was a certified match-winner and could be quite devastating on Pakistani wickets. Imran was playing in Pakistan for the first time in over two years following the stress fracture of his left shin; you just knew that he'd be keen to show his home fans that he was still the fearsome fast bowler of old, particularly in northern Pakistan where so much of our matches were to be played. As a batting side too, Pakistan were at least the equal of India. Pakistan are always hard to play against. There is always a real sense on their part of 'us' and 'them'. It isn't really arrogance, it is just that they feel they can behave and play in the way they wish on the cricket field and nothing anyone says or does can deflect them from their purpose. And when questioned, they retreat behind their particular cultural and linguistic thresholds whenever it suits them. Playing and winning on their terms was the only thing that mattered to them. Whenever Imran was captain of Pakistan he gave the impression, particularly in his later years, that he felt he had the God-given right to lead Pakistan to victory against anybody. And some of us were particularly conscious of the fact that certain Pakistanis felt that Sri Lanka were put on the Test map purely to be beaten.

More so than against any other country, Sri Lanka would always raise its game to play Pakistan, so that made our most high-profile losses to them all the more painful. We lost very close games against Pakistan in the 1987 and 1992 World Cup and the 1988 Asia Cup and 1989 Nehru Cup, games which we should have won, games which would have significantly affected the outcome of those tournaments. In each case we lost because we didn't know how to win, didn't know what to do when we were cruising down the home straight. Pakistan have always known how to either lose abjectly or win heroically, and throughout my career they have been the most consistently watchable cricket team.

Semi-finals have a knack of producing the most intense matches of a tournament. And a game that many reading this book will have seen, would be the epic 1992 World Cup semi-final between New Zealand and Pakistan at Eden Park. A game distinguished by Martin Crowe's assured century and Inzamam's phenomenal 11th hour rescue of Pakistan when Pakistan were so far behind the clock that they'd have had to cross the international date-line just to get close to the Kiwi score. The game was significant for me because it contained the cleverest innings I have ever seen and taught me that, as a leading batsman if you are there to the end your team will win. It taught me a great deal. And it changed the way I played the game for sure. Javed's run-a-ball fifty paced out over half the Pakistan innings made it possible for Inzamam to perform his late heroics. Javed stole the game from New Zealand in broad daylight and they didn't know it until it was too late. He performed with such smartness. Whenever Imran led the Pakistanis, Javed pushed from behind. It was like in those Western movies of cattle drives and cavalry processions, where John Wayne would lead from the front, and with him would be his trusty lieutenant riding up and down the line checking that all the unit was moving in the right direction to their destination. He made an awful lot of noise on the cricket pitch did Javed, but it was all in the cause of doing good for his team. If I had to choose one batsman to bat for my life, it would be Javed Miandad. He'd fight all the way to the end.

In my first meeting with Imran, in Peshawar in October 1985, he came out the distinct winner. Opening the innings in the first one-day international, he had me caught behind in the first over of our innings for no score. In fact throughout our tour, of all the Pakistan bowlers, Imran took my wicket most often. I always wanted to make runs against him, because runs against a great bowler were more rewarding than any other kind. I would always especially try to attack anyone who was rated. This attitude was my downfall and my triumph in the early part of my career. If there had been any doubts as to Imran regaining the pace that he enjoyed prior to his injury they were pretty much quelled as he raced in and unleashed his trademark leap to the crease prior to firing in a thunderbolt. He was back and he was quick. Imran was predominantly an inswing bowler to the right-hander, with a regular vicious 'inshoot' (one that jagged back off the seam). And you'd always have to be ready for the one that went the other way. Typically he'd be at your throat or at the stumps, with the bouncer that followed you being particularly difficult to play. In Peshawar, Imran actually bowled one that straightened after pitching, and I got the thinnest of outside edges. First blood to Imran, and first blood to Pakistan as they beat us in the first one-dayer quite comfortably.

Imran posed a different challenge from the other pacemen I'd faced in Australia the previous year as, not only was he fast, he could also be relied upon to move the ball in the air or off the pitch in almost any conditions. And with the old ball too, especially with the old ball. This was an art beyond the other bowlers on the international stage at that time. Along with the still-improving Wasim, he had already developed the art of what is now called 'reverse swing'. While the West Indies were winning world-wide with acutely angled pace bowling, Imran was the sole practitioner of the 'reverse swing' phenomenon in the early 1980s. With Sarfraz Nawaz (himself predominantly a seam-bowler) winding down, Pakistan had no one of Imran's pace or control to partner him. And with Abdul Qadir taking a swag of wickets whenever Imran didn't, 'reverse swing' wasn't yet established in the consciousness as a genuine match-winning force to be reckoned with. Imran then suffered his stress fracture and was out of the Pakistan attack for two years until he made his comeback to spearhead the bowling with Wasim Akram. In Wasim, Imran found a partner of pace, whip and venom who was keen to soak up everything the great man could teach him. And with Waqar Younis emerging at the end of the 1980s, Pakistani scimitar-swerve fast bowling started to play havoc with the world's batsmen. If you survived the opening salvoes with the new ball and then managed to prevail against the spinners and second-line quicks in the afternoon session, just when you thought that the bowlers would be struggling with a softening ball and fatigue, you'd then have a refreshed Imran, Wasim and Waqar to contend with in the final overs of the day, all of whom could make a ragged ball behave most alarmingly.

There can never be any doubt about Imran's competitive fires, for he would often bowl while carrying strains that would have incapacitated lesser athletes. We noticed however, in this series and in other series against us in subsequent years, how Imran perfected the art of the strategic running repair whereby, having bowled a spell or two with the new ball and done his fair share of fielding, Imran would discover the pressing need for some physiotherapy or at least a shower prior to his ultimate burst with a ball ready to reverse swing. Imran would do this particularly when he played in Sri Lanka, where at 3 p.m. on a blazingly hot day, bowling fast on a batsman friendly wicket can really seem a low-reward occupation. At five o'clock in the afternoon when as a batsman the sweat was running down in streams from your helmet, when your foam and polyester covered body was screaming for air, when your feet were swimming in your boots, you always looked with some amazement, envy and hostility at Imran's ability to not only make the old ball swerve but also for his ability to come back on to the field as crisp and as fresh as a newly-minted 100 rupee note. How very much you wanted to score boundaries off Imran at those times, how very much you didn't want to give him the satisfaction of getting you out.

Plenty has been written about the ins and outs of reverse swing. That it wasn't really noticed until Imran's inheritors, Wasim and Waqar destroyed England in Pakistan's 1992 tour, just shows the power of the

English media to pursue a story and grab on to it like a dog with a juicy bone. However, the bone only has relevance when it is thrown at them. The fact is, 'reverse swing' has been around for a long time. And we international batsmen have been wise to it. From my point of view, a bowler doing something with the ball and posing me new challenges, doesn't bother me one bit. I love the challenge of good bowling. It always gave me far greater satisfaction to make a score against top-line bowling. You play Test cricket to do your best against the best. Winning is a by-product of performing well. What does concern the 'union of batsmen' however, is when a bowler is doing something to the ball. Specifically applying jagged-edged bottle-tops and fingernails, bootspikes and the like on the surface of the ball can bias conditions in favour of the bowler at the expense of the batsman and the spirit of the game. That reverse swing can be delivered without resorting to artificial stimulants to the ball, has been proven by many bowlers around the world. It has much to do with weighting down one side of the ball with sweat and spit so that it is biased to move towards one side. What made Pakistan unique for a long time, was that they alone had the bowlers of pace and control to consistently wreak havoc. And in Wasim and Waqar, Imran had two young men who sucked up his teachings (developed from Sarfraz), as if they were mother's milk. The ability to deliver the lethal yorker became second nature to them. Wasim slicing and dicing it both ways from around and over the wicket, it's like batting against Zorro.

In my first encounters with Imran and Wasim what became apparent was how much care the Pakistani team would take over the condition of the ball. As soon as the ball reached a Pakistani fielder over the rough scuffing outfield he'd start rubbing sweat onto the ball, polishing only one side vigorously until it got back to Imran or Wasim who'd then look at it and perhaps apply some finishing touches. Sixty overs of this and the cricket ball, now biased in weight to one side, did start to behave unconventionally. The shiny side of the ball pointing to the right-hander's on-side has traditionally meant that the bowler is attempting to bowl an outswinger; in Imran's, Wasim's and later Waqar's hands, it meant the reverse. And at 80-90 mph, it meant the ball swung devilishly late at a fullish length. Waqar was so very dangerous when he first burst on to the scene in 1989–1990, getting noticeably quicker and more skilled every time you faced him. And when a season or so later he had mastered his slower ball, he was all but guaranteed to take wickets every time he played. All calculated aggression and venomous confidence, at his supreme peak he was a viper of a fast bowler. I am rarely bowled or beaten for pace or even out for a duck, but early on in Waqar's career in a game at Sharjah, he beat me with outright pace. Yorker. Bowled. First ball – 'Waqared'. Whenever we're out, I think that all batsmen walk off thinking what we could have done to have not gotten out in the way we did. On the way back to the dressing-room you replay in your mind's eye what you saw of the delivery in slow motion: direction and length are apparent pretty quickly (you don't just play the ball as it is released from the bowler's hand you get ready to play the ball as it is set up to be released by the bowler in his delivery stride), next the position of the seam and its rotation of the ball are registered, all the while moving into position to play what you think will be the optimum stroke, and then just before the ball reaches you, you commit yourself fully to play the ball. Following a dismissal it hits you halfway between the wicket and the pavilion, the fatal process of mistakes you have made, and you resolve not to repeat it again.

Every mistake that can be made as a batsman, I've made them; sometimes more than once. The important thing is not to make a mistake as a human being by not learning from one's mistakes. On this blisteringly hot Sharjah afternoon I had made no conscious error against Waqar. An inside-edge was no consolation; my bat just didn't come down in time. Sure, I could have primed myself to face a Pakistani cruise missile homing into toes and leg stump and thus taken precautions – by taking guard further up the pitch, by taking guard outside leg-stump, by simply looking to keep the ball out and thus reducing my backlift – but I have never been one to think too much about what a bowler's doing. He should be concerned about what I'm doing! A guy does his best and bests you, you have to accept it. And make your best even better in readiness for the next time. It doesn't matter what level you're playing at, as long as you think you can get better you've got a future in the game.

When you're used to facing 90 mph deliveries and know what to look for, it's not so bad. Even a tailender with a straight-bat and a modicum of common sense can get his bat in the way, or his body out of the road, of a straight one. But swing is highly unpredictable, no two swinging deliveries behave in the same manner even if they land in the same spot on the wicket. What's important is to cover any late movement and play as late as possible. You have to trust to judgement. And luck. And get on the front foot. Wasim and Waqar, while taking most of their wickets with fullish deliveries, have always had the pace to send the batsmen on to the back foot when he least expects it. Wasim in particular, with his ability to make a ball alternatively skid or bounce when landing on a length, can always keep the batsman unsure of how to play him. Of course the batsman first has to gauge what length this master of deception was bowling! And cope with the regular changes of pace that Wasim, like a racing car changing up and down through the gears, goes through. When Wasim was in his pacey prime Viv Richards used to pay him the compliment unique among bowlers, of not hooking his bouncer. Waqar throughout his career predominantly attacked the stumps, accounting for his relatively high runs-per-over as well as his phenomenal wicket-taking strike rate. I have seen some batsmen, Alec Stewart most particularly and also Ajay Jadeja and Anil Kumble in the 1996 World Cup quarter-finals, make a success of facing Waqar by standing inside the crease on leg stump, reducing their backlift and playing with a straight bat through mid-off for the yorkers on the stumps. From this position too, it only takes the slightest touch to glance a ball on your pads away for runs down the leg-side. These two bowlers were smart, however. No sooner had you shown over the course of a session that you had found an effective way to combat them, then next time you faced them, you saw they had come up with variations of their own to try and defeat you.

By the early 1990s there was no doubt. Wasim was the most complete fast bowler in the world. Curtly Ambrose and Courtney Walsh were alternate match-winners for the West Indies and Waqar Younis had the single most devastating delivery in world cricket – his in-swinging yorker. Actually sometimes that yorker didn't need to swing, sheer speed took it through to the stumps before many front-line batsmen had even brought their bats down. Wasim, however, was the bowler who could do a side the most amount of damage simply through the range and variety of his deliveries.

Wasim sometimes bowls slow at the start of his spells, gingerly feeling his body, his shoulder, his groin, his hip, ankle and back, then, if satisfied that all are up to the strain of all the overs he's going to put them through that day he then gradually moves through the gears looking for the rhythm that's such an important part of his performance. All too often, and I speak as an opposition batsman, he finds that lethal combination of speed, swerve and swing. When his body allows him, when he's in the groove, he is quite simply the world's most dangerous bowler. There is nothing he cannot do, no variation he cannot bowl. And at the other end, Pakistan have had Waqar! In the 1992 World Cup final, Wasim bowled the two most amazing balls back to back that I have ever seen and probably will ever see. I viewed them three times. Once at real speed, where I couldn't believe what the ball had done, and consequently was sure that I must have been mistaken in my perception. Cricket balls do not move like that. I next saw these two deliveries twice each in slow-motion when the fall of the wickets were replayed. I could barely have played them in slow motion. The delivery to the well-set Allan Lamb swinging in, pitched on middle on a fullish length and moved away to devastate off-stump. The next ball to new man Chris Lewis, pitched on a length and swung in, to all effects and purposes curving round his thrust-out front pad. Unplayable.

The first Test of our 1985–1986 series against Pakistan was played on a dead Faisalabad wicket which did much to frustrate both Pakistan and ourselves. Only thirteen wickets fell over the five days of the match. Duleep won the toss and elected to bat. Pakistan kept plugging away and we ended the first day five wickets down, with me coming to the crease just before close of play. Arjuna comfortably outscored me for the duration of our partnership the next day, and never looked in much trouble so it was a surprise to see him eventually go to a catch close in off Abdul Qadir. On such a claypit wicket, the slowest I had ever batted on, I wasn't really trusting myself to drive anything that wasn't a half-volley. And it was with considerable relief that I'd launch myself into the occasional loose ball. It was grim, attritional cricket, played out against bowlers who were doing their best to overcome the conditions. I had been concentrating hard all day, and it was with some relief that I found myself 93* at the close of play.

Overnight, a couple of strokes short of my first Test century, I was really very relaxed. I have never been one to get nervous when approaching a landmark, because personal landmarks are pretty much irrelevant. What matters is the team total; my contributions to the score are just a part of the total. Going to the wicket that morning, and seeing Imran take the third new ball of the innings, I reckoned that a short ball in order to sort out my pretensions to join the ranks of batsmen who'd made Test hundreds against Imran, was pretty much on the cards. Sure enough, when I was on 94, a bouncer from Imran came my way. I could do nothing else but hook it for six. The ball cannoned back from the stands at about the same time Imran's flowing locks came to rest in his follow through. He grunted a 'well batted' as Asantha de Mel came down the wicket to shake my hand. I later managed another six off Imran before he had me caught behind. Rumesh then had some fun on his way to a half century before we were all out midway through the third day for 479.

Two wickets fell in the whole Pakistan innings until the last ball of the final day when Ravi Ratneyeke bowled Qasim Omar. For 206. Javed Miandad and Qasim Omar had put on a stand of just under 400; it was a surprise to see Qasim eventually miss a straight one. As for Javed, he could have batted on forever. We never looked like getting him out. Throughout his career Javed's reputation on the circuit was constantly being burnished by tales of his deeds on diabolical wickets and in desperate times for his team, times when the sheer difficulty of the situation brought out the best in him. Without ever being the kind to 'book himself in for bed-and-breakfast' for such somnolence simply bored him and Javed could never abide being bored, on this Faisalabad wicket against our attack, if Pakistan had batted first Javed would have scored 500. He toyed with us, picking off runs whenever he chose, showing us the full range of his inventiveness. A couple of months earlier I had a masterclass in defensive batting from Sunil Gavaskar, now I had a day and a half's lessons from Javed on how to make bowlers feel absolutely worthless. For try as they might, and Rumesh, Ravi and Asantha were not bowling badly (Ravi Ratneyeke went on to take 8 wickets in an innings in the Sialkot Test), our bowlers could do nothing to disconcert Javed. On the contrary, he would disconcert them.

If a bowler's job is to destroy a batsman's timing on the way to taking his wicket, than a batsman's job is to upset a bowler's rhythm, to not allow them to settle into a groove. Javed, by doing nothing more than occasionally taking guard outside the crease, wouldn't let our bowlers settle into any sort of line and length. This on a pitch where anything short would just sit up and beg to be put away. The secret of his phenomenal run-scoring was that he played the ball very, very late. I like to watch the ball onto my bat, striking the ball a little way forward of me. Javed would let the ball get even closer and play it practically from under his moustache. He would keep all options open to the last possible instant, always looking for the most effective way of using his bat to keep the ball away from his stumps and the fielders.

A combination of cool strategic planning and instant technical improvisation, he foxily thought his way to big scores. During Test matches Javed might play and miss on purpose once in a while in the middle of a bowler's spell, or play a false shot just to keep the bowler (whom he had taken a liking to) persevering, prior to whacking him for several fours a little later. Like all the great batsmen, if any bowler actually had him in trouble, he'd never let it show, but would simply play his normal game. He made the bowlers bowl where he wanted them to. He'd score a boundary and then he would unfurl a grin from ear to ear for the sheer joy of it all. And when he got bored of all this, he'd simply play shots that weren't in any textbook, genius shots of a virtuoso kind. Shots like 'backward-drives' to fine leg where he'd simply bring his bat down from in front of him onto a half-volley moving down the leg-side; shots where he'd simply walk around a chest-high delivery and just lean his bat-defended body into the ball to play it behind square; shots like tennis-type dinks angled away for winners, playing with wrists alone to send the ball into untenanted space. He had plenty of big shots too. He could score a hundred in a hundred different ways. At one-day cricket he was an innovator, a trailblazer of strokes. He was brilliant in tight situations. Javed was really good at working the ball just behind square leg; since the rules say that you can only have two fielders behind square on the leg side, he would always look to exploit that area where he could get singles at will. His appetite for runs was insatiable. He never gave up in any situation; he was a real fighter. Arjuna really reminds me of Javed:

they're both very crafty and very shrewd. They're always looking to legitimately exploit every possible weakness in the opposition and maximise their team's chances. They never make uncalculated moves.

The second Test at Sialkot was played on a livelier wicket, one that favoured the pacemen. Imran and Wasim were always going to be difficult to contend with but given our own seamers' record in recent Tests we were confident of doing well. Javed put us in and we struggled to 157 all out, the innings falling away badly after we had been 99 for 3 at one stage. Imran had a decisive spell after lunch when he took three wickets in two overs including me, hit wicket for 2. Going back to a short ball, I slipped (I wasn't wearing spikes, still not favouring them after playing for so many years on matting wickets) and my back heel dislodged a bail. Pakistan made a good start in reply, both openers, Mudassar Nazar and Mohsin Khan, making fifties. But Qasim Omar went for only 1 and then when Javed was on 11, following an attempted drive to a lifting ball from Rumesh, we appealed with great confidence for a caught behind. Javed was the biggest wicket of them all and how we wanted him. The appeal was turned down but the matter didn't end there. The ensuing backchat between the close catchers and Javed became more and more animated. Indeed Arjuna and Javed, two gentlemen not inclined to back down when the legitimacy of their feelings are questioned, had a coming together and it really got very heated for a while. Three times the umpires had to suspend play, as the jagged comments and gibes flew back and forth.

Javed was perfectly within his rights to wait for the umpire's decision and we should have let the matter rest there, no matter what our feelings were of being hard done by. The way we had all been taught to play back in Sri Lanka was to accept the umpire's word as final. But we were playing Tests now and the stakes were much higher. And it always seemed to us, as it seemed to any touring country, in any part of the world, in the days before neutral umpires, that the touring side would always get the worst of the umpires' decisions. Whether we were right or wrong in allowing the situation to provoke our disquiet, what it did show was that we were no longer the Mr Nice Guy Pushovers of international cricket. We were starting to be competitive and hold our own with the professional cricket-playing countries and that manifested itself in all aspects of the game, including appealing. Which could only be good for us in the long run; we see the results in Arjuna's captaincy record to this day.

It took a great effort from Ravi Ratneyeke to hold back Pakistan from gaining a big first innings lead, and his 8 for 83 was the best Sri Lankan bowling performance in Tests until Murali's amazing 9 for 65 against England in 1998. Our second innings fell away however, after a promising start, and from being 100 runs behind Pakistan at the start of our innings, we only finished 100 runs ahead. Pakistan knocked off the winning runs early on in the fourth day for the loss of only two wickets. On a batting wicket at Faisalabad we had done well, but Pakistan had done better. And on a seamer's wicket in Sialkot we had bowled well, but Pakistan had bowled better. This time decisively.

Overall we were improving and were a much better team than that put out in our earlier Tests. The nucleus of the side had picked up a battle-hardness and every experienced cricketer at some time or another was recording their best figures. We were definitely on an upward curve. But we had still lost. And that hurt. The difference between us and this Pakistan team wasn't that great. Granted, Pakistan had the world's leading pace-bowling all-rounder, Imran Khan, and the world's best spinner, Abdul Qadir, and had a couple of run-monsters in their line-up, but they had to be at their best to beat us. The real difference between us and Pakistan, as it had been in our favour between us and India in our previous series, was that Pakistan's batsmen were able to build crucial partnerships in each of their innings. Partnerships which took the games away from us. On good wickets our basic techniques and capabilities would see us through to big scores but on any wickets that favoured bowlers, we'd be in trouble. We would bat against Imran and Wasim and the others thinking that at any time a wicket could fall at the other end and thus play just that little bit more aggressively or defensively to compensate. But the real problem wasn't the batsman at the other end, it was us. We didn't trust ourselves. Negative thoughts can be replaced by an over-positive attitude – trying too hard – which is equally disruptive to smooth performance. This is another aspect by which cricket becomes a game of the mind.

For example, someone like Javed would bat knowing that as long as he didn't get out, no one else was likely to get out. He batted for himself, his partner and his team. For sure he was an extraordinary batsman, but his essential distinguishing characteristic was that he trusted himself and his ability. As did Imran. They had come through so many crises and had prevailed in so many. As they were to continue to do for the remainder of their careers, perhaps most crucially in their do-or-die batting partnerships in the closing matches of the 1992 World Cup. They were high-definition performers, people who could raise their game when the occasion demanded it. All the 'greats' have this ability. It's what makes them great. They all know how to do enough to stop their opponents from performing at their own best. So many times this factor is the difference between winning and losing; the difference between not-winning yet still not-losing; the difference between a refreshing night's sleep or a waking disquiet that makes you wish you were better at the game so that you could protect yourself further from the agony of defeat. If you can't win, then stop the other team from winning. Losing has to hurt in order for winning to mean anything. For me, the pain of defeat far outweighs the joy of victory. I'd rather contribute a decent score in a winning team than a man-of-the-match century in a losing cause. One-day cricket's a simple game: score more runs than the other team and you win. Test cricket has many more permutations. But the enduring objective remains: if you can't win, then make sure you don't lose. And that is something we had yet to learn. I think it takes at least a few defeats, some of them resoundingly heart-wrenching, before it gets drilled into a cricketer's psyche that winning isn't everything but losing is nothing.

I guess I should admit to the fact that even though I was coming of age as a cricketer and a man, having stopped being a teenager during the Faisalabad Test, my mother still felt it necessary that she should accompany me on this tour. Usefully so, because while a professional cricketer needs talent, mental strength and single-mindedness to reach the top, he also needs people that he can talk to and unwind with and who will help to take care of the important things in life for which he has no time. Having someone who you trust, who shows faith in you and gives you confidence, is more valuable than anything else. My mother and father have always been there for me when I have needed them. I can't share everything with them of course, but they have been nothing less than supportive throughout my career. My mother though, to this day, still wishes I had a proper job. So on this tour of Pakistan (then a much harder country to tour than now), while I was still the acknowledged youngster of the side my mother took it upon herself to ensure that the cricket didn't get on top of me. And her presence established a performance trend that continues to this day: if I'm relaxed off the field, I do well on the field.

We had come to Pakistan thinking that we could win one Test out of three, and maybe even share the series. Thus going down in the last Test to a 2-0 series defeat was greatly disappointing. In the same way that a wet racetrack is the ultimate test of a racing driver, so a turning track is the great test of a batsman. I made 105 in the second innings at Karachi in the third Test on a crumbling wicket against Abdul Qadir and Tauseef Ahmed, the highest score of the match, which gave me great satisfaction although it didn't do much to arouse our team manager Mr Abu Fuard. On my way back to the pavilion soon after play resumed on the fourth morning, after getting out with the score at 221 for 9 in the second innings, with our lead at 88, I walked up the steps back to the dressing-room to hear the other Lankan players start to offer their commiserations and congratulations. But Mr Fuard sternly shushed them all and glowered at me. '105 is not enough,' he said. He was right, it wasn't; but it had been the best that I could do against two of the world's best spinners who had been making the ball fizz and pop and turn and squirt this way and that, like a throat-slit chicken in its last throes of life. Sometimes the 'tough-love' admonitions of an authority-figure can indeed inspire you to do better. And for all his regimented running of the team, for all his dictatorial tendencies, I'm sure Mr Fuard wanted the best for the team and Sri Lankan cricket in general. In this instance, however, his publicly expressed disgust was counter-productive. It took all the pleasure out of doing one's best, not just for me, but for the rest of the team.

One of the qualities a cricketer must possess is the capacity to enjoy his cricket. Someone like Mr Fuard, purely by establishing a standard for performance that allowed little or no room for individual expression, could make you seriously question whether there was any point in trying to do your very best as a cricketer when you were damned if you did and damned if you didn't. He unnecessarily alienated many players who, like him, simply wanted the best for Sri Lankan cricket. Maintaining morale should take precedence over everything else when it comes to running a team. In former years too many of our administrators and their hand-picked managers ran the team on partisan lines, showing undue favouritism to the select few that would hang on their every word. A player didn't have to be outstanding to embark on a career in the national side, just compliant with the prevailing winds. That is no recipe for successful management and it certainly doesn't make for a successful team.

Sri Lankans, at the risk of making a gross generalisation but believe me it's true, are essentially young at heart. We respect our elders (of which there are many), but we are also essentially rebellious. We are receptive to fresh ideas but we don't necessarily like being told what to do. And this is the crux of all our problems within society and with the outside world. I once heard Richie Benaud say that leading a team successfully is all about keeping the five players who hate your guts away from the five players who aren't so sure. But we in Sri Lanka are not always so democratic. For a long time, if a player or even his family or associates didn't see eye to eye with a selector, a Board member or the team captain, he was out of consideration for a place in the team. Even Arjuna wasn't initially immune to this syndrome when he first took the captain's reins. Many were the instances of fine players who were discarded and disregarded as soon as they had the nerve to voice an opinion that didn't chime with the powers that be. It leads to a climate of fear and anxiety when a player can lose his place in the team, not for what he does wrong on the field or simply because someone better is waiting in the wings, but because what a player says and does off the field doesn't meet with the approval of the officials. This approval being founded not on any principles of character or deportment, but on principles of toadying and politics.

Whispers and innuendoes, secrets and lies, with pressmen as stooges. The major problem with Sri Lankan cricket in those years (along with our inexperience and lack of mental and physical conditioning) was that we simply weren't able to enjoy our cricket as much as we should. Players who didn't deserve to be were dropped, players who didn't perhaps fully justify selection were picked in their stead. We were a team playing against other countries on the field and the authoritarianism of some of our administrators in the pavilion. Some administrators would bring their off-field battles in commerce, politics and society into the Boardroom and thus look for support from various players, administrators and the Press to gain sway. There were more cliques and claques in 'our' dressing-room than in a coalition government. There were those on the Board who wanted nothing more than advancement for Sri Lankan cricket; there were some on the Board who wanted nothing more than advancement for themselves. A legacy of the days when being associated with cricket had a certain social cachet and when it was thought that only the elite in Colombo society could play the game properly, to certain administrators it sometimes seemed that Sri Lankan cricket didn't matter as much as their need to have their sway. The hoops one had to jump through before one represented Sri Lanka could make us all forget why we first took up the game. Not for the prestige, not for the power, not for fame and money and not for the chance to make connections, but simply because we loved playing cricket.

I loved cricket, cricket was my life, so I loved life. Buddhist philosophy has it that when a man tries with the gifts bestowed on him by nature to fulfil himself, he is doing the highest thing he can do, the only thing that has any meaning. After an unspectacular start at international level, my batting seemed to have built up an authority that was pulling me forward with excitement. I realized that I wasn't just playing cricket for cricket's sake any more, nor for the prizes a high-profile performance brought along (in this case a Honda CRX sports-coupé from my parents to mark my first Test century), nor even for the sake of fulfilling some of the ambitions formed after 1981. I was playing cricket for Sri Lanka because Sri Lanka wanted me to. I had a purpose in life, a cause. My life had meaning. When you play for yourself, the audience or the record book and don't play for your team-mates, you might be 'successful' but your team won't be. The best measure of success: playing to the needs of the team. The team is what matters. Always. I only really fully understood this eight years after my international debut: since then my performances have become much more consistent. Once the Sri Lankan team became better, so did I. Once I became better, so did the team. That's the secret of our current success.

CHAPTER NINE

The return series against Pakistan, in Sri Lanka early in 1986, saw more gutsy and resolute performances from us, though going by our performance in the first Test you wouldn't have thought so. Pakistan made only 230 in their first innings, and still went on to beat us by an innings and 20 runs! Imran and Wasim removed the top order each time, and then Qadir and Tauseef would do the rest. Like the surf they just kept rolling in, putting the ball in the right place and leaving us to drown and flail. When the bowlers are on top in an innings, as a batsman you have two choices. Either give the bowlers their due and grant them the ascendancy until the end of their spells, refraining from flamboyant strokeplay; or, you can attempt to upset their rhythm and control with a blast of calculated hitting. A quick 30 runs or so can be very useful. The ideal scenario is for one batsman, maybe two, to take responsibility for hitting the bowler out of the attack while the rest of the team drop anchor. With the resolute Sidath out first, that left 10 strokeplayers to take on the turning ball. Who all attempted at one point or another to hit themselves out of trouble. With the net result that 22 Sri Lankan batsmen managed barely 200 runs over the two innings. In our second innings only Roy and Arjuna batted with any authority as Tauseef deceived us all with flight, turn, bounce and guile. Tauseef looked a lot like the singer-songwriter Lionel Richie, but differed from Lionel Richie in one crucial aspect – he often released the unplayable.

At this time in our development, even though we actually were increasingly competitive, a major difference between Sri Lanka and our opponents was that our players kept breaking down injured. A sign of our lack of proper conditioning was that players were invariably pulling up with aches and strains during games, unused to the stresses and demands of international cricket. Mentally we might be getting closer towards the necessary level of professionalism, physically we were amateurs still. For the team, fitness work still meant a few stretches and running some laps of the practice grounds at no particular pace, getting round was enough. It wasn't that we were consciously shirking fitness work, it was just that we had no conception that modern-day professional cricket meant putting your body on the line day after day of play. And invariably to a team of fragile form and fitness, freak accidents happen. Thereby disrupting performances even further. Injury particularly blighted the career of one of our best batsmen, Ranjan Madugalle; he was always desperately unlucky with his fitness. In this instance in the first Test, Amal Silva who had missed the previous Test against Pakistan, to be replaced behind the stumps by Asanka Gurusinha, in turn now found himself recalled because of a broken finger Asanka had suffered while playing against England 'B' in a four-day game a few days earlier. And halfway through the Pakistan innings in the first Test, Amal Silva himself broke a finger. So I took over as wicket-keeper for the rest of the innings. It didn't take too long at all for me to move behind the stumps from short-leg, not long at all. Roshan Mahanama was twelfth man for this Test and after coming on immediately distinguished himself by catching Imran off Arjuna's bowling, setting a standard of brilliance in the field that he maintained throughout his career.

All of these to-ings and fro-ings because of injury, poor form or selectorial disfavour, led to frequent changes in our batting order, with me continuing to be played in all positions from 3 to 8. One loses count too, of all the batsmen Sidath Wettimuny had to partner in his five years as Sri Lanka's premier opener. Not that I was ever in any danger of sharing an opening stand with someone of such judiciousness and serenity! It has been a constant factor in Test cricket that a team without a solid and settled opening pair is a struggling team. Indeed a team where the key personnel are unavailable for selection for one reason or another, is always at a disadvantage. And that was our plight well into the 1990s. Considering that Roy Dias had broken his wrist prior to the start of the second Test, and that Rumesh Ratnayake also had to pull out at the last minute with hamstring trouble, therefore necessitating two of five changes to the team that lost the first Test, it was with some surprise to ourselves that we won the next Test of this series against Pakistan.

Pakistan were the victims of aggressive and accurate seam bowling from Asantha de Mel, Ravi Ratneyeke and débutante left-arm seamer Kosala Kuruppuarachchi (a former DSS schoolboy and young Nondescripts team-mate of mine). Kosala bowled very well to claim five wickets as Pakistan were all out for 132, a little before tea on the first day. Sidath and Roshan weathered the storm from Imran and Wasim, to finish undefeated at the close of play. The next day Pakistan kept plugging away to have us at 147 for 5 late in the afternoon, with the match in the balance, until a sixth-wicket stand of 90 between Arjuna and Ravi took us to relative safety. We ended up with a lead of almost 150, and wondered whether Sri Lankan lightning would strike twice against a supercharged yet surprisingly brittle Pakistani lineup. That it did. Ravi came to the fore, taking all the big wickets – Qasim Omar, Javed Miandad, Ramiz Raja and

Even as a baby I was
looking to hit over the top

My passion for cars
also emerged at an
early stage

Me aged 9

My great-grandfather and
father

Me as a young boy with my father Sam,
mother Indrani and sister Araliya

My mother and grandmother

Araliya with her husband Vasanth and their son Sathya

The family at home watch the team on TV

My 'Aladdin's Cave'
of bats and stumps

Making my début against England at Lord's in 1984 (Patrick Eagar)

On the way to 112 for Kent against Lancashire in the 1994
Benson and Hedges Cup final. It was all in vain (Allsport)

In determined mood with captain Arjuna Ranatunga and Roshan
Mahanama before the 1996 World Cup final in Lahore

Chasing Australia's 241 in the Lahore final
on the way to an unbeaten century

Jayasuriya demonstrates his awesome power (Allsport)

Salim Malik – after Pakistan had recovered from 6 for 2 to 72 for 2. And Asantha took the vital wicket of Imran for 0, inducing him to edge the ball to my midriff at second slip. Pakistan ended the fourth day with a lead of 13, 9 wickets down. Eventually we only had to knock off 32 to win. Credit to Imran: his fire was raised and when he and Wasim bowled, they gave it everything, looking to show that they were fighters and assert themselves against our debutant opener Roshan and the two-Test veteran Asanka, who was batting first-wicket down. Imran was decidedly quicker than Wasim in this instance, and he really made life difficult for the top order with deliveries of searing pace and sharp bounce. He reminded us that he was again the lead-from-the-front captain of Pakistan, and that he hated losing. In those days Pakistan just didn't lose games it was felt they should win. Having resisted Imran mightily to bring the scores level, Roshan was then unfortunately caught behind, leaving me to score a highly pleasurable single (a sentiment I have rarely felt for singles). Tying the series, we had won our second Test by eight wickets against the mighty Pakistan, proving to all that our victory against India wasn't a fluke. It was a victory all the more credible for the fact that no one had given us a chance of victory. With so many fine juniors in the side, it heralded the start of an era of success for Sri Lanka.

Or so we wished. In fact, we didn't win another Test for almost seven years. Having played a major part in our victory, Kosala Kuruppuarachchi was unfit for the next Test a few days later. So many of our cricketers made promising debuts, when they'd really impress, only to have their careers come to a premature end. Fast-bowlers particularly suffered as the strain of bowling to the best of their ability took toll on bodies unused to delivering sustained spells of aggression over the five days of a Test match, over the three Tests of a series. Their youth was both their asset and their weakness. And once they did get injured, there was precious little that these youngsters could be offered in the way of sophisticated medical support or physiotherapy. In the mid-1980s sports medicine was only just beginning to make an impression on the international cricket scene and the benefits were slow in reaching Sri Lanka. Rest was our young fast bowlers' only cure and as they rested, they became forgotten. Ravi Ratneyeke alone of all our pacemen stood out for the care and attention he took of his physique. He really was a fine athlete. A relative giant amongst us at over 6ft in height, and as broad as a banyan tree, he kept himself on a self-directed fitness regime which included running, weights and plenty of squash for stamina and strength.

So for the third Test against Pakistan, another eventual two Test-tyro Kaushik Amalean made his debut in place of the injured Kuruppuarachchi. Imran put us in, and though Sidath fell to Wasim for no score, all the other batsmen made decent contributions until we were all out just after lunch on the second day for 281. From being 158 for 5 at one stage, Pakistan thanks to Ramiz Raja's century and solid support from the tail, eventually gained a small lead on the first innings. When play finished a little early because of rain at the end of the third day, we were 24 for 2. Still seven runs behind, Asanka and myself at the crease. We batted through the morning session after the rest day undefeated, and then it rained. A draw became the most likely result. Though there wasn't much play after tea on the fourth day, Imran did manage to have me caught in the slips just before the close. Which brought Arjuna to the crease first thing next day.

Throughout that 1985–86 tour, Pakistan fielded poorly (not that we looked good ourselves in comparison) but with Imran and Wasim firing on all cylinders in a desperate attempt to win the match and take the series, Arjuna was dropped five times before he passed 30. And his habitual playing-and-missing and then belting the next ball over the boundary, really frustrated Pakistan. Throughout the final day chances were put down off Wasim's bowling as, finding his peak form, he starting generating extra yards of pace. His short run-up and flurried action typically produce deliveries of immense variety. He has been one of the greatest bowlers ever: he can do whatever he wants with the ball. Wasim's always been a rhythm bowler. He can bowl an awesomely fast delivery with no obvious change in body-action from delivering his stock fast-medium ball. He can be incredibly difficult to face. From nowhere can come a scorching lifter which considering its length, rather than rising to no more than stump height, suddenly climbs to threaten your shoulder. All you can do is trust to judgement and hope to survive as you ever so hurriedly attempt to get bat on to a ball which is suddenly on to you a couple of yards sooner than you expect. It's not easy. And in this instance, after two and a half Tests without ever reaching express velocity, Wasim suddenly unleashed whiplash-fast deliveries as he strove to break Asanka's and Arjuna's partnership. For no discernible reason the ball was suddenly just flying from Wasim's hand and he took the batsmen and his close-catchers by surprise. Slips and the wicket-keeper were several yards too close to the stumps to give themselves enough time to react to the scorching chances that came their way. So Arjuna and Asanka rode their luck and carried their bats to the close of play, both recording valiant centuries. In spite of the chances they inadvertently gave they really batted very well and displayed the vital qualities necessary at this level of competition: grit and determination.

Arjuna really got up the noses of some of the Pakistanis for, not only did he never back down from any verbal or physical confrontation, he had also shown a series of sterling performances that often stood between Pakistan and victory. In this series alone he scored two half-centuries and a century against them. During the second Test Arjuna had a coming together with the mighty Imran himself. Two individuals who think they are right (and they mostly are) until proven wrong, two individuals perceptibly proud and noble, two individuals who are de facto leaders in any environment. Confrontation between these two really became primal, tapping into a basic desire to assert supremacy that wouldn't be out of place in a jungle.

Imran like any fast bowler considered intimidatory bowling at tail-enders perfectly legitimate and, like any fast bowler finding tail-enders able to keep out the straight ones but missing the ones that moved away, was apt in his frustration to overdo the throat-ball in his search for wickets at the end of an innings. During our first innings in the second Test, with us clawing ourselves to a vital first-innings lead, Imran brought himself on to make the vital middle-order breakthroughs. 130 for 4 soon became 137 for 5 when Duleep Mendis was gutted by Imran, to be caught at slip. Our lead was just 5 runs on a result wicket: the match was in the balance. The destiny of the game would be decided over the next couple of hours. Ravi Ratneyeke came in, stuck around, played some bowler-enraging smears to Imran and Wasim and along with Arjuna was soon subject to some serious bouncer-attention. None of our umpires were particularly experienced at that time, indeed it was one of the officials' first Test; the laws of the game on repeated short-pitched bowling were unclear too. Certainly Imran didn't expect to be hauled up for his actions, not by a Sri Lankan umpire. Not by any umpire. For all the prowess of batsmen such as myself and Duleep Mendis at the hook shot, the stroke itself was very rarely played by Sri Lankan batsmen at the time. On our pitches and with our bowlers the ball really didn't tend to get up very high, so as schoolboys and club cricketers there really was very little call to play with the horizontal bat unless you were particularly short and greedy for runs. Ravi was a competent batsman, but in this instance with repeated deliveries being aimed above the stumps it was clear that Ravi was struggling to get his head and hands out of the way of Imran's and Wasim's leather air fresheners. It really didn't look like cricket was being played out there, it was more like 'get this joker out of here – don't care what it takes' on one side and a funky dance routine, all jerks and bizarre body movements on the other.

After one delivery had Ravi in a lot of trouble, bowed but unbloodied, Imran unleashed a torrent of Anglo-Saxon abuse at the end of his follow-through. Arjuna from the non-struck end decided to step in with his own choice phrases as Imran turned his back on Ravi and started walking back to his mark. Imran was visibly shocked. A Sri Lankan cussing him and one, moreover, that looked like a boy? It went against all laws of Imran's known universe. Imran prided himself on being like a tiger, and while I'm sure some can think of a number of animals to whom Arjuna could be superficially compared, in essence Arjuna is a 'Singha', a lion. Like a lion at the head of his pride, on this occasion Arjuna felt the safety of all depended on his ferocity. Enraged, Imran swore some more. Interspersing his adjectives with something that went along the lines of 'I'll knock your head off with the ball', Imran with one hand on his hip like a prima donna, the other bearing the ball and a furiously gesticulating finger, laid into Arjuna. 'You've got the ball, I've got the bat. Take me on why don't you ?', Arjuna replied. Arjuna hit upon a simple truth. Take away all the sound and fury, take away all the crowd and the umpires, take away all the nation versus nation element and cricket simply boils down to this contest: Bat against Ball. Nothing else matters. It must have been something about the way Arjuna stood with bat in hand that showed Imran cricket really was a batsman's game in Sri Lanka, and that all he had was a ball to play with. Ravi and Arjuna went on to complete a vital 90-run stand and put the game right back in our favour.

I think I should mention at this stage something about the umpiring controversies which raged between the two sides throughout this series – invariably either Javed or Arjuna were at the centre of these disputes. Like any side touring the sub-continent in those days of non-neutral umpires, Pakistan felt unjustly treated by the local umpiring. Similarly, we were not without our concerns when we took the field in Pakistan and India. As competitors we never felt that the home umpires were unduly biased in any way to the home side, but what was undoubtedly true was that any repeated doubts about an umpire's judgement became seen by the bowlers and fielders as an opportunity to press their luck by zealously appealing whenever the slightest chance presented itself. And for sure, the same attitude which saw our opponents consider us as international novices naturally led them to think our umpires as insufficiently experienced too. In the early stages of Pakistan's second innings in the second Test, Ravi took the ball to the umpires requesting a change as it was out of shape. On inspection, the umpires did change the ball, and a new one was brought out onto the field. Naturally, this new ball has to replicate as near as possible the condition of the ball it is replacing. After near to an hour and a half of play, the original ball was obviously a little scuffed and faded. So the umpires, not having a spare ball in this condition, took a new ball and in full view of everyone, started rubbing it vigorously on the ground in order to take the pristine shine off it. The Pakistani batsmen Ramiz Raja and Qasim Omar protested and soon after Javed Miandad, padded up and ready to go in at the fall of the next wicket, came on to the field along with the Pakistan manager and a copy of *Wisden* in order to point out to the umpires the error of their ways according to the rules that govern the game. Pure Javed! If ever he felt wronged on the cricket field, he'd go out of his way to correct it. Not many batsmen would take on opposing fast bowlers the way he did throughout his career, even fewer would take on umpires. But that was Javed. He had the courage of his convictions and there aren't many of whom that can be said.

Javed believed passionately in himself and his side. Both as a captain and as a player, he wore his heart on his sleeve. An attitude which I see has continued into his tenure as coach of Pakistan. Off the field, he is an immensely charming man, deflecting any gambits with a laugh and a joke, but while he was on the field he was a tiger. He became the man the Sri Lankan crowd loved to bait for not only was he the biggest wicket in the Pakistani lineup, he was also someone who when he batted gave the impression that he was taking on the crowd as well as the bowlers, fielders and umpires. Truth was, when Javed was at his supreme best, umpires had absolutely nothing more to do than signal boundaries. From the time of his debut, a great player like Javed was never playing for his place. He could be short of everything but fitness, and Pakistan would always pick him. He was the promise of runs. However, in this 1986 series against Sri Lanka, he was actually not in the best of form.

It is when a batsman is just a little bit off his game that he can get frustrated and try too hard to compensate before soon self-destructing in a frenzy of attempted big shots (believe me, I know). Or, an off-form batsman can get confrontational and try with sheer presence to bluster and bluff his way to a decent score (believe me, Arjuna knows). Apparently this was also Javed's policy. It is another of cricket's great mysteries why an out-of-form batsman is never put out of his misery straight away. He always seems to get out the ball after he feels he's played himself back in form. It can be so frustrating. And this was what happened to Javed in that Test at Colombo, setting him off on another of those incidents that made him so notorious. Given out lbw to Ravi after a painstaking 36 (following his first-innings 0) to leave Pakistan 131 for 5 and still some runs short of making us bat again, Javed shook his head at the umpire in big, slow, side to side movements, said a few words, and pointed to his bat before making his way back to the pavilion. And then, amidst all the jeers and cat-calls that were directed at Javed, some fool in the VIP section adjacent to the pavilion threw a stone at him. Javed charged towards the crowd, bat raised like an axe, challenging all and sundry to at least a frank exchange of views. Javed with a bat in his hands against a boorish mob? In form or not, I'd back Javed every time.

In the aftermath of this incident, the beleaguered Pakistanis felt that with the umpires and the whole of Sri Lanka against them, they should cancel the remainder of their tour. Sri Lankan Board officials had to work long and hard to persuade Pakistan to stay. Had they not stayed on, not only would it have been a huge disappointment to Sri Lankan cricket lovers – and an embarrassment to the country as a whole – but it would have scuppered the honorific staging of the Asia Cup a couple of weeks later, which it was Sri Lanka's turn to host. Citing political reasons, India had already pulled out of the tournament at the last minute, so New Zealand who were going to be Sri Lanka's and Pakistan's opponents (along with India and Australia) in the Australasia Cup in Sharjah the week after the completion of the Asia Cup, were invited to compete in a hastily arranged triangular with Pakistan. This event was sandwiched in between our games against Bangladesh and Pakistan in the Asia Cup, our game against Pakistan in the John Player Tournament counting towards the teams' standings in the Asia Cup and vice-versa etc etc etc. The ingenuity of tournament organisers sometimes knows no bounds.

So from March to April of 1986 in the space of three weeks, Sri Lanka competed against three different countries in three separate tournaments in two different nations. And completed a Test series too. The Asia Cup we won, for what it was worth without India's participation, comfortably beating Pakistan by 5 wickets to win both the Asia Cup and the triangular series. A good result especially after we'd lost the one-day series that accompanied the Tests against Pakistan by a long way. Significant wins were still so rare for us that President Jayawardene, as he'd done for our first Test victory, declared another public holiday. It was our first ever tournament victory and it was our last until the Singer Champions Trophy in October 1995. We flew to Sharjah for the Austral-Asia Cup a few days after Pakistan and New Zealand, because as holders of the Asia Cup we were given a bye through to the semi-final. Sri Lanka lost the semi-final to India in the last over and with Pakistan reaching the final, the stage was set for the match which made Sharjah's name: India vs Pakistan in April 1986. The response given to Javed's heroic last-ball six in that final against India brought home to me how passionately the game is followed in the Indian subcontinent. Watching the live satellite feed on television back home in Colombo, like any other fan of the game, I was gripped by the ebb-and-flow drama of a great one-day match. India played Pakistan far less often then than they do now so each game between them meant a hell of a lot to their fans. More engaging than a Bollywood-type movie, with more spectacle, colour and death-or-glory combat, Javed with this innings in this titanic match made cricket on television an event to watch throughout the subcontinent.

Our one-day game against New Zealand in Colombo had actually been my first encounter with Tony Blain the batsman/wicketkeeper and John Bracewell the off-spinning allrounder, who were both to become coach and manager of the Auckland Aces during my season playing New Zealand domestic cricket ten years later. None of us could have even imagined that happening way back in 1986. I, for one, had no concept of playing cricket for that long and these kinds of opportunities just didn't exist back then, certainly not for a Sri Lankan. That it happened ten years later was just a small example of the symbiotic relationship between sponsorship and television. In 1996-1997 the newly formed Auckland Aces were a team reliant on success, and therefore maximum television exposure, for patronage from the sponsors who underwrote the team's operating costs. And I who had become prominent because of the 1996 World Cup, which was a huge television event in New Zealand (TVNZ paid so much for the television rights it couldn't be anything but), was seen as someone who could boost the Aces' chances of achieving that success. So Auckland's administrators got together with the sponsors and offered me a contract to play in New Zealand's Shell Cup one-day competition. After being flown over by Air New Zealand, and put up at the Auckland Sheraton, and given to drive a Toyota Previa estate with more sponsors' logos on it than a Grand Prix racer, it was readily apparent to me that my success would be Auckland's success would be the sponsors' success, should we reach the nationally televised semi-finals and final of the Shell Cup. This is how television has changed the game. We cricketers are the vehicles for commercial activity. We've always been interesting but now we're marketable, especially when we're playing one-dayers.

CHAPTER TEN

There are times when you're not in any particular form and can still scrape together a half-century and bowled off the inside-edge going for the big one, or you are just plain and simple beaten by a marvellous piece of bowling or fielding. String a few of those together and suddenly you're perceived to be in a slump. All those happened to me in our tour of India, late in 1986. I never looked like getting out until I was out, and when the Tests and one-dayers were finally over black and white statistics painted a pretty disappointing picture. In five Test innings I'd scored 94 runs and there are times when you're feeling in good form but don't trouble the scorers for too long. Umpires' decisions go against you, or you get caught one-handed on the boundary, or you get in three one-dayers had scored 57 runs. A poor total for a month's work. And yet I had really felt in good nick. Coupled with my lack of runs, around me for one reason or another, the rest of the team mostly struggled too. Time and Test-match tensions were catching up with Duleep and Roy though they still had much to offer, Arjuna was a little below par, Rumesh and Asantha weren't the force they once had been with the ball, and it was asking too much of Ravi Ratneyeke, well though he performed, to open the bowling and the batting and not have either aspect of his game compromised. The batting could never settle; I went from No. 3 to No. 5 to No. 8 in the three Tests and Ranjan Madugalle who could be relied upon to steady things and who had made a hundred in the last Test series against India didn't play a single Test. And when he was picked for the one-dayer at Baroda, he unfortunately injured his hand in the field and thus didn't even get to bat. (CHORUS: Ranjan really was unlucky with injuries.)

In this 1986–1987 series against India consistent with Sri Lanka's performances in Tests, on a good wicket no team other than the West Indies could have bowled us out twice in five days but on any wicket favouring the bowlers, in this case the Indian spinners Maninder Singh, Shivlal Yadav and Ravi Shastri, we were put away with ease. Perhaps we did attempt to play too many shots against the spinners, perhaps we could have played with softer hands, used our pads more, used our heads more, and simply hung in there to grind out draws. But we simply didn't have the bowling to trouble the Indian batsmen, and that had put our batsmen under pressure whenever they batted following a big innings by India. Granted, in this series as batsmen we weren't great, but as bowlers we were worse.

Back home following the tour, I did my usual thing in domestic cricket for Nondescripts, made some quick hundreds and then 'retired hurt' mid-innings once my appetite had been sated. Making easy runs in domestic cricket has never seemed important to me. I had been playing for Sri Lanka for three years and I felt I had done a reasonably good job. Runs at international level were what counted and I had made quite a few. So it was with some surprise that I heard the week before our Tests against the New Zealand tourists was due to start, that I wasn't in the team. There was no real reason given, but the whisper was that the selectors wanted a steadier batsman. Cavalier play was no longer tolerated. It was the first major rejection of my life (I had yet to be rejected by girls because I was still too shy to approach any, but that would happen in time). Such a categorical rejection made me think that my future as an international batsman might be at stake. For if I was dropped when I wasn't feeling out of form, how could I ever work myself back into the team?

On hearing the news at the SSC, where I'd been practising, I didn't want to face my parents who would soon enough know like the rest of the country that I had been dropped from the Test team. I simply jumped on my trail bike, bat and bag strapped to my back and roared full throttle down the Galle Road until I found myself in front of a friend's house. It was siesta time, the time between lunch and tea, when Sri Lankan households after a frenzy of domestic activity in the morning, settle down for a kip following a big lunch and a day's work well done. Seeking sanctuary, a shoulder to lean on, moral support, a cold drink and some of my friend's mother's life-enhancing sweet potato pie, I entered to find the whole house quiet and my friend, Richie Keith Colin de Silva (named after Benaud, Miller and Cowdrey by a cricket fanatic father), apparently snoozing. I was left to my own devices. Having raided the fridge, I found my friend asleep in his room. Like me he had a full-length mirror on his wall and from the time we were youths it was in front of these mirrors that we would, like boxers shadow-boxing, repeatedly practice our strokes in front of the most critical and congratulatory of audiences: ourselves. Bat in hand I drilled myself in front of the mirror on the strokes I would need to play if I wanted to be a great batsman. I played Sunil Gavaskar leg-glances, Allan Border punch-drives, Greg Chappell on-drives; not hitting the ball but guiding it, using its own force against it. All maximum percentage strokes, strokes to which these batsmen never ever got out, strokes which brought them thousands of runs in all conditions. I was determined to rehearse these, embed into my body and mind the feeling and form of these strokes and lay the basis for their future employment by me. When we were younger, we'd replay and rehearse only big attacking strokes. Now I saw for the first time the need to broaden my game. I was determined to never ever let anyone accuse me of only being a dasher, of not being a complete batsman. I was determined to get back into the team.

While Richie slept I played cameo after cameo of class batsmen's strokes, murmuring my mantra: 'Gavaskar like this . . . Border like this . . . Chappell like this.' But my friend hadn't been asleep. My motorbike had woken Richie (and quite probably all the neighbours) but in sympathy for my eccentricity and not having heard the news, he had decided to leave me be and let me continue in this frenzied practice. When I did turn round to see him awake, he maintains that I had tears running down my face. If I was really crying, they were tears of frustration. Three years an international cricketer, and the team that I made my debut against was now the team I wasn't good enough to face. I hadn't changed, but the way I was perceived was changing. That was the problem.

Brendon Kuruppu, once a regular wicket-keeper/batsman in our one-day side a few years earlier, made his Test debut in this game against Hadlee, Chatfield and co., and proceeded to surprise himself and everyone else who knew him by batting for over two days to score the slowest ever double-century in the history of Test Match cricket. As a counter to Hadlee's threat it was admirable, but it just wasn't the way Brendon normally played! It wasn't the way anyone played in Sri Lanka. But the word from on high was that over-ambitious strokeplay was frowned upon, so Brendon like everyone else knuckled down. In Duleep Mendis' case, this meant not trying to hit Hadlee out of the ground until he'd settled, or had scored 50, whichever came first. The last day of the Test match brought home to me in the most humbling manner, how the supposed agonies I was going through, by not being able to play Test cricket, really didn't amount to much. Like my father says, a man with no shoes is upset until he sees a man with no feet. On the morning of 21 April 1987 around the time New Zealand were resuming their first innings at 214 for 5, chasing Sri Lanka's first innings 397, four buses loaded with military personnel were machine-gunned near Kandy and later that evening a bomb exploded near New Zealand's team hotel in downtown Colombo ripping through a bus terminus, maiming and killing hundreds. The civil war between the Tamil separatists and the government forces in the north had reached Colombo and the peace of the whole country was threatened. No one could feel safe any more.

With the next Test match scheduled to have been at Kandy, the New Zealanders' tour was abandoned in the light of the growing unrest throughout Sri Lanka. The bomb-blasts were a relatively new phenomenon back then, people in Sri Lanka hadn't yet got used to living with the threat of terrorist attacks. For a while it looked as though law and order would break down as the civil militia struggled to comprehend the scale of potential unrest in the country. The politicians worked hard to keep the human conflict from becoming even more murderous. Naturally no team wanted to tour Sri Lanka until the terrible situation calmed down. And for a good few years, all domestic club cricket competitions were suspended. It was to take five years before we played another Test at home.

These were the wilderness years. The years spent playing every international game away from home, lurching from country to country like cricketing refugees. Our playing schedule became erratic to say the least, a few Test matches here and there, along with one-day tournaments whenever and wherever possible. Playing away isn't easy at the best of times, but with under-prepared and under-confident transitional teams, these years were particularly hard for Sri Lankan cricket. Losing so many games, some by huge margins, pretty soon we would take the field expecting to lose, and of course with this latent attitude we couldn't do anything but fulfil our expectations. Playing so infrequently we forgot what winning felt like.

Simultaneously our front-line bowlers, so combative in the earlier part of their careers, were now struggling against the world's best batsmen. Rumesh and Asantha though still young men in their twenties were finding the strain of having to be stock and shock bowlers too much for their aching bodies. And it was asking a great deal of Ravi Ratneyeke, manfully though he performed, to have to combine the roles of opening bowler and front-line batsman. Speaking as a batsman I know that more often than not, it is bowlers that decide matches. One individual, one spell, can totally alter the destiny of a game. Teams that set winning trends in Test cricket do so on the back of their bowlers making things happen. A batsman or two might be the decisive factor in winning or saving a Test Match but bowlers win Test series. If a team is weak, however, if it isn't playing very well, the first thing you notice is that the bowlers aren't that aggressive. And our bowlers weren't aggressive any more. Worse, no attacking bowlers were coming through the ranks. Hence we had to attack with our bats.

The one-day game therefore, has always favoured our style of play. Generally, in the late 1980s bowlers around the world were struggling to intimidate batsmen as much as they used to. International one-day cricket now being standardised to fifty overs a side, with fielding restrictions and penalties for short-pitched bowling, had become significantly more batsman-friendly. A trend which continues to this day. In the old days, with the exception of Desmond Haynes who set the pre-Sachin record with seventeen hundreds, even great batsmen didn't score centuries too often. Hundreds really were harder to come by what with no fielding restrictions and less specially designed audience pleasing 'one-day wickets'. And less jaded bowlers it has to be said. Nowadays teams don't mind giving hundreds away so much because there is the feeling in the side that has to bat second following a run-bath, that anything the opposition can do, they can too. Batsmen seem to be scoring hundreds more frequently. I had only scored three one-day centuries before the 1996 World Cup, Sachin Tendulkar had only scored four. Since then I've bagged a handful but not as many as Sachin who once he started opening the Indian innings and rightfully so, has accelerated beyond all others to become the all-time highest limited-overs century maker.

Rare is it to see a bowler be awarded Man of the Match in a one-day game. Certainly the once all-conquering West Indies bowling-machine was finding towards the end of the 1980s that being restricted to one bouncer per over was seriously hampering their attacking style. A fast bowler in order to be fully effective has to try to intimidate the batsman just a little. Just one time can work. As long as the possibility of a repeat dose exists, the batsman will always have it in the back of his mind. But once under the one-bouncer rule, with his quota of one bouncer in the over safely negotiated, the batsman now has conditions in his favour. Line and length, line and length, 'corridor of uncertainty'(?!) became the bowlers' philosophy for a time and Qadir aside, spin bowling was dying a death with slow bowlers bowling flatter and flatter trajectories. Batsmen were starting to adopt particular one-day tactics to the longer game too, as they sought ways to break free of the bowlers. Playing in the 'V' wasn't enough anymore. And once all batsmen, from nurdlers to flashers, learnt to improvise it was all a line and length bowler could do to stop them from scoring in all manner of ways. The introduction of heavy bats led to more boundaries being brutally clubbed than there were baby seals in the Arctic.

Salim Malik, Azharuddin and Javed Miandad have been distinctive for the way in which they could score off any ball in any direction. They could blast broad-battedly too, but on the slow and low wickets where they've played so many subcontinental one-dayers, they showed that there were as many angles of deflection off the face of the bat, each potent with runs, as there were stadium ball-boys to retrieve their hits beyond the boundary. The downswings of their bat can be way off the perpendicular, their feet splayed in the most unorthodox manner as they give themselves room to either blaze or nuance a ball in the direction they choose. Azhar especially likes to flash the ball through the off-side and this he often does amazingly with nothing more than a bat angled so sharply that to the bowler it looks as if Azhar is playing only with a sliver of wood. Playing slow bowling, it almost defies belief how Azhar manages to keep the ball on the face of bat a little bit longer than the rest of us, as he nuances the ball into the gaps.

We cricketers are always eager to learn from each other and given these batsmen's example, the wide expanses of field opened up to anyone with an eye for the ball, a still head and deft wrists. In the way that in recent years the best soccer strikers have started to aim for the extreme sides of goal, aiming not just for the corners of the net but for the inner side of the side-netting, so as to maximise their target area (and simultaneously reduce their margin for error), the best batsmen have started to exploit more angles of attack, playing with more wrist and subtle deflection in order to beat a particular line of bowling and setting of fielders. There was a time when the last ten overs of a limited-overs contest were an absolute bloodbath for the bowlers, although I can recall just how effective the then fast-medium Steve Waugh could be at the death with his changes of pace, yorkers and clinical precision of delivery. 'The Iceman' had cometh. In the years either side of the 1987 World Cup the one-day game was very much establishing itself as being in the batsman's domain, and the game started to get quite formulaic; as I feel that in between the World Cups of 1996 and 1999 it has threatened to become again. It almost doesn't matter where you play, under lights or not, white ball or red ball – for the side batting first 250 off 50 overs is almost a given, 270 is par, and 300 might still not be enough to defend.

Then sometime in the early 1990s bowlers around the world, following the lead of Wasim Akram and Waqar Younis, rediscovered the fact that yorkers are not the easiest to keep out for batsmen. Runs were now at a premium in the closing stages of a limited-overs contest. When batsmen had developed methods to combat these yorker-closing tactics, in the mid-1990s a fresh theory developed along with the rise to prominence of Mushtaq Ahmed, Shane Warne, Murali, Anil Kumble and Saqlain Mushtaq, that slow bowlers would be most effective at the down-to-the-wire squeezeplays that are the hallmark of a great limited overs match. In those situations, the ball always gets thrown by the captain to the bowler with the most confidence. Waqar and Wasim were the world's most confident bowlers during the period their yorkers reigned supreme, nowadays Shane, Murali and Saqlain are the ones who feel they can be match-winners. Sure, they'll lose a game here and there, but inevitably the guy who thinks he'll take wickets is the guy who will.

The game itself changes all the time. And each World Cup seems to highlight new shots and tactics, the best of which are carried through to Test matches. It's like those car manufacturers who experiment on the racetrack with certain technical features before adopting them into their road-cars. World Cups concentrate the mind wonderfully. The first World

Cup I played in was the one India and Pakistan hosted in October-November of 1987. Played on pitches devoid of grass with fast outfields, this tournament saw the death of the merely medium pacer. Only fast or slow bowlers could get any purchase out of the conditions, and the slow men, including the dinky-dobblers, bowled a lot of overs. The sweep and the reverse-sweep became the modish shot. So rare had been the sweep shot in one-day cricket until then, that England's deliberate adoption of the sweep shot in their semi-final against India on a turning Bombay wicket took the Indians by complete surprise. With this one stroke, played from outside off-stump if need be, Maninder Singh's and Ravi Shastri's threat was nullified and they were milked for plenty of runs by Gooch and Gatting on the way to an English victory. It's not that these strokes are any more successful in the long run than any other, but one-day cricket is not about the long run. It's about gaining an advantage for a couple of overs. In the time it can take for a captain and his fielders to react to a batsman's advantage-gaining unorthodoxy, a game can be won and lost. In the 1992 World Cup it wasn't so much one kind of shot that came to the fore but rather the policy adopted by Pakistan of keeping wickets intact until the final ten overs when batsmen could hit out in the knowledge that there were others to follow behind them who could play with freedom. That tournament was also significant for Imran's insistence that wicket-taking bowling was the key to victory; the loss of a wicket being seen to do more to put the brakes on a side than any number of line and length deliveries. Whereas in the 1992 final, England's bowling strategy was much concerned with 'attacking corridors', Pakistan's bowling strategy much rather concentrated on breaking into the batsmen's chambers. But in reality Imran's emphases on his team's bowling strengths – Wasim Akram, Mushtaq Ahmed, Aqib Javed – in spite of his own shoulder injury, were made to compensate for his recognition of the frailty of Pakistan's batting line-up. Outside of Javed (playing with a sore back), Ramiz and himself, Imran felt he couldn't rely on anyone to play a long innings. That's why he felt it necessary to anchor the Pakistan innings and go in first drop.

In the 1996 World Cup, we took this evolutionary process one step further: in a team packed with versatile batsmen, the loss of any one wicket at any stage didn't really matter. Our seven-man bowling attack was certainly capable, but batting was our strength. Batting would win us matches. And the strategy of our coach Dav Whatmore and Arjuna was to play to our strengths to the max. Jayasuriya and Kaluwitharana therefore wouldn't have to take the customary openers' look at the bowling for a few overs and rocked bowlers from the outset of any Sri Lankan innings. The loss of Sanath or Kalu would just bring Asanka to the crease, next wicket down was me, then Arjuna, then Roshan, then the unflappable Hashan and Kumar Dharmasena to be followed by the lusty Wickremasinghe and Chaminda Vaas. Subcontinental run-filled wickets helped make this policy practicable: any one of us were interchangeable, any one of us could adapt to any situation. The dismissal of one just brought another batter up in the rotation – 'batter up'. If anything this is where the baseball analogies should have properly been brought in to describe our style of play during the 1996 World Cup. 'Pinch hitting' as in bringing in a specialist batsman to do a specific job was never our intention. Our intention was to maximise the runs from first ball to last. Any batsman could do it; we weren't overly dependent on anyone.

Successful cricket at the highest level is all about playing the vital innings when it matters. And stopping your opponents from doing the same. It took Sri Lanka many years before we could do this. One thing that the first World Cup I played in, the 1987 competition, did reveal to me was just how unforgiving high-stakes cricket could be. A big win between two evenly-matched teams is almost always due to a team's habit of punishing single solitary mistakes. I have noticed that each team that wins a World Cup is distinguished not by having the tournament's top run-scorer or wicket-taker, but by invariably being the team that takes its catches, that makes run-outs, that holds its nerve in the tightest of situations. The teams that win the World Cup are not the teams that necessarily do anything spectacular in the qualifying rounds; the teams that win World Cups don't make mistakes when it matters. Every match-changing chance is taken. No decisive chances are given. Each World Cup winning campaign is due to any number of factors, but there are moments when the fate of the whole campaign lies in the balance, times when a game irrevocably swings the way of the team that will ultimately become the World Cup champions.

Those who saw the first World Cup final in 1975 as it happened can probably vividly recall their feeling that they had just witnessed something incredibly significant when they think of Viv Richards' run-out of Ian Chappell; the same would be evident following Viv's stepping-back to leg and then the off to *coup de grâce*-edly smash the last ball of the West Indies innings for six over square leg in the 1979 final; the same for Kapil Dev's amazing running over-the-shoulder catch of Viv in the 1983 final. I saw the 1983 final at Lord's as the beneficiary of a Singapore Airlines sponsorship for being the Sri Lankan Schoolboy Cricketer of the Year. I've only seen the first two World Cups on videotape with knowledge of the eventual outcomes, but these truths are self-evident: World Cups were won and lost in those moments. The 1987 World Cup final, if it would come down to one decisive incident in favour of Australia, it would be Mike Gatting's misplaying of the reverse sweep that had brought him so many runs in the semi-final at a point when England, batting second, were cruising comfortably towards the Australian total. He was such a big wicket for Australia to take. The 1992 World Cup's 'significant moment' in favour of Pakistan? Graham Gooch's dropping of a swirling skier off Imran's bat, early on in the Pakistan innings in the final. The decisive moment of Sri Lanka's 1996 triumph? No one particular incident in the final against Australia although it was heartening to catch Steve Waugh early on in his innings; for 1996 I would rather cite Kaluwitharana's phenomenal leg-side stumping with a split-second to spare of Sachin Tendulkar in the Calcutta semi-final. For sure, Sachin like the other Indian batsmen would have found it increasingly difficult to keep going on a wicket taking more and more spin, but up to the point of his dismissal Sachin had been batting brilliantly. Reaching 50 in no time, had it not been for a momentary over-balancing, Sachin could well have carried his team through to victory. No total looks safe when Sachin's chasing, ears pinned back and eyes ablaze. With his dismissal India were derailed and everything we had done in recovering from 1 for 2 was vindicated. We knew we couldn't lose, not with this team, not with this attitude, not with this momentum. Thing is, these incidents are not just significant in retrospect. Every game has its turning-points, when the fate of the match rests on the outcome of a single moment. As soon as they occur and are resolved in one team's favour, one team knows that the gods are smiling on them, and one team knows in its heart that it is not meant to win. It doesn't have to be said. The players just know.

A major attraction of one-day cricket for the spectator must be that the destiny of each game hinges on these supreme moments of confrontation. And from the player's point of view you know that every action can play a significant part in the final result. As a batsman you've just got one chance to have an impact on the match, as a bowler you've real only got two spells. A fielder may only get one chance, if that, to effect a potentially decisive run-out or catch. Test-cricket is the greater game undoubtedly; I'm still more thrilled by a Test match when five days of intense hard work result in a well-earned victory or a hard-fought draw, but it is rare for the final day of a Test Match to produce the dramatic goods as often as a one-day match. One-day cricket is a zero-sum game. You either lose or you win. Every run conceded is one that has to be scored, every run scored is one that has to be defended. All within the space of seven hours. One-day cricket forces you to play so that your whole life becomes one big now. Big matches are all about pressure: who can take the most and who can apply the most. Once you're out there in the middle everyone knows you can play. It comes down to whether you think you can do the business. It becomes a mental game. When you start thinking positively you play positively and you start making things happen. You become proactive rather than reactive.

Fielders gain an extra yard's worth of anticipation, turning half-chances into run-outs and catches; bowlers attack with zip and fire, knowing wickets are just around the corner; batsmen start opening their shoulders and finding the gaps. The opposition can be overwhelmed by a tidal wave of surging, irresistible cricket. There's no better feeling than riding the crest of that wave.

If a team is winning more close games than it loses, it isn't just because it is good and collectively cool in a crisis. More than loving the thrill of victory, it just hates to lose a game in the final over after having given it everything in the previous ninety-nine. A team that wins more close games than it loses hates with a vengeance that feeling you get as you walk off the pitch, feeling like all your insides have been sweated out of your skin, when not even a glass of the coolest water tastes of anything but bitterness back in the dressing-room, when a post-game shower can do nothing to wash away your disappointment and tears. It's only when you get hungry again, as your body rhythms kick in and you realise that life does go on and that you have lived to fight another day, that the feeling of despair fades. 'So we lost. We won't make the same mistakes again.' A team that thinks like that is made of the right stuff and will always win more close games than it loses. Examples? Pakistan in the Imran and Javed days; the West Indies when Clive Lloyd was playing; an Australia with Allan Border. Once these guys taste defeat, they know they will do everything in their power to stop it happening again. On the right kind of team-mate, these players can be inspiring examples.

The only comparable figure in the Sri Lankan dressing-room was Arjuna. Arjuna came to the captaincy in 1988 early on in our period of haplessness. He had known for a long time beforehand, we had all known, that he'd be Sri Lanka's captain in due course. The way he carried himself on and off the pitch, I was a teenager in comparison. He wore the Sri Lankan cap with pride, there was a set to his jaw and a flinty sharpness even to his stubble that told everyone of his determination to do well for the team. And his eyes, his eyes, always watching, observing, learning the ways of the world and his opponents. Arjuna's body has always anatomically suggested his right to lead and competence to supervise. Father of contemporary Sri Lankan cricket, the messiah to the masses, Arjuna is saved from saintliness by his hot partisan temper. Scallys have started to call him 'Napoleon' and 'Benito' (i.e. Mussolini) nowadays and Arjuna can certainly seem incredibly dictatorial at times, wanting to run the world according to his precepts. There are youngsters in the squad who are rather fearful of him and not even I as senior pro have escaped the occasional fierce reprimand from Arjuna. Arjuna leads from the front, and thus receives on the full all the slings and arrows of outrageous fortune, umpires, opponents, media hatchet-men and foreign crowds. He does this all in the interests of his players. When a player deserves praise, Arjuna's the first to push him into the spotlight, when a player is under the cosh, Arjuna's the first to offer protection.

In return, he never asks any more of a Sri Lankan player than to be the best he can be. He may play the game with a rare intensity, pushing himself to be the best he can be, every ball a matter of life and death, but he is also able to wisecrack and look for the joke in the most pressured of situations. Poking his tongue out at Shane Warne (imitation is the sincerest form of flattery) after smacking him for a six in a World Cup final, is just the kind of thing Arjuna likes to do. He came to the captaincy as a young man but the fact that some of the ultra-patrician elements of the Board thought he was an 'uncouth upstart hooligan' counted against him, and he was removed from the team after just a couple of years in charge. Arjuna had the support of his players, we really needed him with us. Deprived of a natural leader the team thus struggled even more. In looking to the fill the gap until Arjuna's return to the helm the selectors even turned to me, they were that desperate.

It is wonderful to be trusted, even more wonderful to be led. Someone like Arjuna can carry a team, a Cricket Board, the establishment and the media on his back with a mixture of strength and adroit leverage, all the while maintaining his form. But I have never found that easy to do without compromising my personal game. Whenever I've captained Sri Lanka, I have struggled for runs. The first time I captained, on the 1991 tour of England, it was sudden, following the fall from favour of Arjuna and I don't think I was ready for the extra responsibility at that stage. It might be a coincidence but the consequence of leading the team (which is a 24-hour job) and of being the leading batsman, appears to be that I leave a lot of my runs in the dressing-room. Leadership is wonderfully fulfilling, but captaincy is somehow confining for me.

Captaining any team is a job for none but the most centred of individuals. Captaining Sri Lanka, a job where you need the judgement of Solomon, the compassion of Lord Buddha, the sense of responsibility of a mother with her first-born, the megawatt charm of a Hollywood star, the political savvy of a UN Secretary-General, the motivational skills of an ayatollah, the ability to read an opponent like a CAT-scan, the assertiveness of a quarterback, the roar of a lion along with the hide of a rhinoceros and no little cricketing ability, is a task beyond most people. Which is why Arjuna must stand out in the history of the game as a great captain. He has won many battles on many fronts. Initially he led a competent side combatively, saving matches was the most he could expect from us. In recent years Arjuna has led a competitive team that is expected to win every limited overs game it plays, when even Test Match defeats are thought of as disappointing by the fans. Before 1996 we were playing catch up with the rest of the world, now they are playing catch up with us. Winning and losing mean a great deal more than they used to. And the focus is always on the captain, it is to his name that the team are always attached. Now the pressure, the weight of expectation, on Arjuna is far greater than before. The remainder of his career may well cement him in the history of the game as one of the all-time great captains.

From the start of the 1987 World Cup to the start of the World Cup in 1992, the number of times Sri Lanka snatched defeat from the jaws of victory are almost too painful to recall. More so, because wins were so rare for us anyway. In 53 One-Day Internationals in the four and a half-years between these two World Cups Sri Lanka lost 41. Some by a very long way: Viv Richards' 181 at Karachi, when in reply we scored 169; the time when Simon O'Donnell and Dean Jones set about us in Sharjah to the tune of 332 runs; the time when Australia chasing 204 had beaten us by 9 wickets at Perth with ten overs to spare. There were other occasions when the game would be over as a contest, before we'd even finished batting or bowling against our opponents in the first half of a game.

That 1987 World Cup game in Karachi against the West Indies, prior to Viv's innings we were actually doing pretty well. He came in to bat with the West Indies on 45 for 2 after about 10 overs with Ravi Ratneyeke on a hat-trick. Viv's first ball, he played back calmly to Ravi After that it was pure carnage. Our fast bowlers were at just the right pace to suit Viv's aggression and our slow bowlers could only toss up what they knew to work against other batsmen, flighted spinners. On the front foot throughout, the length of delivery mattered little as the bowling was either swung high over midwicket or smacked on the up through extra cover. I think Viv's first fifty was quite tame, but his second fifty took him about half an hour and his last 80 runs, well I think they only took him a few overs from both ends. I was patrolling deep mid-on, right on the edge of the rope, and the closest I got to fielding a hit from Viv was when it was thrown back from over the boundary. Mark Waugh, Sachin Tendulkar, Brian Lara and Saeed Anwar are the most talented batsmen amongst my contemporaries, the criteria by which all others are measured nowadays. It's not just that they can make Test Match scores in one-day matches, but they never look to be in trouble; they can make the difficult look so easy, oozing style all the while. But Viv was the best batsman I have ever seen. He had all the shots and all the time in the world to play them. He could make great bowlers look absolutely powerless. He made you want to be 'a batsman'.

This kind of whipping at the hands of a great like Viv was one thing, any of our bowlers who'd been blasted around the park could feel that it wasn't their inexperience or ineptitude or lack of fitness or physique that put them in line for such punishment. The best bowlers all over the world suffered repeatedly too. But when our bowlers and our batsmen struggled against anything less than the superhuman, it did prey on their minds. Our one consolation as individuals during those years of flying in to a country, taking a beating and then flying out again, was that it does take a hell of a lot of ability to be an international cricketer. We might not be the best in the world but we were the best in Sri Lanka. If we couldn't cope then few other Lankans could. But when you keep getting beaten, when you keep showing up just to keep getting shown up, when very little of what you try succeeds, when your best efforts come to nothing, defeatism sets in. And it is so horribly infectious. Success breeds success but defeat doesn't half spawn a few bastards. As batsmen we felt we couldn't rely on our bowlers to defend any kind of total, and as bowlers we felt that we couldn't rely on our batsmen to bat us through to victory. So each section of the team felt it had to compensate for the shortcomings of the other. Good for team spirit possibly; bad for team performance definitely. From going into games with no plan at the start of Sri Lanka's international life, we were now formulating game plans with our weaknesses in mind rather than our strengths. Nowadays we play to our strengths — Sanath, Murali, depth in batting and variety in bowling — aspects of the game unmatched by most other teams. There is nothing Sanath cannot do to a cricket ball, there is nothing Murali cannot do with a cricket ball. Of course, it took us a long time to discover our strengths and then develop them. Indeed it took us fourteen years of struggle to become the 'overnight sensations' of the 1996 World Cup.

CHAPTER ELEVEN

To put our Test performances in those years when we were only playing away from home in context, England finally ended their own run of eighteen Tests without a win by beating us at Lord's in 1988. We were that bad. When top-flight cricket in Sri Lanka between 1987 and 1992 with no teams touring was all but a handful of semi-official squad games between local contenders for the national squad, when the only quality time out in the middle was when we were playing a Test or one-day international abroad, it was wholly understandable that a Sri Lankan player should feel himself out of his depth when making the leap from domestic to international cricket. Every time one of our players crossed the threshold into international cricket he was entering new territory mentally and physically. More was to be asked of him than ever before. It was sink or swim. Naturally it took each of them several consecutive matches, the equivalent of a year or three with our haphazard schedule, to find their bearings.

Part of our upturn in performance in the mid-1990s did arise from the simple fact that we were starting to get paid a little better. It is one thing to feel a second-class cricketer in comparison to those opponents who are hammering the life out of you, it is another to feel second-class off the pitch because you don't have the money to lead a decent life. I've been lucky undoubtedly, my parents supported me during my early years and from the outset my business ventures have proved successful. But for many of my team-mates who were unable to work full-time in a proper paying job because of their cricketing commitments, life was lived on the margins. They'd come into the side as young men and remain in a limbo of half-hearted employment in the off-season, unsure of their prospects in life or in the national team. Some were even married, and had to support themselves and their families on whatever small stipend they received. It was painful to witness, but some of my team mates would find themselves having to wash their own kit while on tour because their daily allowances didn't stretch to paying for meals (invariably Chinese takeaways), telephones (calls to the folks back home? Forget about it), travel (we're walking, guys). All these little niggling concerns add up and can be a distraction to the necessary focus you need to perform in the top class. To put matters in context, on Sri Lanka's first tour of England in 1984, each player received 150 pounds sterling for the whole two months of our stay. Each England player received 150 pounds a day for playing a Test. For the next ten years as the salaries of international cricketers climbed steadily, our pay levels clumped along. Playing a man's game we were paid like boys. And it wasn't as if we were receiving much in the way of prize money either, obviously.

Obviously we were playing for love, not money, but the seeping effects of impoverishment meant that for too long too many of us felt like second-class citizens playing a first-class game. The season before the 1996 World Cup, with our tours of Pakistan and Australia, the pay situation became a little better thanks to the trickle-down effect of television revenues. There just wasn't much money in the game for Sri Lanka and it was only after, and I stress 'after', we won the World Cup that a whole load of local and international corporations started seeing us as prime marketing opportunities. Even now the players do not receive a fortune by any means; getting paid better only makes us play better in the way that gaining self-esteem makes every aspect of your life better. You become more self-confident, more self-assured, more willing to take the initiative in every situation on and off the pitch. Winning respect has meant that we are treated with more consideration than before by the international press and public; by all those who when speaking to us in English, speak with just a little bit more slowness and with words of fewer syllables than normal, and by all those who follow cricket and for whom too long 'Sri Lankan cricket' was synonymous with 'minnows'/ 'pushovers'/and 'little fellows'. It's simple; the more you win the more respect you get.

Back in the bad old days our batsmen only really knew one way to play: see a target and chase it. All this about building an innings couldn't really be believed with any conviction by our batsmen. There was so much evidence to the contrary. One or the other of our openers would invariably fall early on, our middle order was inconsistent and we had a tail longer than a peacock's. In Tests especially, our weaknesses were exposed. If a bowler's unthreatening for ten overs in a one-day game, chances are he won't go for more than sixty runs give or take a few. If a bowler's unthreatening in a Test match, chances are he'll have to bowl thirty to forty overs and go for plenty. As a batsman, if one particular bowler is giving you trouble, you just can't avoid playing him for too long in a Test match. In one-day cricket we were a better side. Our batsmen could have more impact. They had more scope to play to their strengths. We actually were a team packed with batsmen of flair and application but the surprising thing was we never managed to play well together. So many times Arjuna would be left not out at the end of a one-day innings or Asanka or Roshan would make a vainglorious fifty in a losing cause. So many times a bowler would find catches off his bowling not held, so many times a bad ball every couple of overs would undo all a bowler's good work. So very many times a fielder would gift away a run or two to an opposing batsman. So many times our best wasn't good enough.

Rookie cricketers like the all-rounder Athula Samarasekera, the slow left-armer Don Anurasiri, the seamer Champaka Ramanayake, our paceman Graeme Labrooy, the batsman Hashan Tillekeratne worth a place in the side for his fielding alone, the leggie Asoka de Silva, the offie Ranjith Madurasinghe, the wicket-keeper Gamini Wickremasinghe, the fast-medium Kapila Wijegunawardene, a certain Sanath Jayasuriya, the strokeful Marvan Atapattu, the opener Dammika Ranatunga, the hard-hitting wicket-keeper/batsman Romesh Kaluwitharana, the off-spinner Jayananda Warnaweera, the opener Charith Senanayake, the nuggety all-rounder Chandika Hathurusinghe, the fast-medium Pramodya Wickremasinghe, and the off-spinning allrounder Ruwan Kalpage all made their international debuts during these wilderness years. And while all tasted occasional victory in the one-day arena, all too often they, like the rest of us with more experience, found themselves outgunned, outperformed, out-thought and outclassed. Somehow we were never a whole cricket side; just a collection of individuals playing cricket. When we were bad we were diabolical and when we were good we were average. The Sri Lanka of 1982–1987 had been a road-worthy mixture of experience (Mendis, Dias, Wettimuny, D.S. de Silva) and youth (Madugalle, Ranatunge, Ratnayake, Ratneyeke, de Mel et al). But the Sri Lanka of 1987–1992 was a melange of unduly suffering bowlers, inconsistent batting (P.A. de Silva) and hapless fielding. During these years players were pushed to the front while still learning. And while there can be no better school than the international arena, the lessons learnt were often very harsh and painful.

It wasn't that we weren't trying. We were. It was just that we didn't know what else we could do. We were ignorant more than incompetent. Cricket is the kind of game you can only learn by doing. The game is the teacher. Other countries, apart from playing more international cricket than us, were playing a lot more competitive cricket at domestic level. Purely through being in an environment where a lot of good cricket is being played, players and teams get a sense of effective tactics and what is or isn't possible in the context of a game. For example, when a team needs 80 runs with 6 wickets in hand with 10 overs to go in a one-day game, enough batting teams prevail to show that it is very gettable. If a team is defending 30 runs in the last 5 overs, enough bowling teams have prevailed to show that this too is very achievable. As a bowler you learn what balls not to bowl in the light of having anything short and wide smacked away; as a batsman you learn how to use the wrists and the angled bat to nip and tuck runs at leisure. As a fielder you learn that the one thing a batsman hates and a bowler loves is the brilliant stop that registers a dot ball and saves a certain four. Other teams learnt these principles in domestic cricket, we had to learn them at the highest level. Learning how to bat properly in Tests took us longer than learning the lessons of one-day cricket, but slowly and surely we were growing into a good side. Ripeness is all.

Technical faults persisted to an unfortunate degree amongst our players purely because once the faults had been exposed – a vulnerability to the balls that come back on to the stumps; a vulnerability to balls that bounce and move away; a vulnerability to anything Wasim Akram bowls – they couldn't be remedied immediately. An emerging technical or temperamental fault takes just a few innings to become common knowledge on the circuit and there is practically no time to effect repairs during the middle of a hectic series of games against international competition. So we Sri Lankan batsmen would go home following a tour fractured in spirit and technique and would then have to modify our game for future matches possibly six months ahead. Proper practice is about ingraining in your mind and muscles the best way to play, if you're not playing proper matches it can all become a waste of time. In those wandering, talent-squandering years we'd lurch from good to bad to good in a haphazard cycle of play-rest-play. You either overcame your defect, and sometimes it really took a batsman no more than standing more upright in crease and playing just a fraction closer to his body, or you learnt to live with what you couldn't rise above. And exposed your weakness to the world the next time you played, hoping it wouldn't be picked on. Fat chance.

Nowadays with so much cricket being played, international players can carefully assess their schedule of playing commitments and aim to maximise output when it really matters. We're almost becoming like professional golfers and tennis players with their never-ending calendar of events. You're never more than a few weeks away from playing somewhere. You have to prepare your mind (and your loved ones) to the demands of playing a full season home and away, and of course you have to train for it physically. Which means pushing through innumerable pain barriers in daily training. You have to be able to deal with this kind of pain to the point where it doesn't affect your performance during a game. One of the major reasons we would drop catches and make unforced errors when batting or find that our bowlers weren't able to maintain pace and enthusiasm throughout a day in the field, was because we would tire easily, certainly more easily than our opponents.

Cricket is physically demanding but it is not as demanding as boxing or running a marathon. The stresses and strains come from pushing tired bodies with tired minds. I think all of us find that our brains consume most of our energies on the field. Like golf, like tennis, cricket is a particularly mental game: a series of one-on-one duels within a framework of team competition, any stroke can decide the fate of a game. Every game is a fight from first ball to last, and the teams who understand this are the teams that win the most. For some series and tournaments you know you have to be at nothing less than your very best, for others you feel that maybe you can relax a little bit and just ride with the punches, giving yourself a chance to recharge batteries, to experiment and develop more skills in less intense environments. The year is now a marathon of sprints. Always you're attempting to tune your body and mind to a certain level of performance. Always you're looking two months ahead. Not trying too hard, not trying too little, just trying hard enough in order to peak at the right time. And when you're in the middle of a limited-overs event playing back-to-back games, only pride and a hunger to assert oneself keep one trying to give of one's best when one's body and soul are crying out for rest. The prize money, the gongs and baubles, welcome though they are, are a minor spur. You play to win because if you do win, then the other team don't. Golf and tennis have their 'majors' in the midst of other less prominent events, we have 'majors' too: currently, contests against Australia, Pakistan and South Africa. Playing England too, is a 'major' irrespective of how well the England team are doing, because English cricket attracts so much attention in the cricket world. And the World Cup of course. These are the contests you want to win more than any other.

With Sri Lanka playing so little cricket in our barren period it was worth nobody's while to coach us on a regular basis, although eminences like Dennis Lillee, Frank Tyson and Sir Garry Sobers would make fleeting appearances. In lieu of regular play and practice, players were left to their own devices until a few weeks before each tour when we'd all gather for nets and practices. A far cry from now when even in the few off-periods from cricket each national squad member receives detailed instructions from the management on particular diet and exercise regimes to uphold. The first days back after a long break are agonising for many players as all leisurely indulgences are exposed under the rigorous testing of the team physio Alex Kountouri. The Cricket Board did an honourable thing in our fallow years by giving national squad-members 'pay-or-play' contracts so that even if no cricket was being played in Sri Lanka the players would have at least a little income coming in and wouldn't be tempted to move abroad for work or play. But let there be no mistake. Money, useful though it was, has never been the reason why we played the game in those days. Many cricketers while playing in their back-yards and progressing to playgrounds to school games have dreams of being great, of being popular, of being winners. But as soon as they reach a certain level of competence and find that the next stage up is proving difficult to achieve, many lose heart. Why expose yourself to public ridicule, why risk disappointing others? I started a modest import/export trading business in those years and quickly realised that my commercial goofs and triumphs were only important to me. But a goof or triumph as an international cricketer meant so much more to so many others. You performed in full view of the cricket world. Playing international cricket is like going to work each day in the biggest open-plan office there is, with the sneaking suspicion that your flies might be undone.

From being impressive in sub-first class conditions back home to being given the chance to combat the likes of Imran, Viv, Gooch, Hadlee, Border and Kapil, really is a huge leap for a youngster to have to make. The support of mentors is vital. Pakistan can just launch cricketers with little or no first-class experience into the world because there is always the support group of hardened veterans in the side. I am sure that Wasim and Waqar, and even Inzamam wouldn't have had quite the enduring impact on Pakistani cricket they have had were it not for the presence of Imran and Javed. It was not unusual to hear Imran call out to Wasim what kind of ball to bowl, or for Javed to come running from the deep to offer advice to a bowler or, whilst he was batting, to give coaching to his junior partners in between overs. Conversely, nowadays whenever Wasim and Waqar are not in the side the Pakistani pace attack just flounders in a mess of loose deliveries. For Sri Lanka however, some of the retired players whose experience and insightful opinions would have been useful in these traumatic times were alienated by the attitudes of certain administrators, and their valuable insights were not able to be heard by the youngsters in the team. In these years, I might have been establishing myself as Sri Lanka's leading batsman with 167 and 267 in Tests against Australia and New Zealand respectively, but it was all I could do to get myself psyched up to do my best without having to worry about the performance of others. Looking back now, I'd rather have scored half the runs I did if it meant the rest of the runs would have been scored by the others.

In fact we were all on this massive arc of potential, but as soon as we gathered enough momentum to reach a certain level of competitiveness – a win against the West Indies in Sharjah in 1986, the final of the Asia Cup in 1990, a string of competitive performances in Tests against New Zealand, England and Pakistan in 1991 – we'd slip back. Between the middle of April 1987 and December 1989, while the rest of the world played 57 Tests between them, we played just two. Both of which we lost by big margins. There wasn't quite the volume of Test cricket then as there is now of course, but during the whole period of our enforced five-year exile from playing in Sri Lanka we played only twelve Tests, six of them in 1991 alone. England played the most Tests (fifty-two), New Zealand played thirty-eight, and India played the least (twenty-six). Erratic as our schedule was what with only being able to play abroad, we did play a fair number of one-dayers however. We may not always have been able to last the course in a five-day match, but one-day tournament organisers have always loved to have us on board. We could be relied upon to show some entertaining strokeplay and pile on a decent score and when it came to our turn to bowl, opposition batsmen could be relied upon more often than not to beat the blazes out of our bowling. Big box-office either way. And doing both the entertaining and the winning is the best of all.

When Ranjan Madugalle captained the team to Australia in 1987–1988 our primary objective, in lieu of any self-delusional desires to be the best batting and bowling team, was to establish ourselves as the best possible fielding team in the world. Much of Australia's renaissance following their loss of the Ashes for the second series in a row and back-to back series defeats to New Zealand in the 1985–86 season, a climb that took them to the winning of the 1987 World Cup, was credited to their redeveloped fielding prowess. Physical preparation is a great way to create confidence and fielding has a terrific effect on on-field attitude and overall team performance. 'Catches win matches' and dropped catches don't win anything. To be a great fielder you just need to work hard and be committed to succeed. A brilliant fielder by himself is like another bowler, who with a catch or a run-out or a series of run-saving stops can take wickets. Look again at what a batsman does right after he plays a good shot for no runs as the result of a terrific save in the field: feeling that he is owed some runs, the very next ball the batsman tries even harder to beat the field and can simply end up in losing his wicket. It happens time and time again. A brilliant fielder can also go into bat with anything up to 20 runs in credit as the result of all the runs he's saved in the field. Allan Border, David Gower, Roshan Mahanama and Mark Waugh have been some of the very best fielders I've seen but when Jonty Rhodes retires just add 10 runs to his batting average. That'll be a truer measure of his worth to South Africa and the game of cricket.

Fielders don't impinge too much on my consciousness: if I hit the ball, I aim not to see them anywhere near it. But people like Jonty make you take notice. Watching them is an education and a delight. Jonty brings off the impossible (for me at least) and makes it look so ridiculously easy. If he has a secret, it's got to be that he's moving towards where the ball's going before it hits the bat. Roshan Mahanama, with Murali and Upul Chandana the best of our fielders, often tries to explain to the rest of us how they 'anticipate' the ball's movement off the bat. They're cover/mid-off/mid-on typically and they explain their uncanny powers of anticipation as thus: the ball having left the bowler's hand, its trajectory is already in their peripheral vision, simultaneously, they have their eye on the batsman and observe his initial reactions to the delivery. They read the batsman's feet and hands, the speed of the swing, the angle of the body, and some other almost subliminal things which all add up to give them a picture of where the ball will be going. They note, in a compendium that builds up every game, where the batsman likes to play certain kinds of deliveries. And Murali as a bowler keeps an eye out for what areas of the field the batsman's been eyeing in-between deliveries. It can be a real giveaway, he says.

No matter what level a cricketer plays at, he is witness to some extraordinary catches, catches taken with such speed of thought and motion they can scarcely be believed. Human beings never cease to amaze me. It's just that at the highest level the reactions are the sharpest. A couple of years ago (at Gwalior in a Pepsi Independence Cup game in May 1997), Roshan took a catch at mid-off 25 yards from the bat that simply defied belief. To the rankest of long-hops (the kind that has '4' written all over it as soon as it leaves the bowler's hand) delivered by Sanath from around the wicket, Ijaz Ahmed drilled a flat-bat smack straight back past Sanath's left-hand side. It was hit so hard that Sanath didn't even have time to raise an arm to wave the ball goodbye. It was the kind of drive that bursts through boundary-boards. The kind of ball that is hit so hard that if you're not within a couple of feet of it, it's past you before you can get down to it. It was the kind of drive that you actually don't want to be in the way of. From nowhere, Roshan flung himself to his right to catch the ball as it was screaming into oblivion. Sanath had his eye on Ijaz Ahmed. Ijaz's mouth fell open. He couldn't believe what had happened. Sanath turned round and saw the ball in Roshan's hand. Sanath couldn't believe it. Ijaz couldn't believe it. None of us could believe it. Roshan pulled a comet out of the sky that day, and he literally flew a couple of yards to do it. Sanath ran up to Roshan and hugged him, and bouncing him up and down in his Tigger-like way, just asked Roshan 'How? How? How'd you do it?' Roshan's reply: 'It was the only place Ijaz would hit a ball like that!' Which was true, a lesser batsman than Ijaz would have pulled it, an accomplished aggressor like Ijaz hit the ball from well in front of him; he hit it straight, all his weight moving onto the front-foot, maximum power dictating that the ball still be climbing ever so slightly as it blazed past the bowler.

Fielding is a team effort, one unnoticed by many observers. They say that fast bowling and patient batting are alien features to Sri Lankan cricketers, but fielding really does tap into our best 'country before self' mentality. Like the many measures of character in this world, few of which are ever posted on a scoreboard, so many features of fielding go unrecorded in the score-book: the saves, the run-outs, the whole contribution to a bowler's figures in stifling the opposition batsman and creating the right environment for wicket-taking. Just one brilliant piece of fielding can lift a side. So with the tacit knowledge that in the short-term we could never become the world's best fast-bowling nation or the world's best batting team, we embarked on collectively improving ourselves in the field. But it's one thing to express a desire and another to know how to go about achieving it. In the absence of full-time coaching, fielding practices were still unstructured and while the flesh was willing, the spirit was still weak. Nothing drains a team mentally like a long losing streak. We just didn't know what to do nor how to go about using fielding to raise ourselves out of a slump. Our practices were very tame compared to what Bobby Simpson, the prototype for the modern breed of former-player coaches, was putting his recently-acquired Australian charges through. As to actual batting and bowling, for players like myself, Ranjan, Arjuna, Roshan, Asanka, Rumesh and Ravi, the perceived 'seniors' of the side: it was all we could do to work out how to hold on to our own form, fitness and motivation when we were playing so little cricket. So in the absence of any kind of support from anyone who really knew how to get the best out of a player, our young players saw no way out from under the shadow of their difficulties. A few played league and club cricket in England like any other off-season professional, but the majority stayed at home twiddling their thumbs.

Diplomatically too, Sri Lanka was becoming more and more isolated for its perceived human rights abuses against the domestic insurgents; whenever we toured England and India particularly, there would be politically motivated demonstrations and a protective police presence very much in evidence. The whole concept of international cricket became problematic. There were scare-mongering whispers of another 'rebel' Sri Lankan tour of South Africa to follow the one of 1983, which would have been absolute death to Sri Lankan cricket with the resulting bans on participating players that would have been imposed by the Board and the ICC. That South Africa would suddenly be welcomed back to international cricket in the summer of 1991 no one could envisage at the end of the 1980s. The first time we did play South Africa, in Sri Lanka in August 1993, both teams observed a minute's silence for the victims of political repression and violence in South Africa and, by analogy, Sri Lanka.

During these years of being cricketing wanderers the possibility did cross my mind, but not for long, of going to live abroad. My sister Araliya was married and settled in Auckland at this time prior to her later move to Sydney, and as an adviser to my business affairs she painted an attractive picture of the opportunities for competitive cricket and investment in the region. Eager to play anywhere, I took up an offer to play cricket at District level in Australia for Prahran, a club in the Melbourne suburbs, in the 1988–1989 season and was pleased to discover that even a little below Sheffield Shield level, the standard really was quite high. At District level it was quite common to find Australian cricketers and even some from England on their way up to, or on their way down from, international level. The skills might not be consistently topflight but there was no doubting these weekend cricketers' competitiveness. Even the practice sessions were intense blood-and-guts affairs. They are a fine breeding-ground for competitive and mentally-tough cricketers.

The motivation to get up for a single one-off Test as so many of our games were is difficult enough; you cannot pace your game nor properly channel your adrenaline. Nor can you train in the interminable off-season with any great enthusiasm. Away from cricket, I was sick with unused self. Simultaneously, in the light of continuing political unrest at home which in spite of all diplomatic efforts didn't look like abating, I really couldn't see myself playing cricket for Sri Lanka for too long. Emigration offered me a chance to make a decent living outside of cricket and also a competitive playing structure. At this stage I had no idea that I would be playing three more World Cups-worth of international cricket, and seeing the scale of our ethnic troubles at home I had no conviction that Sri Lanka would ever play international cricket at home again. So emigration did cross my mind as it did some other players', and I invested in some property in Auckland. But the lure of playing full-time for Sri Lanka in the hope that we would soon enough again be playing cricket year-round kept us at home.

South African and Australian rugby players and cricketers all seem to have the same attitude. You win by making things happen. The motivating forces for sporting performance in the southern hemisphere seem to tap into the original settlers' desires to carve a way of life out of an environment not totally supportive of human habitation. You'd think that New Zealand's cricketers would have the same consistent success as their All Black confreres but there's something about the deeply personal nature of cricket performance that seems to consume the New Zealanders' introspective souls. New Zealand has almost been like a second home to me at times and part of my fascination with the people there is based on the essential contrasts between them and Sri Lankans. You only have to spend a little time with the very best New Zealand cricketers of the modern age, Richard Hadlee, Martin Crowe and Glenn Turner to realise that their insularity and isolation from their team-mates is the result of their own alienation from anybody else in New Zealand who could completely support them in their iconic life at cricket's peak.

To be a champion in any sport demands intense focus on a goal; to play cricket consistently successfully requires a psychological stamina known to only a few. It takes so much out of you, that there are times when you have nothing left to give to others, nothing left to recharge your batteries with. To fill that void some seek attention and approval from outside themselves. And that's when team-mates can feel their needs overlooked. Everyone is a hero to themselves and it is very easy for a star performer within a team to upset the feelings of team-mates by withdrawing into himself. Prior to drawing in all the media attention. When the team is winning all anxieties are forgotten, it is only when the team is losing that tensions begin to surface.

Until the re-organisation in 1990 of Sri Lankan club cricket into a district and provincial competition, the President's Trophy, the remedial school of domestic cricket was all but worthless to our cricketers; consequently the rookies had to suffer the slings and arrows of world-class opponents for longer than necessary. Things started getting better for Sri Lankan cricket when teams from abroad resumed playing in Sri Lanka, first with a hastily scheduled popular visit by England 'A' at a time when the full Sri Lankan side were touring New Zealand in early 1991. The reason why England could come at such short notice? They were playing in Pakistan in the midst of the Gulf War crisis and what with all the rioting and mayhem with the England team being prisoners in their hotel rooms, a generally calm Sri Lanka seemed like a safe haven for England 'A'. In these games Marvan Atapattu and the schoolboy Muttiah Muralitharan were particularly impressive against an England team which included Mark Ramprakash, Graham Thorpe, Nasser Hussain, Neil Fairbrother, Richard Illingworth, Mark Ilott and Ian Salisbury. Once again popular with European tourists in search of an idyllic tropical paradise, Sri Lanka was now being seen as a safe place to visit and the Cricket Board started making plans to host tours in the following season. But our civil war troubles hadn't all gone away to the north of the island. During the last 'A-Test' against the English, the Sri Lankan Defence Minister was assassinated by car bomb two miles away from the P. Sara stadium where the teams were playing.

Until the time of our World Cup win, even though to much of the outside world Sri Lanka might have seemed to be a collection of the unpronounceable doing the unremarkable, the emerging players of this era were actually all valiant cricketers. To a man they all improved as their careers progressed. As their careers progressed they grew as men. They stuck in, gritted their teeth and held on. They were amongst Sri Lanka's best and they wanted to show they were amongst the world's best too. Their desire to play top-class cricket was so great that they would happily risk repeated public exposure of their failings as long as they thought it was improving their skills. We all know of quite how far Hash, Sanath, Marvan, Kalu and Wicky have come on, but even now Don Anurasiri having made his Test debut in our win against Pakistan in 1986 as a 20 year-old is worthy of playing in Tests, as he showed against Zimbabwe in 1998. Ruwan Kalpage and Chandika Hathurusinghe are often asked to step in. Even that doughty competitor Champaka Ramanayake is perennially threatening to make a comeback.

A major factor in Sri Lanka's weakness then was perceived to be the small pool of talent it had to choose from. Though we didn't realise it at the time this actually proved to be a strength. Like wood seasoned by exposure to the elements, our emerging talent was toughened up the hard way. Just by playing you would get better. And in the absence of much competition for places, once a player had broken into the side he had every chance of enjoying an extended run. The Zimbabweans 'enjoy' the same circumstances too, with an even smaller talent base to choose from. And from the outset they have never really been a bad side. All a country needs to consistently compete at the highest level are twenty or so seasoned quality players, two XIs worth, with a top junior coming through every couple of years. Right now Australia (even with its small population) has them for sure, the other nations possibly.

You'd think that England with its sophisticated and elaborate professional game would be at the top of the tree when it comes to talent. But a player coming into the England side where there are two hundred or so professional cricketers to choose from, has to prove himself very quickly because there is perceived to be so much talent waiting in the wings staking a claim for a place. An England debutant has to be a hero – the 'next Botham/Gower/Gooch – from the off, or he is quickly and undeservedly seen as a zero. Any selection policy that doesn't back a player after he has been selected, hobbles itself. The sight of talent being picked and then quickly discarded sends a dispiriting signal to all those on the fringes of selection. It should be hard for a player to break into the side yes, but it shouldn't be easy to drop him either. The media, fans and partisans might clamour for a player who has had an initial disappointing run to be replaced, but if that player was considered good enough to be selected then surely that player should have it in him to shine. A player always knows, in his heart of hearts, whether he really has what it takes to play at the very top. Next to oneself, one's peers are the best judge of talent, and if colleagues in the dressing-room think a player is made of the right stuff, then a modest run of performances by themselves should not be grounds for being dropped. Foundations have to be as deep as the heights to which you aspire and if a player has the basics – footwork, technique, reflexes – then the rest is all in the head. If a quality player doesn't set the world on fire from the start of his international career, then

Brothers in arms – embracing Arjuna on reaching my century
in the 1996 World Cup final (Pradeep Mandhani)

A drained group of players gives thanks after winning
the World Cup (Prasanna Hennayake)

Relaxing with the World Cup trophy

The merry-go-round of international cricket is not all glamour!

The love of my life, a Ferrari 355 Spyder

The other love of my life, fiancée Sarita Rajendran

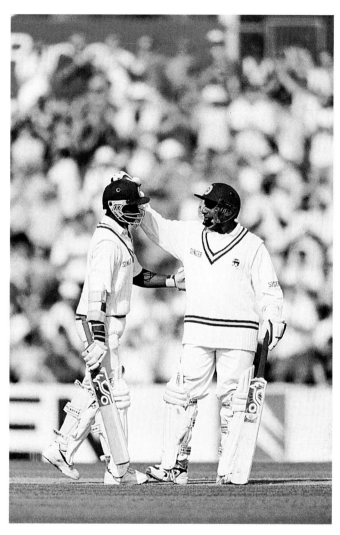

Congratulating Jayasuriya on reaching his century against
England at the Oval in August 1998

The unique double-jointed action
of spinner Muralitharan

Murali (9–65) celebrates bowling Sri Lanka to
victory against England in 1998 (Allsport)

A remarkable shot from a remarkable player
– *that* flat-batted six over cover

Where it all begins, and ends

there has to be a way to keep his talent and desire from burning out.

Of course it took a while for these international rookies new to cricket, new to life, to find out what their strengths were especially when, in the absence of domestic competition, all that was being revealed were their weaknesses at international level. And technical and temperamental weaknesses were exploited with relish by the opposition. The need to constantly learn the game is a given, it is just a shame when the lessons taught are the harshest truths in a classroom big enough to fit in a school the size of the world. And it was just so upsetting to keep having the same lessons drilled into us over and over again. We thought we'd gone beyond that through our experiences in earlier years. But just knowing what's needed isn't enough, a player knowing he can do the necessary is what counts. Let's not overlook the fact that during part of the period when Sri Lanka was playing all its cricket abroad, Sachin Tendulkar the 'boy wonder' of those days was simultaneously playing twenty of his first twenty-one Tests outside India. He too has had to learn the game the hard way. Good as Sachin was then, he has become even better since. Even with Sunil Gavaskar as a constant mentoring presence off the field and the support of his seniors on it, Sachin has worked very hard to achieve greatness and all credit to him. Only when a cricketer's comprehensively tested himself in all conditions against all contenders and known he's worthy to play at the highest level, has he truly 'arrived'. Maturity comes in many forms: emotional, social, financial, professional. When everything off the field combines with maturity on the cricket field then a player's career really takes off and he goes on to the field knowing he will have an impact. You start saying to yourself what would you do if you were the most confident cricketer in the world? And then you are that person.

Once it's in your head no one can take it away. The secret key to making it: you learn from success, not failure. We would touch success rarely and then only in the one-day arena. But what with the media and our vaunted opponents considering each of our wins a fluke or the result of a distinctly sub-par performance by them, and with us (ever-hospitable) buying into that to some extent, it took a while for us to learn the importance of properly valuing our wins. Of dissecting and analysing them. And really, in the middle of a tournament what with the travelling, the back to back matches and the sheer mental and physical strain of having to be at your best, post-game analysis would be overlooked. But the unexamined life is not worth living. After a win, let alone a loss, a professional cricket team has to understand the reason for the result. You have to find out the whys, and the hows. That's the key. Success is never easy, but the more you taste it, the easier it gets. No different with failure. The more you taste it, the more you get it. Which is why the taste of even one defeat has to be so upsetting as to make you determined to not experience it again.

With our hit-or-miss, death-or-glory batsmanship we could never be relied upon to prevail. Whenever we won, it was because a top-order batsman like Roshan settled down to play a long innings around which someone like Asanka, Arjuna or myself would push it along. There were times when Arjuna's form was such that the only way he could get out would be through run-outs. And he'd get out that way quite a bit. We didn't understand then how vital it was to build partnerships. One batsman batting well makes it easier for his partner, who simply needs to support him not just by giving him as much of the strike as possible, but by approximating his partner's strike-rate. With both batsmen doing well, the fielding team is really struggling. Too often it was down to our stroke-players to play a lone hand. If Asanka would do well, neither Arjuna or I would, and vice-versa. I now know how much strike-rotation is essential in a one-day innings. You have to make the bowlers work as hard as possible, put the fielders under as much pressure as possible. Both batsmen have to see the strike, stay alert, get into a rhythm of run-getting. But in those days, we were diabolical runners between the wickets, and whenever we were tied down by the fielding side, our solution would be to try and compensate by playing over-aggressively. So we'd either hole out or look for quick singles when none were there. The number of run-outs we suffered was staggering. Asanka especially, was a master of turning ones into two desperate scrambles for the crease. Averaging over one run-out per game in this period, we were even worse between the wickets than Pakistan and that's saying something. For example, four run-outs in one innings against India (myself included) cost us the Asia Cup final against India in 1988.

Switching back and forth from Test cricket to one-day cricket game was never a big problem for us because we played like one-day cricketers over the duration of our Tests, (not that many of them lasted for five days). Boundary-hitters all, we thought throwing the bat was the solution to everything in a crisis. It's not. Finding the gaps is most important of all, be it with a push or a shove. Winning batting is not about playing shots, it's about runs. It's not just about scoring runs, it's about contributing a score that has significance. It's not just about big scores, it's about substantial partnerships. It's not just about major partnerships, it's about an innings as a whole. It's about playing for the team. It's about playing to a plan. As soon as we understood this we came good, we became a team capable of achieving any score. And with the emergence of a new generation of batsmen and bowlers, Chaminda Vaas, Muralitharan and Marvan Atapattu to the fore, we have become consistently capable of winning Tests as well as one-dayers.

CHAPTER TWELVE

It's been a learning process since I started, and I've only recently started putting it all together. 'Brilliant but inconsistent' . . . 'talented but immature' . . . 'possessed of all the strokes but injudicious in their application' . . . these are all the ways in which I was described for quite some many years after my emergence on the scene. And for a long time, yes, there was a 'but' when it came to my game. In spite of scoring plenty of runs in Tests and limited-overs internationals, I didn't consistently make the most of whatever talent I have. Cricket, like baseball, has a statistic for just about everything and according to studies of baseballers, thirty-one is the best of all possible ages to be if you're a ballplayer. That's the peak. The skills of youth and the knowledge of experience meet there. I was in my thirty-first year when we won the World Cup in 1996. I'd been playing at the highest level for over ten years and had realised that I needed to combine my youthful exuberance with wily maturity. Once youth and maturity are combined a player becomes luckier, smarter and more of a winner. For a youngster to have a great captain and a good coach on his side is a terrific advantage, but only when he works things out for himself is he completely developed.

In cricket, conditioning the mind is as important as conditioning the body. In the middle you need your mind to be working perfectly, not reacting to the pressures. You need to be able to read the game and read yourself. You can reach a state when what everyone else does doesn't matter; you're playing your own game out there. It's a heady state to be in, fraught with the dangers of being so far up yourself that you forget that twenty-one others are competing desperately to impose themselves on the game too. But there are those times when you are so in control it's awesome. The fastest deliveries come to you in slow motion, the spinning seam visible in every rotation: you know exactly what's going to happen before you make it happen. The World Cup final and semi-final of 1996 were such times for example, times when everything came together for me. It had happened a few times before, and several times after those games, but those two times naturally stand out in retrospect for me and all those who saw me bat during them.

There used to be so much racing inside my head in the old days.

Delight, desire, hunger, determination, anger, frustration, insecurity, so much grinding of the gears. I had so much to prove: that I could bat, that Sri Lanka could compete. I just didn't know how to maximise my talent. I would walk out to bat, and only during the walk to the middle it would occur to me whether I would bat well or not. My performance could depend on how I felt emotionally and physically, on how my hands felt inside my gloves as they gripped the bat (the 'feel' of hand in glove is so important to me), on how my life was off the field. I had any number of different stances and grips, for the spinners, medium-pacers and quicks, top of the handle, bottom, mid-handle, top-hand loosest, bottom-hand heavy etc. etc. I remember during the 1989 Nehru Cup (when I scored plenty of runs in a six-nation tournament), during every game I had to change my grip and stance because I hadn't settled on the one combination that made me feel most comfortable. So I just settled on something that felt right at that moment. I just did what felt right on the day. I made runs that fortnight but I couldn't rely on myself to come up with the goods consistently. I was one of those 'on his day . . . ' batsmen.

I still have the ability to improvise as the ball comes to my bat, but I am now master of my talent and not its servant. The difference between the Aravinda of then and the Aravinda of now is that I've reprogrammed my mind to react to my emotions differently. I have no time to think 'original/fresh' thoughts at crease, relying instead on conditioned reflexes developed over hundreds of days of competition. The education has been as much physical as psychological, learning has come in increments. Most importantly I learned to love the details of the game. You do small things and they lead to big things, and big things lead to huge things, and huge things lead to team success. You are not fighting alone out there, there are a bunch of guys who are learning with you and as you demonstrate your development, they're watching you and learning too. The best teams need only have eyes for each other.

Most of the times I have scored runs easily, I haven't enjoyed them; they do not give anywhere near the satisfaction that comes from innings that are hard-earned in a tense, pressure situation. Playing lower middle order or even further down in the early days didn't give me a chance to develop a sense of regret – a very necessary sense – on losing my wicket. For invariably, soon after I was out, my team's innings would end and we would all go back out to field. I had played my part as a free-swinging batsman, what more could there be to my part in the game? But as I developed, became older and was given more responsibility and started to come in either first down or No. 4, I developed a greater love for crease occupation. Time and front-line batsmen were now my partners and I finally discovered for myself the simple truth that the longer I spent at the crease, the more runs I would score, the more fun I would have, and the more significant a contribution I could make to the team. You never really understand this until you suffer unto yourself the most diabolical of self-inflicted dismissals — caught in the deep — and then troop in to the 'pavilion' to watch the remaining batsmen either pile up the runs or fight the battles that were originally yours. All that fun for the having, all those runs for the taking, all those challenges to be risen to and you can't indulge. Why? Because you're out. Nothing to do but sit and watch and play the game in your head. A terrible place to be. Immersed in international cricket, I had deprived myself from its pleasures by the simple fact that I didn't think to marry my talent to my appetite and the needs of the team.

The way I liked to play was to always attempt the most positive shot, knowing full well that I would always give bowlers and fielders a chance to snare my wicket. Delight and danger went hand in glove, adding to the thrill of performance. There is a risk-reward ratio to almost every positive stroke, and I always went for the reward. My response to the threats of the bowlers bowling to a field and people in catching positions, were immediate and unsubtle. I reckoned that bowlers weren't just sending down deliveries, they were throwing down the gauntlet, challenging me to do my best. And I'd take them on every single time. Sucker! Sure, I'd win some battles but I'd also lose a great many wars every time I was out for less than what was needed to hurt the opposition. Success is hard enough when you've got to take on atmospheric conditions, the state of the wicket, off-field influences, the rub of the green and the efforts of others, but shooting myself in the foot on a regular basis didn't help.

All batsmen, bowlers and fielders live with the prospect of failure, batsmen especially, as their fates rest on the impact of a few square inches of moving bat on moving ball. The slightest half-inch of miscalculation can mean the difference between survival and dismissal. And this placing of bat on ball depends on so many things. But the prospect of failure never bothered me, I just wanted to succeed. Particularly in those years either side of 1990, I had so much 'juice' in me, so much of a desire to show the world what I could do, that whenever I went in to bat I wanted to attack at every opportunity. I carried two thoughts with me out into the middle: the bigger the reputation of the bowler the better I wanted to play against him and, secondly, something I picked up from what Boris Becker once said on his way to winning Wimbledon for the second time (as an eighteen-year-old!), 'first you destroy an opponent's strengths, then his weaknesses'. If a bowler's main weapon was his bouncer then you could be sure I'd go all out to play the hook-shot. If a bowler's most devastating delivery was the yorker then I'd do my utmost to drive him back down the ground. It was bloody and relentless, and I didn't always come out on top, but for as long as I was at the crease the opposition all knew that I was someone they'd really have to compete with. They'd call me 'Mad Max', 'Quick Silva' or 'Metal Mickey' for my tendency to swing the bat from side to side at full speed. My aggression was rampant and uncontrolled, my mind filled with the thought of runs. In concentrating on 4s and 6s I forgot the bigger picture, and lost just about every mind game I was challenged to play. At the time I probably didn't even realise there were mind games. My hands were always clasped round my bat, leaving me no room to keep hold of the initiative once it was in my grasp.

The 267 in Wellington (against a Hadlee-less New Zealand attack in 1991) is notable only for the fact that on the day in which I scored over 200 runs, I didn't make a single mistake against an attack that didn't ask too many questions. The 167 against Australia at Brisbane the season before that, I still rate as one of my best Test innings, for the team had a lot riding on the outcome of the game. It was our first Test for fourteen months, only our third in two years, and the match came at time when many in Australia and around the world were questioning our right to be playing Test cricket. After a large innings defeat against Victoria just before the first Test, some in the Australian team had already written us off as no-hopers and were just looking on the Test fixture against us as an unfortunate interruption to their more important playing schedules. The last time we'd played Australia we'd lost by an innings with almost two days to spare, my contribution being 6 and 7. Against Sri Lanka, the thinking went you could only pick up some cheap runs and wickets or a stupid injury. Either way it wasn't worth playing Sri Lanka. After this two-Test series against Australia we had no idea when or where our next Test was going to be. No Tests at home, the possibility of precious few away and with none on the immediate horizon, when we took the field against Allan Border's team at the Gabba we were playing for more than our pride. We were playing for our status. We were out to prove we were worthy of playing Australia, worthy of playing Tests. To many, Sri Lanka was, to all intents and purposes, a Test team in name only. This tour of Australia would conclusively resolve the issue of our future playing schedules.

Brisbane is an unusual wicket and has played differently each time I've played there. Sometimes it can be almost as bouncy as Perth, on other occasions it can be pretty slow. The practice pitches on the edge of the Gabba's outfield this time were playing pretty hard, however, and we knew that Australia were going to field an all-seam attack. So the day before the Test we were all rather grateful to receive a local sportswear representative in our midst and spent a good deal of time trying out all the latest protective gear combinations he had to offer. We weren't taking any chances against Merv Hughes, Carl Rackemann, Geoff Lawson and

Terry Alderman. The Australian team, fresh from a 4–0 routing of England, was on one of their periodic surges of excellence in those days and whereas they still lacked a front-line Test spinner, their seam attack was pretty strong and their batting was formidable with Boon, Taylor, Border, Jones and Steve Waugh all sure to feature. With particular regard to Allan Border, at this stage in his career he had played twice as many Tests as our entire 16-man squad put together. Even after eight years of international cricket Sri Lanka still appeared like novices.

The widely reported words of Simon O'Donnell, the Victorian captain, after our match with them, where he seriously questioned our ability as a Test team to even challenge Australia's state sides, and the comments of his team-mates during our match, had really stung deeply and we were motivated not to appear as no-hopers in this Test. Australia, batting first, comfortably made 367. Which doesn't sound like much of a triumph but it was the first time Australia had scored less than 400 in their first innings in nine Tests against the West Indies, England and New Zealand earlier in the year. And considering Ravi Ratneyeke couldn't bowl after lunch on the first day because of a side-strain, we were happy with our efforts. Next to hostile bowling, pride is the strongest weapon a team can have.

Rain on the first day seemed to quieten the wicket and the expected zip off the pitch didn't quite materialise for the Aussie fastmen. As a batsman against pace-bowling you have to half anticipate events. Terry Alderman bowled his wicket to wicket medium-fastish groovers, moving the ball both ways; the best way to play him, I thought, was to get as close to the pitch of the delivery as possible, coming down the wicket to him if necessary. The closer you are to the ball, the less room it has in which to move. Terry Alderman, outstanding bowler that he was, may have been a little flattered in his career by bowling so often to Englishmen who wouldn't take him on, content to play him from the crease with a half-hearted bat. That is just asking for trouble in my opinion.

There is a grey area between a batsman's hip and his shoulder in Australia, which can turn black and blue whenever a batsman encounters sudden extra pace. Squaring up to the short deliveries, I did get pinned quite a few times on the arms and ribs, rather than play a hook which I might have done at any other time. For me, the hook and pull shots are maximum percentage strokes: maximum runs and minimum outs. The most steepling deliveries sail way above my head and are a waste of energy for the bowler, the deliveries that I choose to hit are the ones that simply climb into my torso. It feels so much easier to play them with a cross-bat rather than a perpendicular one. I always aim to hook downwards, unless there aren't any fielders in the deep, when I fancy collecting maximum runs for the stroke. The tussle with Merv Hughes was particularly invigorating. It has to be said that Merv Hughes wasn't perhaps at 100 per cent fitness, that much was clear from seeing him with ice-packs strapped to both his knees, front and back, after close of play on the third and fourth days. Not that he gave any sign of discomfort during his jousting spells of bowling. He was a monster competitor and would run down hits to the boundary when in the outfield with the same drive and determination that he showed in his bowling.

For this innings, anticipating a bouncy wicket, I made a conscious decision to adopt Sunil Gavaskar's technique of going back-and-across to anything on or short of a length. In fact it was my initial extreme concentration on this as opposed to being properly responsive to reading the length of the delivery from the bowler's release point which caused me to be stuck in 'two man's land' and play half-cock to a full-length ball from Merv Hughes and spoon a chance back to him. Which I'm delighted he dropped. From the pace of the subsequent deliveries I think it must have really upset him to drop a relatively easy caught and bowled chance from me when I had barely got off the mark. Alerted to the danger of premeditation, I then played the right shot to the right ball on just about every instance – playing away from the fielders at every opportunity (Allan Border put men in front of square and on square-leg for my favourite lofted shot), keeping the ball on the ground on all but one gloriously tempting occasion, until I was last out with the score on 418 (I lofted that one too). It had been my best Test innings to date; one that really helped to redefine the team and Sri Lankan cricket. Our performance had won a lot of critics over. Australia were now behind on first innings for the first time in a long while and, had David Boon and Tom Moody not been dropped early on in their innings late on the fourth day, perhaps we could have really taken the upper hand in proceedings. As it was, Mark Taylor went on to yet another one of his big hundreds on the final day and the match petered out to a tame draw. We hadn't won overall, but we were light years away from losing and that meant a great deal to all concerned.

Within the space of a few days, Sri Lankan cricket emerged with new self-respect and the respect of others. International cricket is a highly public game and cricketers are seen to represent their teams' philosophies, their countries' national characteristics along with even their upbringing and background. No criticism can have the impact of self-criticism but outsiders' disparaging comments can really cut us to the quick. Maybe it is because we are a small nation with small people in a big world with big people, maybe it is because we have only just started to have an impact on the world stage with our athletes and statesmen – we are very quick to carry what some would call a 'chip' on our shoulders in our response to our opinions being overlooked and our feelings disregarded.

Sometimes we have thought that we are just not understood or treated as equals by the rest of the cricketing establishment. Whenever we cricketers (Sri Lanka's most visible export) take to the field, we are representatives of a way of life that is very different to those of our opponents, India, Pakistan and Bangladesh notwithstanding. Whenever we Sri Lankans play we are very conscious that we are playing for ourselves and our families, our culture and our way of life. Any criticism of a player we take to be a criticism of a player's background, the way he was brought up. That's just the way it is: a player is the sum part of all his influences. Naturally, critics who are just plain wrong are easily laughed off, but those who would touch on our personal characteristics with all the subtlety of a power-drill really get our backs up. Sure, in 1989–90 we weren't a great Test side but half of that team went on to win the World Cup, and win Tests and tournaments around the world.

For years we would play well in one game only to subside haplessly in the next, and even though we did go on to lose the following Test to Australia at Hobart, we did put up a good competitive fight. Winning the toss, Arjuna put Australia in and, with the revitalised Rumesh to the fore, Australia were dismissed after tea for only 224. Coming on first change, Rumesh took four wickets in five overs with his off-cutters and away swingers, finishing with six wickets in all. You could even say he did Ian Chappell with one that he wasn't expecting when, in response to Chappell's post-match questioning he gave the reason for his success with the ball as being 'Almighty God' and not anything mundane like 'putting the ball in the right place etc. etc.'.

Rumesh has been the most deceptive personality I've ever met. His roguish smile and voguish dress, his absolute disregard for anything like timetables and wake-up calls told of a life lived on the edge of both cricket-club and night-club. Yet he could be up all night and still be the most enthusiastic at practice the next day. He was a brilliant balladeer and with his songs and open-necked shirts could melt the heart of any lady who heard and saw him sing, and yet he was the most God-loving and wife-fearing, or even God-fearing and wife-loving, man you could ever meet. His performances were the toast of many a Sri Lankan and yet never a drop of alcohol passed his lips. An all-out competitor, he could yet faint at the sight of the batsman's blood that he so aggressively spilled. He was almost childlike in his pleasure, a big joyous kid who believed he could do anything on a cricket field, and whose enthusiasm was infectious for his team-mates, for the fans, even for those he played against. He is the world's most innocent playboy, a man infused with love for the game and a fine example of attitude and aptitude to the Sri Lankan 'A' team currently in his care.

Starting an innings towards the end of a day is always difficult, and the last hour's play on the first day of the Hobart Test saw us lose three quick wickets to catches in the slips. Not out overnight, Roshan and I took our partnership past lunch on the following day, both of us with hundreds in our sights when I played back to a ball from the mouthy Greg Campbell and was out lbw for 75. Roshan was out soon after for a well-composed 85. Scenting blood, the spinner Peter Sleep and Merv Hughes clawed up the rest to leave us all out for 216. A major disappointment considering that at 148 for 3 prior to my dismissal we were again contemplating taking that all-important first-innings lead. Still, we hit back almost straightaway and took two Australian wickets before close of play. The game was obviously headed for a result, the only question was which way. The bowling and batting of the two sides up to now had been pretty even and there was the distinct thought that, given a total of 250 or even 300 as a fourth-innings target, Sri Lanka could win the Test match. That must have really motivated the Australian batsmen. As it was, when it came right down to it, the real gulf between the sides became apparent on the third and fourth days when, on a wicket that was flattening out all the time, Taylor, Border, Jones and Steve Waugh simply piled on the runs before Allan Border declared the innings on 513 for 5. Leaving us to score 522 runs in ten hours.

You know, we really thought we could do it. Of course no one had come anywhere close to it being achieved before apart from England's drawing a 'timeless' Test against South Africa in 1939 with a score of 654 for 5. Not that we knew it in the dressing-room at the time. I have yet to meet the cricketer who carries a *Wisden* in his kitbag or even one who's ever read 'The Laws of the Game' in their entirety. Ours is very much an orally and visually absorbed game and what gets said and what gets done is what is understood. One advantage of being quite new to the game is that you don't really know what is or isn't possible and batting in the fourth innings for a day and a half on a good wicket did seem within our capabilities. A win was unlikely, a draw a definite possibility. A conviction that was strengthened by us proceeding to close of play with only three wickets down. Four runs an over for 90 overs with Test match fields isn't impossible, we've come close to it a number of times in recent years as have Australia. Arjuna and I were the not-out batsmen overnight, and we knew that attacking batting was the best way to play because it would keep the bowlers and fielders on edge, and playing 'nothing' cricket could only lead to loss of concentration. Our plan was to stay together all day for as long as possible. We hadn't counted on the wiles of Allan Border though. The day before, I had found run-scoring pretty easy as, fired up by a desire to assert myself against the overbearing Campbell in particular, I had pushed the field back so that there were plenty of singles for the taking whenever I couldn't hit a four.

Opening the bowling on the final day, Peter Sleep partnered Merv Hughes and whenever I was facing, Allan Border had changed the field placings to both bowlers from the day before. Square-leg rather than being on the fence came up by the umpire, and mid-on and mid-off were moved wider. If I wanted runs square of the wicket on the leg-side, I'd now have to hit over the top, or if I wanted runs in front of square, I'd have to play pretty straight. I saw the plan, I saw the possibilities of the trap, and I decided I wouldn't be dictated to and would rather keep the great man dancing to my tune. It is always difficult for a batsman to adjust his gameplan mid-innings but not even a miscued drive that went off the leading-edge short of mid-on taught me the error of my ways and before the first hour was up, I misplayed another on-drive as I came down the wicket to Sleep and the ball ended up in Greg Campbell's hands of all places. Those days, if I had a brain I'd have been really dangerous. The direct result of my wicket falling was Arjuna's instant departure for no further score and in spite of game and valiant resistance from Rumesh and Asoka de Silva who had a big seventh-wicket partnership we were all out in the final hour to give Australia their sixth victory of the year.

Immediate post-mortems on the series with the waiting press showed the beginnings of Arjuna's staking of the moral high ground in Australia with his revelation of 'racial comments' directed at us by one Australian player (whom, it must be said, Rumesh was not averse to body-checking in retaliation late on the fifth day) and his absolute disgust at the antics of bowlers and fielders (Ian Healy in particular) in claiming non-existent catches as the minutes ticked away on the final day at Hobart. Bobby Simpson in reply said that Sri Lanka needed to 'grow up' if it wanted to play the game and perhaps a mountain was made out of a molehill by all. On the field a lot gets said, most of it in the heat of the moment, to alleviate boredom and frustration, but some of it is pretty calculated stuff. There is no doubt that Australia are the world leaders in verbal provocation. This can take the guise of overt hostility – 'You can't effing bat, you bastard' – or the honeytrap methods of Shane Warne who might teasingly say to opposing batsmen, 'Why aren't you trying to hit me over the top? Don't you think you're good enough?' Either way, the intention is clear. The Australians want opposing batsmen's games to be upset, and once they sense you're vulnerable they don't let you go until their mission's accomplished. The fall of the batsman's wicket by hook or by crook.

Australia aren't alone in these methods, everyone does it. Even England, heaven forfend. We do it too, but in Sinhalese and are perhaps more sardonic than aggressive in our heckling. Arjuna might say, for example, of a batsman to the rest of us, 'this one's no good: he can't even hit Aravinda off the square'. Still, Arjuna has such eloquent body-language opposing batsmen soon find out what he thinks of them. But the Pakistanis are the worst. In the days when they were justifiably kings of the hill as World Cup champions they were the most inanely chattering bunch of guys you could ever bat against. It was just non-stop. Mushtaq Ahmed would bowl, Moin Khan would go 'well bowled, Mushy, well bowled', irrespective of the quality of delivery, and then a relay of close-in fielders would start chirruping and laughing amongst themselves, rhythmically tossing around Urdu and Punjabi verbals and the occasional pointed English comment, until it came time for Mushy's next delivery. So much talk had to be counter-productive. We get sledged a lot, all the resentment that gets built up against Arjuna is directed against his followers. And we take it as a compliment. It concentrates our minds and inspires us to play better. The game gets ever so personal for a few minutes and you raise your game just that notch higher so as not to give your opponents the satisfaction of getting you out. If a guy's reduced to trying to talk you off the field, he's down to his last weapon. That should never be forgotten.

It wasn't heckling that caused us to lose our next hastily arranged Test to India at Chandigarh late in 1990. It was an underprepared wicket that was spitting gobbets of turf from the second day, an unprepared team and a pretty decisive spell of bowling from left-arm spinner Venkatapathy Raju who took five middle-order wickets in quick succession to send us tumbling all out for 82 in our first innings. Seven runs short of the follow-on target. Our second innings saw us lurch to 198, with my contribution being 7 runs (for a grand match aggregate of 12) and we lost by an innings. The game was also notable in retrospect for being the start of the unfortunate Marvan Atapattu's run of ducks in his first three Tests. He did notch up one single in his second Test, but rumour has it that it was in reality a leg-bye mistakenly not signalled. But the lad (Marlon Vonhagt's nephew) had so much talent he had to come good eventually, which he has since done with a flourish.

Our next Test series was in New Zealand, starting with the first Test at Wellington. A remarkable game, featuring one of Test cricket's amazing comebacks. All out for 174 on the first day in the windiest conditions you could imagine – the umpires had to use steel-weighted bails – New Zealand were sliced apart by Rumesh and Graeme Labrooy. In much gentler conditions for the remainder of the match we then scored 497 and, in needing 324 to save themselves from an innings defeat, New Zealand then went on to score 671 for the loss of only three wickets until the very last ball of the game. The reason for their rise from the ashes: Andrew Jones and Martin Crowe. John Wright had set them on their way with an assured 88 and a century opening partnership but after he went we didn't see the shadow of a New Zealand wicket for another nine hours. Andrew Jones and Martin Crowe just piled on the runs in their then all-time Test record stand of 467. They never went crazy, but were particularly hard on my offies for a while. In fact we bowled steadily and fielded well throughout. They just piled on the runs on a flat pitch.

On my subsequent visits to New Zealand, friends have always brought round videos of the match to while away the hotel hours and I can admit to having seen highlights of Martin Crowe's epic innings in Wellington quite a few times now. Some wonder why I don't just keep replaying highlights of my 267 in the same game for them, but in reality for all Danny Morrison's, Willie Watson's and Chris Pringle's and Grant Bradburn's efforts I don't really feel too roused by the innings. Somewhere along the line I passed 1,000 runs in Tests. It had taken me seven years for the first 1,000; I scored 4,000 in the next seven, which is testament to the fact that Sri Lanka has been playing more Tests and that I have really developed my game. The innings of 267 was significant as a demonstration of my fitness, as I had never before batted through a whole day's play and walked off the field feeling pretty fresh, but really it has no great resonance for me. What I found more significant about the game was Martin Crowe's innings. Andrew Jones in his time at the top showed himself to be one of the world's great accumulators and had a pretty good record overall, but Martin was the batsman who was the leader in the partnership, the one who completely neutered the bowling. If he had fallen early I am sure we could have forced the win. I had seen glimpses of him before in visits to Sri Lanka and World Cups, but he stood out head and shoulders above the rest of the world's youngish batsmen for his sheer class, composure, grit and determination. He blunted the teeth of the most hostile fast bowling, regularly converted fifties into hundreds, played spin bowling as if it was schoolboy stuff and had the most classical technique of all the batsman then playing the game. So I loved watching him bat. It was an experience I'd rather not have lived through on the field, especially when he was smashing my own off-spin around, but it was nevertheless a pleasure to observe a master batsman at work. If you can't accept it when someone plays very well, then deep down you're not really a player.

Hashan Tillekeratne kept wicket throughout the New Zealand innings without conceding a bye, which in itself set a world record and which also shows how straight we were bowling. Arjuna set an attacking field for the most part, figuring that wickets and not containment was the only way for us to get back in the game (some you win, some you lose). If you observed Martin closely you could sense the supreme concentration with which we applied himself to his innings. He'd talk to himself between deliveries when batting, you could hear him sometimes saying 'keep still, keep still, watch the ball, watch the ball'. The noise inside his head must have been deafening at times but, judging by his record, he obviously kept himself at just the right pitch to achieve his goals. I might have played smart a couple of times in my life until then and thought my way to big scores, Martin did it on a regular basis. He was the prototypical modern-day cricketer, programming his brain to channel his talent and aggression into concentration on a single objective: scoring runs in all conditions all around the world. Plus he had the added responsibility not just of the New Zealand captaincy but of carrying the New Zealand batting in the same way that Richard Hadlee had carried the bowling. It wasn't that New Zealand was ever a one-man or two-man team, whenever they'd win it was a total team effort, but people like Martin Crowe and Richard Hadlee made it easier for others in their team to do well and if they ever did fail, then the team failed too.

You always got the sense that Martin's mental focus was hard-won and came at great physical cost. His brain must have physically tired out his body, so highly strung was he in his intensity. Every one is liable to get injured but only the relaxed heal quickly. In Wellington, having passed what must have been many mental milestones on his way to 299, confronted with the last ball of the day to reach his ultimate target of 300, Martin jabbed at a wide one from Arjuna looking for a single to third man. Springing full length low down to his right almost before Martin had completed his stroke, Hashan took an amazing catch inches off the ground. Even better than the one he'd taken off Rumesh to snare Martin in the first innings. Hash had been concentrating pretty hard too. Martin was obviously gutted and his head was so full of disappointment I don't think he heard us or the crowd applaud him all the way off the field. We did hear him do some damage to the stadium walls on his way back to the dressing-room though. It had been a pretty good innings, and my only consolation in being overlooked in terms of monumentality was that if Martin had scored as fast as I had done, he'd have scored 400.

With respect to me and every other young batsman during the years he played international cricket, Martin was the one who could have made us all look silly, could have shown the rest of us youngsters up for what we were – too often fallible, too often self-destructive. Martin Crowe could make you feel that he was never going to give the bowler a chance, he almost always seemed to play the right shot at the right time; when he set his stall out for a big score he wouldn't let anything defeat him. While not lacking in flair and bold shots, Martin was a very self-disciplined batsman. He knew his strengths and concentrated on them. He was mentally and physically organised; he arranged the component parts of his game in the way that would let him score the necessary runs. Fitness, form, net practices, the necessary understanding with batting partners, game strategy – he'd worked it all out.

Martin Crowe always played under a lot of pressure, self-inflicted and imposed from outside. He always had to play with a lot of responsibility. It made him a grown-up batsman at a very early age. During Martin's playing career New Zealand were always more than a side that depended solely on him and Hadlee for results, but undoubtedly Martin was greatly influential on his team-mates' batting performance. His attitude to the opposition bowling rubbed off on his team-mates. Many's the time Martin's batting partners would be emboldened by his confidence and composure when confronted by the best that the world's best bowlers could offer. He scored Test centuries against all but South Africa, and he was consistently the Kiwi wicket opposing bowlers found hardest to take. Martin retired all too early from the game, forced out by a cruel knee injury. If he was still playing he'd be up there in the hallowed atmosphere of the very best, rated amongst the most all-round accomplished batsmen, batsmen who can adapt their game to any conditions. I admired Martin Crowe so much. If I had understood what made him great earlier in my career, I would have scored a lot more runs by now.

In fact, during the years Martin and I played together, you could say he was the complete opposite of me! I had been in awe of batsmen like Javed and Sunil and Viv ever since I was a boy, and I came to respect and admire Allan Border and David Gower very much, but Martin was the best batsman in the world nearest to my age when I started playing international cricket and he was the one I secretly compared myself to. I looked at his strong points, his authority, arrogance and assertiveness at the wicket and recognised them as necessary attributes for survival and success as an international batsman. The knowledge Martin gained about himself as a batsman, the vital self-knowledge you need about your own strengths and weaknesses and how best to apply all this in match conditions, Martin acquired much earlier in his playing career than I did. It's only in the past four years that I've truly understood myself – hence the surge in consistency, form and runs since the 1995 English season.

CHAPTER THIRTEEN

To be successful in international cricket a country needs a great batsman, a great fielder and a great bowler on which to build a team. We weren't quite able to boast such a complement, but we were certainly on the way up and could feel confident of challenging all our opponents. Prior to the 1992 World Cup we were playing with greater confidence. We weren't winning too many games but we were much more competitive as a team than we had been in a long while. Sanath Jayasuriya and Pramodya Wickremasinghe were amongst a batch of youngsters staking their claims to be in the team on a permanent basis. In Hashan Tillekeratne (another D.S. Senanayake old-boy) we had perhaps found, for a while at least, the solution to our perennial problem of fielding a wicketkeeper of international class. Which was testament to his ball-playing ability because before he put on the gloves for Sri Lanka, Hashan had never even kept wicket in domestic club cricket. Our bowlers were steady, if unspectacular, and our batsmen were all coming to terms with foreign conditions and quality bowling. Not even the fact that Arjuna kept finding himself either in selectorial disfavour, injured or in bad form could stop us being thought of as a team that could beat anybody on their day. And, in particular, players such as Sanath and Hashan were showing big-match temperaments and pulled many an innings out of the fire. Ironically, they were both to miss the Test – against Australia at the SSC in 1992 – where their gutsy talents would have come in most useful.

In Tests against England and Pakistan in 1991 and 1992 we certainly came close to victory, only losing at Lord's against a resurgent England (who had just drawn their five Test home series against West Indies 2–2) late on the final day, and then against Pakistan losing a highly charged Test by only three wickets to cede the series 1–0. In our first match of the 1992 World Cup we scored the highest ever total by a side batting second in a limited-overs international, 313 against Zimbabwe (a record until we later broke it against the West Indies three years later). For the remainder of that World Cup we always competed at full throttle without ever really threatening in the final stretch. Halfway through the competition, with wins against Zimbabwe and South Africa, we still had a chance of qualifying for the semi-finals as all the other teams, with the exception of

New Zealand and England, seemed to be losing as many as they won. But we then lost by a long way against England and West Indies and subsequently lost a close game to Pakistan by 4 wickets with 5 balls left. I captained the side for all these encounters and the 1992 World Cup and, for all our efforts, the worrying trend that these games revealed was how we lacked the killer instinct. We certainly weren't quite as gormless as in the old days, but what we didn't have was that ability to go for the throat of opponents and to impose our grip on games.

It was not a matter of ability. Sri Lanka simply did not have the mental toughness to play three consecutive weeks of cricket against the best in the world. The one-day game is a great leveller not just because it sterilises fast-bowling and gives equal weight to an inside-edge as it does to a straight-drive, the one-day game is a great leveller of abilities because it can reveal the fragile psyches of any player when matches reach their do-or-die climaxes. We are athletes ruled by our minds, and our minds aren't half as well trained as our bodies. Pakistan, for all their mighty fast-bowling and great depth in batting, were always liable to be beaten, never more so evidently than in the preliminary rounds of the 1992 World Cup. But what they had, which precious few other teams had at the time, was an absolute belief that they could win when they most wanted to, when they absolutely had to. And to the win they would give of themselves completely. It wasn't the kind of clinical professionalism of the best of the other teams, it was just desire run rampant. The one-day game is a great leveller of physical ability, but the mentally tough win the most games.

My own form as a batsman in these times was a little lacklustre; presented with plenty of opportunities, I only managed one half-century during the World Cup and no score of consequence in six Test innings against England and Pakistan. It might have been the added burden of captaincy, it might have just been the implacable rules of the game, it might have been a combination of any number of things but I wasn't quite the force I wanted to be out in the middle. I wasn't like Martin Crowe, Javed Miandad, Allan Border or Graham Gooch, the most eminent in the world at that time, batsmen who could be relied upon to do a job for their team. I was a batsman viewed with curiosity rather than fear every time he walked out to the middle. After eight years at the top I was starting to see that if I wanted to be anything more than a mercurial talent plumbing the highs and lows of my ability, I would have to modify aspects of my game, modify aspects of my mind. Not that I quite knew exactly what needed to be modified. What makes a batsman great is not necessarily the fact that he has all the shots and makes big scores, but the true criteria for greatness is making runs when they matter, time and time again. With so much cricket played nowadays, so much high-stakes cricket, a cricketer's capacity under pressure is regularly tested. The ones who come out best most often are those who play without a thought for the consequences. Let me qualify that: positive actions have results, mistakes have consequences. Strokes and deliveries executed more in hope than in calculation have a habit of going wrong. Of course there are times when a particular individual rises above the circumstances of a game and everything that can be thrown at them, and is simply almost single-handedly the match winner. When I was younger, I always wanted the team to be successful and I wanted to be the main cause of that success.

Cricket is as much a test of self-management as a test of skill. There are so many days to beat yourself in so many ways. I wanted to be good, I wanted to be great, I wanted to win games for Sri Lanka. And yet, out in the middle, I couldn't translate my constant hunger to succeed into consistently dominating performances. Bowlers, fielders and opposing captains, once so disregarding of my capabilities, now started to wise up to my game and raised their game accordingly. When I stood in the crease, the idea of what was expected of me, what I could be, affected the way I swung the bat every time. There were smatterings of success which excited people, and excited me, to the point where I never really found the time to develop a really professional workaday attitude. To my mind, one match-winning innings would cancel out a run of ineffectual scores. I always knew that I could do better. I hated just being 'potentially dangerous'. I hated being a batsman who could just as easily get out as stay in. When I started it playing strokes was a challenge, then it became difficult, until finally it practically became a burden. Cricket stopped being fun. The game was always the master, but I didn't like the lessons it was teaching me.

I had to start applying all that I'd learnt; start using my head. I've gone from being a dasher to dangerous to dependable. Now I'm less prone to slumps amidst the streaks and am better under pressure. I can play the right shot to the right ball according to the dictates of the match situation and that's the way the game should be played. You have to rise above the frustrations of the moment. You have no idea what it can do to a batsman's run-hungry psyche when, tied down by accurate bowling and tight fielding and unable to assert himself, with all his normal avenues of scoring all blocked off, he has to start having to think about things that he doesn't usually have to think of. Overs tick by, the scoreboard's constipated, the runs just aren't coming. All the time, with every dot ball, the batsman is conscious of more and more opportunities lost, of falling further and further behind expectations. The one-day game is such nowadays that two maidens in a row are considered a disaster for the batting team. The smart fielding team will just whistle through the overs in these situations. Even in Test cricket the principles remain the same:

wickets do fall as the result of containment. You wouldn't think that grown men playing the game at which they are world masters could ever be reduced to self-destructive flailings of the bat, tortured prods and twitches, premeditated shots that bear no relation to the ball being delivered, and desperate running between the wickets, but it happens. It's a mental game and in this instance the bowlers have imposed their will on the batsmen.

Speaking as a batsman, frustration causes so many mistakes. Frustration closes a switch in the brain. Your concentration is lost. The eye is taken off the prize. Over-anxious and pressing, it is easy for batsmen to start either hitting impatiently ahead of the ball or swinging too late. The best course of action in this situation is to play smart and be sensible. If a fielding side's on top of a batsman like a fog on a swamp, then the batsman has to do what the fielding side doesn't want him to do. With the seed of doubt sown in the batsman's mind, the fielding side want him to take risks, they want him to attempt to break free by hitting over the top, they want him to chance the risky single. They want him to get out. What they don't want to see is the batsman playing 'percentage cricket': keeping the ball down, calmly rotating the strike, not forgetting to punish the inevitable bad ball. The only real alternative to continued frustration is guts. Even if the salvation of a bowling change, the next boundary or the next interval seems ages away and the will to win begins to disappear: the will to survive has to prevail. You have to guts it out. As difficult as it seems out in the middle, it will seem even harder for the next batsman burdened by your pressures. In fact, the game will only look easy once you're out prematurely and back in the pavilion. And then it doesn't matter. You have to be sensible in your positive approach. If the ball's tossed-up on leg-stump, with fielders in catching positions and runs needed, you don't have to hit over the top, instead you can step out and play it along the ground. In these situations, batting really becomes a partnership game. Both batsmen have to look for the single, halve the pressure and support each other with talk and insight whilst remembering that getting out in this kind of situation could have serious consequences for the team. One batsman playing a lone hand is self-destructive. Something else: the great batsmen are never intimidated by any clock. If I only knew then what I know now . . .

I've already referred to Sri Lanka's 1992 series against Australia as being particularly significant for me, as it was for the team. It was our first Test series at home in five years and a huge event on the island. A re-emergence out of the shadows, a furthering of our legitimacy as a Test nation, a chance for the fans to forget all the troubles for a while and just enjoy the spectacle of seeing their boys play at home. Floodlit cricket too was introduced at the newly built Khetterama stadium, a symbol of national progress, and all matches drew big crowds. Australia has always played a special part in our cricketing history. Ashes teams from England and Australia would always stop off in Colombo in the days of the long sea-voyages to play island XIs and many friendships were struck between the players and administrators. Actually, Australia's championing of our cause in the late 1970s ensured that Sri Lanka was accorded Test status earlier than some other countries thought appropriate. Ironically it is against Australians that we have had our most titanic battles on the field. If not the strongest Australian team to leave their shores, Allan Border brought a talented team with him: strong in batting, the fast-bowling spearheaded by Craig McDermott along with an unproven spin-bowling department led by Greg Matthews. It couldn't have been easy for them as tourists because our island was still rumbling with gunfire and discontent, but I believe they really enjoyed themselves throughout their stay. Especially as they won the first Test in the most incredible circumstances.

Fired up by a desire to perform to the best of our abilities in front of our friends, families and fans after such a long time away from them, we had Australia at 124 for 7 after lunch on the first day, before they recovered to 256 thanks to Ian Healy and a wagging tail. Then on the next two days we piled on the runs, Roshan making an assured fifty, Asanka a patient hundred, Arjuna a brisk hundred, and the debutant Romesh Kaluwitharana making a blistering hundred. Arjuna and Kalu were particularly harsh on the Aussie leg-spinner Shane Warne playing in his third Test and with hitherto only one wicket to his name. His team having scored quickly, Arjuna was able to declare late on the third day with a lead of 291 (having posted our then highest total in Test cricket). Australia themselves then played some fine positive cricket, scoring at a good clip to finish the fourth day with a lead of a hundred runs and three wickets in hand. Overnight we all thought that if we hadn't won by lunch, we'd definitely win by tea-time on the next day. Apparently everyone else thought so too, for well before start of play the SSC started filling up with fans and musical bands all looking to be there at the epochal moment of our first Test win in over six years. National holidays were sure to be announced for the day following our victory; there was a real carnival atmosphere in the stadium orchestrated by our two most loyal and devoted supporters Lionel Nawaragegodera and Percy Abayesekera. Lionel and Percy come on tour with us often too; they are practically our team mascots. Win, lose or draw they keep the Lankan flag flying and that day, like everyone else in the stands, they thought that victory was inevitable. The bands in the stadium were playing all the most popular baila tunes and the crowds were singing themselves silly with patriotic anthems. And even though the last three Australian wickets put on a further hundred runs, nothing could dampen the enthusiasm of the Sri Lankan support packed into the stadium. There is a positive aspect in realising the public's wishes, it can be mutually uplifting. Chasing 181 in two sessions was eminently within our reach and we looked forward to the post-match national rejoicing.

We started well and I joined Asanka at the crease with us needing 101 to win, eight wickets and all the time in the world remaining. The thought of having that many wickets in hand didn't even feature in my thinking. Asanka and I, maybe Arjuna too, would be able to see Sri Lanka through to victory. I was bursting to win and raced into overdrive, the target shrinking all the time until it was almost halved within an hour of my arrival at the crease. I used to think I was smart when younger, you only needed to show me something once and I'd remember it. But something would happen to me on the cricket field and I couldn't override the mental programming which said to me 'don't be dictated to – attack – be positive'. I would ignore the possibilities of failure, and throw caution to the wind, probably in reaction to the mental subcurrent within me which said fear was a bad thing. I took bowlers and fielders on. That was my mission in life. That was how I could serve my cause and my country's. Admittedly it wasn't always the optimal course but it worked often enough, I thought. Overcompensating, my competitive fire would push any feelings of vulnerability to the side and if I misplayed a shot even to the extent that it almost cost me my wicket, I'd simply set my stall out to hit another shot in the same manner, but with even more emphasis as soon as possible. If my team had runs to score, having hit one boundary, I felt I could hit another and then another. People tried to warn me, they told me to be more careful but they might just as well have been asking a teenager to change his spots. Now, with the wisdom of experience and the stern admonitions of those who truly only want the best for me and the team, I know that it takes twenty times the guts and class to restrain 'natural' impulses than to cave in to them. As in batting as in life: the subsequent rewards are so much greater and so much more frequent.

Sometimes just one ball can change the course of a Test match and the one that saw this Test against Australia swing their way was the delivery that saw my dismissal. Allan Border had reintroduced Craig McDermott after tea in a bid to break Asanka's and my flourishing partnership. I whipped one ball which pitched leg-and-middle on a length, way over the head of Allan Border at mid-on for a boundary. The crowd went wild. I tend to hit my boundaries in bundles and one boundary is normally the prelude for more. It all just clicks into place: the bounce off the wicket, the pace of the bowling, my timing and sense of the gaps in the field. I live to score runs. The following delivery from Craig McDermott was

149

dealt with in exactly the same manner, Allan Border for one instant looking like he might get near it, but ultimately trundling to the boundary to retrieve. The crowd were delirious. The next delivery received the same treatment, with me coming down the wicket and pulling the ball towards the mid-on boundary from outside off-stump. The result was different from the other strokes only in that it flew a little higher in the air off the bat, and that it saw me lose my wicket.

Close to the wicket, Border was brilliant. But I've never seen anyone (though Roshan doing a Spiderman to catch Ian Healy off the last ball of the 1996 Singer World Series final comes close) take quite so breathtaking an outfield catch as Allan Border's that afternoon. It was awesome. The ball flew off my bat sailing towards the mid-on boundary and Allan Border ran after it full tilt, when few would have even thought a catch was possible. First his floppy white hat came off, then his Oakleys; throughout he never took his eyes away from the ball which he was running at full pace towards. He was running to the spot where he expected the ball to drop: the only point at which he could possibly lay a hand on the ball. I had almost grounded my bat at the other end when I, along with the crowd upon whom such knowledge was simultaneously dawning, realised that a catch just might be taken. It was. Inches from the turf, with one hand outstretched to its utmost reach after a race to the ball of thirty yards. I couldn't believe it. The Aussies couldn't believe it. AB had done it for them.

It was a huge blow. The oomph was now all Australia's. Back in the pavilion I felt as shredded as a tyre blown out at high speed. And worse was to come. Arjuna, first-innings centurion and just the man for this kind of situation, was snared by Border close-in off the invigorated McDermott for no score. Back in our dressing-room, players for whom thoughts of batting had been distant, were now starting to frenziedly put on their kit. There are two responses to pressure: fight or fold. Marvan came and went, Kalu smacked a four and then played around a Matthews off-break and the next man up didn't last too long either, trapped right in front by the cock-a-hoop Matthews. Seven down for 147, 33 runs still required. An Everest of a target. Asanka did his best, trying to play sensibly and win the game in singles or paddled fours as there were still almost twenty overs left to play, but every time he took a run he merely exposed a palpably nervous tail to the Aussies. Pressure – the walls of the dressing-room start to contract, your field of vision is reduced; all you can think of is not losing. McDermott was starting to tire, however, and the other Australian seamers hadn't looked like taking wickets throughout the whole Test. Neither had Shane Warne for that matter, but Allan Border in his infinite wisdom gave the ball to his front-line leg-spinner. A great latent talent was therefore given the chance to decide the destiny of a Test match for the first time. Even in homoeopathic doses responsibility is an exhilarating drink and the emboldened Shane Warne spun Australia to victory, picking up the last three wickets in the space of as many overs. The last seven wickets had fallen for only 37 runs in less than an hour. Australia had won by 16 runs after being up against it for almost the whole Test.

Back in the dressing-room we were speechless. A spreading numbness mixed in with flaring jabs of remorse spread over us all. None of us could bear to look each other in the eye. It had all happened so quickly. All of us felt we could have won the game given another chance, all of us were personally embarrassed by our defeat. We all felt that we had let each other down. Australia had won the game, but we had lost it. As with Sri Lanka's inaugural Test in 1982, we'd lost a game we should have won. Ten years of Test cricket and we still hadn't learned how to win. The crowd of 10,000 jeered and hooted us at the post-match presentations. The drums had stopped beating. In contrast, the cacophony emerging from the delirious Aussie dressing-room reminded us just how joyous winning could be. Winning meant so much to these guys. Winning meant something to us too. But it was a feeling we had gone without for a very long time, and the thought that we were so close to achieving that elusive win made the fact of this defeat even harder to bear. I have never been one for 'If only . . .' but I knew that the collapse had started with my dismissal.

Whether I did well or badly on the field I never brought my emotions home. At home, once I was a full-time cricketer we talked of every subject other than cricket. My life didn't intrude on my parents' any more than it had to. They'd given me everything I could possibly want or need on my way to becoming a national cricketer and shared none of their grown-up concerns with me. It was the least I could do, not to share my problems with them. And when things were going well, what could possibly need to be discussed? My parents don't know that I know that they know this because I never showed my emotions at home win, lose or draw but that night after going home, I just shut the door to my bedroom and cried tears of frustration, anger and regret. I reckoned to hole up in my room and stay there forever, unless there was something really good for dinner. In fact I only emerged the next day after deciding that never again would I put my team in that kind of position. Never again would I be the cause of a problem. The only way we can improve in cricket and in life is to be self-critical. I didn't want to let Sri Lanka down ever again.

Sometimes just one ball can change the course of a career. After that innings I realised that if I did not change my attitude I would be remembered as an ordinary player. We are all heroes of our own lives, I came to realise I was a bit of a villain too. I had made a habit of getting out too often with too many runs being left unscored. As a result of that Allan Border catch I've become a much better batsman, more consistent and more match-winning. This new found 'maturity', 'soundness', 'understanding', call it what you will, has come at a price, however. The audacity and flamboyance that marked the first ten or so years of my career has been curtailed, as has my father's desire to watch me bat in the manner to which he had become accustomed. If you think I play plenty of shots now, you should have seen me in the old days. My father still comes to every game he can, however. And after a satisfying innings, I'm happy for me, the team, and for him.

The following day's newspapers were united in their feeling that my 'unforgivable carelessness' cost Sri Lanka the match; opinions they were entitled to air, not that they were even halfway to being right. There are only a small number of people in cricket whose opinions I value and if any one of them praise me, I am delighted. But I have always judged myself by my own standards. I know when I have done well and I know when I have done poorly. I know exactly who to turn to for advice: it is never the newspaper pundits. I hadn't lost the game all by myself. Though I wasn't being 'careless', what was undeniably true was the comment of someone close to me: 'I thought you'd have been able to assess the situation a bit better by now,' he said. It was only a game of cricket that we had lost, and as much as we felt chastened as cricketers for letting victory slip out of our hands, it wasn't as if we'd humiliated the nation, bankrupted the exchequer, or committed any crime. But in a country where the armed forces have had to be drafted in to keep the peace at schools matches, cricket at national level has a hell of a lot riding on it. More so nowadays, when Sri Lanka is expected to win every home encounter. What had happened back in August 1992 was that a populace starved of cricket, strangers to the prospect of a winning Test team, infused by the grim realities of civil war, economic problems and a constantly simmering atmosphere of physical and material danger, desperately wanted the tonic of a top performance by the national team at the national game to make life feel better for a while. We were the prospect of escapism pure and simple. If we had won we would have made all the country's troubles disappear in a euphoric high, for a little while at least. For four and a half days our plucky bowling and blazing batting had fanned flames of expectation. To be moving so close to this kind of nirvana session by session of this Test match only to be dashed at the last was a downer few could bear with any equanimity. Some had staked on our success in this Test match their very heart and souls.

Some had also staked quite a bit more besides apparently. Abusive letters from strangers started coming in stacks and in the next few days after this result people kept ringing my parents house with death threats for me. My father would answer most of the calls, coming as they did late at night when everyone was in bed. They hardly seemed to bother him, in fact, I think he rather relished the opportunity to fire back a few verbal volleys of his own. But I am sure they upset my mother. She didn't so much fear for my life at the hands of these cranks, but I know that she wondered if such nastiness from these so-called 'fans' would lead me to question my appetite for the game. I quickly put her fears to rest. Nothing could make me give up playing for Sri Lanka, not when there was so much left to be accomplished.

I myself am a gambler. I gamble on myself, using my talent as the stake. The pay-off is personal fulfilment. For a long time I would only play 'all or nothing' shots. As a young man I had gambled my life on 'cricket or nothing', and when cricket became nothing I staked all my money on my first business venture. Sri Lanka is one part of the subcontinent where gambling is sanctioned by law, and we have plenty of enthusiastic punters. There is nothing like the chance of easy money to get the most apathetic sports fan excited. On the subcontinent itself, it's a mania. There are those who scream for my head – invariably losing punters and punters will believe anything rather than admit their judgement is wrong – thinking that when I underperform it is because I am taking money to do so. The same morons then started thinking I started to play well again because it paid me to do so. I don't want to dignify their existence by commenting on them any further but, in complete contradistinction to their feeling that money won is twice as sweet as money earned, for me a victory won is far more sweet than any prize-money earned. And the same goes for all the Sri Lankan team. People make money off us, we don't care. And if they lose money on us we don't care either. We're not in the business of making money, our job is simply to play cricket to the best of our ability. Punters only wager money, players wager a piece of their lives.

Undoubtedly, the fans new to the game need to be better educated. They have to understand that even if you do try your hardest, sometimes it's not good enough. I don't make promises to fans, not even to my family or my friends. Not even to my team-mates. Basically you just try to keep them to yourself, and then you hope it works out for everybody else. You think about what you want to do before each innings and there are days when achieve your ambitions and there are days when you do not. Everybody struggles with that part of themselves and my performances map out that struggle. As much as the world loves a winner it reaches out all the more for a contender; I don't always win but I always try to give my best shot. I think that to many onlookers I represent the spirit of adventure: the maximum tension and the maximum pleasure. Playing out the hopes of the audience, it is immensely heartening to experience the sensation that in the eyes of a multitude one is, for a short while at least, a hero. I play the shots everyone would love to, and I get out the way everyone would hate to. Mine is a very public job and the public can help me to perform. But I can't do any more for them than I do for myself.

Still, cricket can be hard work for both the players and the fans. Particularly whenever I've played abroad, many Lankan expatriates have come up with their best wishes and stories about themselves and their families, and made me realise that there are people who have driven maybe 100 miles to see me play and then they hang around just for a smile and maybe an autograph. It's very flattering. And if you're lucky and take it in the right spirit, it makes you a better person. Their support represents national hopes and dreams, the pride of a community in one of its sons. It's very humbling and emotional. It makes you want to be as good as you can be. It makes you want to win as a Sri Lankan. Only my exceptional ability at cricket separates me from the people who come to watch me bat. Nothing else. The best supporters, and they are supporters in the best sense of the word, understand that every victory is hard-fought and every defeat a disappointment. Just as in life itself. If my occasional successes make them feel good about themselves, then that's great.

That infamous innings of 37 was understood to have revealed my essential character to all. I was like a heavyweight hitter with a knockout punch who yet had a glass jaw, the glass jaw being thought of as my temperament. My 'temperament' problem wasn't skittishness, nerves or gracelessness under pressure as thought by so many, it was actually over-confidence. In my youth I thought anything was possible, that fortune favours the brave, that who dares wins, that Derek Trotter really was a successful businessman. I never contemplated the possibility of failure. But the game is greater than any of us. Muhammad Ali once said that when a fighter is beaten, everybody who believes in him is beaten too – his family, his friends, his children, the people who cheer him on, who give him their hope, their love, their pride. We Sri Lankan cricketers walk amongst our fans on a daily basis, everyone knows where we live, who our parents are and what we do socially. Our culture of openness and hospitality, of regular family gatherings and social get-togethers, mean that we see and hear everything that is said about us. Certainly those closest to us do. I was determined to never let my well-wishers be embarrassed again. This Test series was the first one that left me looking inside myself, where before I had been concerned only with the outside. Change had to come from within. Batting was no longer a matter of being seen to challenge each and every bowler, batting was now a matter of carrying the team to its goals.

'Change is inherent in all component things. Work out your own deliverance with diligence,' said Buddha to his disciples. When everything you do is subject to unwarranted scrutiny, when any action can be misunderstood by those watching from a great distance who then, to make their reactions heard, start spouting off at great volume fouling the air around me, my family, friends and team-mates, then you soon learn to pay such things no attention. I love this game. I play for the team and myself. No one else comes into the equation. If losing doesn't hurt, then there's no joy in winning. But once the pain starts to ease and you admit to yourself that the defeat or dismissal was the result of your own ineptitude, then you are well on the way to learning from the experience. If any good came out of this débâcle against the Australians, it was that I learned to value my wicket a little bit more. With my penchant for scoring runs quickly, I had forgotten that one can't score runs from the pavilion. And the team itself became that much stronger; it takes extreme pressure to create diamonds. I have learned to be patient and have learned to keep my adrenaline from racing ahead of the situation. And by following my rightfold path, I have taught myself how to prevail.

Allan Border's lesson took a while to bring to fruition but the immediate effect of this Test match on our performance was that we became scared to chance losing again. I made 85 in our first innings of the second Test, batting with a painstaking slowness in a stand of 107 in 41 overs with Chandika Hathurusinghe; my two fingers to all those who thought I was incapable of patience. Point proven, I went back to my normal game. Allan Border declared once Dean Jones reached 100 on the final day, leaving us 62 overs to score 286. I didn't even get a bat as we didn't even attempt to go for it. The third Test saw a repeat of the trend of the previous two when having made the initial breakthroughs and piled on the pressure we couldn't come up with the killer punch. It was as if every time we had Australia in trouble we'd simply remind them that that such a state of affairs was not meant to be. They'd dig in and play a greater game. Dropped catches never help either and from having Australia at 58 for 5, with Allan Border and Greg Matthews at the wicket, they recovered to 337 all out. Border was dropped when on 44 by the wicketkeeper Hashan (Kalu had been dropped by the selectors for having a nightmare behind the stumps as opposed to in front of them) and went on to his first Test century in four years.

Not that Allan Border was ever in bad form or anything, for he had scored twenty-one fifties in the intervening period, many of them undefeated. Javed Miandad himself had only scored one Test century in three years until his 153 against England at Edgbaston in June of 1992, and even Viv hadn't scored any centuries in his last two years in Tests. What these guys in these relatively leanish years had done was score a bagful of half-centuries and any number of important runs. Batsmen like that, having achieved greatness, don't need the bolster of hundreds to make a significant contribution. Rather it is the younger batsmen in their midst whom they encourage to score runs and pass milestones on their way to establishing themselves. What these batsmen brought with them every time they walked to the wicket was a threat of achievement. They still had an appetite for the ruthless physical and mental examination that Tests and limited-overs internationals provided. Javed told me once that the 'other team knows I won't give up, and that is something that puts a lot of pressure on my opponents'. You always knew that they were capable of a decisive score. What someone once said of the great Jackie Robinson, the first black player to be allowed to play major league baseball – 'This guy didn't just come to play. He came to beat ya. He came to stuff the goddam bat right up your ass' – could be applied to Border, Javed and Viv. Looking back, how often can we remember the sight of them walking off the field undefeated?

The best make it look so easy, but failing's easiest of all. Whenever their teams won through in a run-chase or whenever they were batting to save a game, invariably it was these guys would see it through to the end. It is a middle-order batsman's privilege and responsibility to decide the course of a game and I very much wanted to be like these titans. So once more I went back to remedial school. I had to unlearn my satisfaction with myself, become less of a strokemaker and more of a batsman. With this experience I stepped for the first time over the threshold of maturity.

Following Australia's 337 we replied steadily with Roshan, myself, Hashan and Arjuna all notching decent scores. Having lost five hours to rain and bad light over the first three days, an imaginative declaration by Arjuna left us 63 runs behind on the fourth morning and Australia started their second innings in conditions responsive to our seamers. The new boy Dulip Liyanage bowled excellently to dismiss Taylor, Boon and Mark Waugh. With Champaka Ramanayake also having Moody caught behind, Australia were 9 for 4, a lead of only 72. Dean Jones then went with the score at 60, bowled by Anurasuri. Early on Border was dropped twice by Hashan and Sanath, normally two of the safest hands in the country, and then with Greg Matthews calmly proceeded to save the game for Australia and take the series 1–0. Liyanage was particularly impressive in the two Tests he played in this series but for the next few seasons he was to find that he was scheduled to play on spinners' wickets and as the most junior paceman, in spite of his potential, coming into a home Test he would be the one to make way for the extra spin-bowler. He's always been hovering on the edges of the team and, still a young man, he last represented Sri Lanka in Pakistan in 1997 where he performed creditably.

Everybody is given as many chances as they need to succeed nowadays. No one is overlooked.

We had lost a series we could have easily won, and Australia undoubtedly left our shores thinking themselves rather fortunate to have prevailed. The investments the Board had made in ground facilities and player back-up were the first steps on the upward curve that has taken Sri Lankan cricket to the level where it is at today. The Kandy-man Murali made his debut in this series, another example of us starting to source talent from previously overlooked pockets of the island, and Frank Tyson in the week that he was with us had shown how useful it was to study videotape of opponents before taking them on. A direct result of this was Mark Waugh's untypical run of two pairs in successive Tests. Analysis of the videotapes of his innings had shown us that, with a backlift towards second slip and a bat which was very much out of the perpendicular whenever he was forced back on to the back-foot, Mark Waugh was pretty vulnerable to the incoming ball. And so it proved. He had struggled against India in his previous series, a five-Test series which Australia had won 3–0, but whenever you're part of a winning team personal faults can easily be overlooked. It took the investment of bringing someone who had first-hand knowledge of the Australians from the facilities of the commentary-box to point out to us whatever technical faults the Australian players might have and to give us the ideas to exploit them. I have to say that batting should remain a largely spontaneous affair but having a bowling plan is infinitely better than just bowling and hoping, as we were wont to do. It was just a pity Greg Matthews hadn't played in any of those games against India for his unorthodoxies, especially as a leftie batsman who favoured using his pads, took us by surprise. On the field you have to think quickly. Proper practice and good coaching is all very well but on the field players have to read and react to constantly shifting situations. You have to be able to cope with things not going to plan. Like the Chinese warlord Sun-Tzu said, 'no plan survives contact with the enemy'. The more experience you have, the more aware and responsive you can be. We'd get him out quicker now.

Long-term, the benefits of this series went deep into all the players' psyches, for the enduring good of the team. Australia themselves have shown a recurring tendency in the last twenty years to lose Tests when chasing a small fourth-innings target. The pressure that we found ourselves under in those last breathtaking minutes of the SSC Test taught us that of all the ways of losing, the most common is forgetting that the other team haven't won until you have lost. Having been reinstated to the captaincy, from this series Arjuna learnt how not to trust the press and public; he learnt to believe in himself more and, with the following of the side, he became even bolder in the future. The ultimate mystery is one's own self. In the days that followed, I pondered and probed through what had passed, and came up with some answers.

Cricket is such a simple game: do what your opponents don't want you to do. Of all the symptoms of pressure the most common isn't playing below the level of your natural game, but trying to play beyond your abilities. Almost every time that we have faltered in the final stretch, from our very first Test to our most recent tour of Australia where we played a limited-overs triangular along with England, it has been because our response to pressure was to try too hard, to be too brave and to play too hurt. Granted, previously we just didn't know how to win because the only significant cricket we were playing was against the big boys with inexperienced teams. But with experience came a greater awareness of our capabilities. Mastery of this game is so elusive I have come to believe sustained winning is very much due to mental ability. And at our best we realised that we weren't that much short of being able to beat any of our opponents with accurate seam-bowling, adroit spin-bowling and gutsy batting. The important thing was to be able to concentrate our minds to perform at our best as often as possible. Such a realisation was the beginning of the end to all those many years of disastrous indiscipline for me and the team.

CHAPTER FOURTEEN

Another big bomb blast in Colombo in mid-November of 1992, the explosion spraying civilians' and naval officers' blood, guts and body parts across the front of the touring New Zealanders' hotel, raised the prospect of yet another period without international cricket. The New Zealanders were badly shaken and were ready to call the whole tour off, but the majority were persuaded to stay by the New Zealand authorities who had one eye on maintaining sporting relations and the other on trade relations. I think by now all of us in the Sri Lankan team were able to put the troubles in perspective. Like my father often says, 'a man without shoes is unhappy until he sees a man without feet'. With so many dying year after year as a result of the separatist conflict, our position as cricketers at the forefront of national life didn't matter a great deal. We were only entertainers after all, a temporary distraction from the problems of living. If we had any merit it was that we united the island and all its warring factions behind us whenever we did actually play. Maybe having Murali (he being of Tamil descent) in the team helped; certainly the Tamil Tigers were adamant that no cricketing establishments would ever be targeted by their bombers. But you could never be sure.

Some have thought that the bomb scare may have helped us to overcome a severely shaken New Zealand as we proceeded to win a foreshortened series by one Test out of two. Five of their original squad did go back home, heeding the calls from family and friends for self-preservation, but the ones that did remain were united by a kind of Alamo spirit, and the five hastily flown in replacements were keen as mustard to seize their chance to impress in the remaining fixtures. The second Test of the series which we won was memorable for being the first in which our policy of loading the team with spinners worked to our advantage. Anurasiri, Muralitharan and Warnaweera bowled us to victory with fifteen wickets in the match between them. The game was also memorable for an Aravinda-like innings, if I do say so myself, from Martin Crowe who with some aggressive strokeplay raced to an excellent rearguard century in his side's second innings. Ours was a bittersweet victory, only our third in 42 Tests, but heartening nonetheless.

England were our next opponents at home a few months later and we were well up for them. England landed in Colombo weary in mind and body following their five-Test series in India, captained by Alec Stewart in place of Gooch. The warm-up one-day international was won comfortably by us and we moved on to the Test match confident that we would win. A feeling all too rarely enjoyed; it sure made a difference. England made 380 in over a day and a half without ever looking comfortable, and we replied with 469 which owed much to Hashan. Coming in at the fall of my wicket on 330, frustratingly caught glancing down the leg-side by Stewart (falling to a good catch is never any consolation) just before the tea-interval on the third day, Hashan saw five further wickets fall quickly around him. With only Murali and Warnaweera left and with us still behind England's total, after having looked for so long as if we'd take that vital first-innings lead, Hashan took things into his own hands and played an innings of ingenuity and belligerence to add another 90 or so runs to our total. Murali, who like many a tail-ender is as ambitious for his batting as he is proud of his bowling, batted cleverly to keep his end up as he and Hashan took their partnership well into the next morning.

We ended with a lead of 89, Hashan finishing undefeated on 93. Warnie, Murali and Sanath then chipped away at England with spin, Asanka's seamers contributing in addition the two important wickets of Atherton and Emburey. At one point it looked like we might have to chase a total close to 180 in our second innings, but eventually we were left with only 140 runs for victory with practically a whole day in which to get them. The memory of what Australia had done to us six months earlier, or rather what we had done to ourselves, was still something in the crowd's minds and the media's. John Emburey was in the England attack too, as he had been in our inaugural Test where he had triggered a second innings collapse. The whole of Sri Lanka feared a repeat; their pessimism made us in the team just that bit more determined not to fail again.

Arjuna and Emburey were the only survivors from that Test, and the thought of that disaster simply hardened Arjuna's heart against all possibility of defeat. In our team talk before the start of play, Arjuna drew us all together in the SSC dressing-room and said the following:

'They think we're a young and immature side, one that freezes in sight of victory, one that doesn't know how to win. It's common for them to patronise us and to call our victories flukes. Well, they're wrong. They don't know us. They don't know what we can do. We are a good side, don't let anybody tell you different. Now we have a great chance to beat England, a chance that we have earned through superior batting, bowling and fielding. The way we have played, West Indies wouldn't beat us. Now go out and play like the best Sri Lankan cricketers you are. Play positive, play for each other, play for the honour and self-respect of the country.'

Eyes blazing, he looked us all in the eye and transmitted to us his determination and confidence. There was no way we were going to lose. We all wanted to be the ones to hit the winning run.

When we batted, even though the wicket was slow, England should have bowled the seamers in rotation with Emburey the bogeyman rather than persist with the twin-spin attack. Tufnell offered flight and guile, but we felt he wasn't as much of a threat as Lewis or Malcolm who from anywhere could bowl the amazing wicket-taking ball. But I guess Alec Stewart as wicketkeeping captain, felt that he saw enough from where he stood to persist with the spinners pitching in the rough against our preponderance of left-handers. We were glad he did. It made the left-handers facing the Emburey and Tufnell deliveries that spun away all but immune to lbws, thus making batting that much easier. Plus with Emburey, you always got the sense that he wasn't looking to take wickets from the outset, merely to keep things tight, as he fired them in flat and quick. If he'd tossed it up he might have been hit for more runs, but he would have had far greater chance of taking wickets. Malcolm and Lewis, purely because of their erratic nature, you had to play with more attention. Blasting us out had the better chance.

It isn't always possible for a player to live up to his captain's advice or indeed his own desires to play to his potential, no matter how hard one tries. Some days you just don't get it right. No sooner had I settled in after the fall of Asanka's wicket, and having hit one four, with good fielding depriving me of another, I then proceeded to belt the tamest of Emburey long-hops into the fielder's hands at deep backward-square-leg. That was carelessness. Hathurusinghe then fell the next over, for no further score. From 61 for 2, we had lapsed to 61 for 4 and Emburey and Tufnell were threatening to stifle us; 140 started looking problematic. A buzz of concern spread across the ground. I started to hate myself. But we all took consolation in the fact that Hashan and Arjuna were at the crease and they wouldn't let it slide. England were canny enough to make things as difficult as possible for us but their hoping that we would self-destruct after losing a few quick wickets was never a viable option, not with Arjuna batting as if his life depended on it and with Hashan in the form he was in.

England crowded the bat, while they attacked with their spinners. Avenues for glancing, cutting and driving opened up, and the runs slowly but surely started accumulating. The total went past 100, then the 50 partnership was posted, then Hashan and Arjuna doubled the score to 122, then they were within a boundary-hit of victory. Unfortunately Arjuna was then snaffled by Gatting at silly point off Tufnell and the honour of hitting the winning runs went to Sanath who came in and hit his first ball for six. Two Test wins in a row. Unprecedented! We were on a high and felt that at home with Tests against India, West Indies and South Africa scheduled we were a match for anybody. Especially if we played them on spinners' wickets.

With the policy of high-profile attacks by the separatist terrorists, the most prominent being the assassinations of our Prime Minister Mr Ranasinghe Premadasa and India's Prime Minister Rajiv Gandhi, whenever we toured India in those days, and vice-versa, armed security forces were omnipresent. On the field it was a different story. With only two umpires on the field and in spite of a match referee ensconced in the pavilion, all the seething tensions between the players – invariably centred around Arjuna (he might not run too much but he certainly never walks) – were able to be vented. There is a great fraternity amongst the subcontinental teams, we make friends amongst ourselves very easily. But there is also great sibling rivalry, and India and Pakistan, having been first on the cricketing scene for some considerable time before our emergence, used to think of us as their juniors in all matters cricketing. Nor, until they beat us and we beat them some more times, could they ever sit comfortably with the fact that our first ever victories in Tests were against them.

Like ourselves, India in this series were a mixture of youth – Tendulkar, Kambli, Kumble and Srinath – and experience – Kapil Dev, Azharuddin, Sidhu, Kiran More and Prabhakar. Building up a head of steam, they were particularly keen to prove that they could actually win Tests away from home. They had won four in a row at home prior to this tour but hadn't won an away Test for seven years and, as ever, Sri Lanka seemed the easiest place in the world to secure a victory. India were really fired up in looking for that win and validation as an international cricketing force. With Arjuna leading the way, we fought fire with fire. The weapons used by both sides weren't pace, tactical gambits or ferocious batting but backchat, querying of dismissals, accusations of ball-tampering, boundary-fielding controversies, rancour and recriminations, running down the wicket and plain and simple bad manners. In a word: gamesmanship. Whenever sides are so evenly matched, each captain looks to exploit every opportunity to gain even the smallest advantage and particular strategies are developed for performance and behaviour.

We Sri Lankans are a polite bunch of guys, it's the way we are brought up as anyone who has visited the island can observe, but we are not ones to turn the other cheek. Arjuna gave as good as he got out in the middle. Throughout his various innings some of the Indians would 'chat' to Arjuna, and he'd 'chat' back. A spell from Prabhakar, for example, was just an excuse to indulge in some conversation. It was a good thing that Prabhakar hadn't yet developed his 'accidental' beamer, for Arjuna would surely have stirred things up further by calling Prabhakar a word that rhymes with 'f★★★er'. During these times, the quietest place on the field was by the square-leg umpire and it was there that I'd wait on many an occasion prior to taking strike.

The first Test was a washout but in the second Test India gained their precious overseas victory when in chasing an unlikely 472 for victory we fell in between the two stools of aggression and defence and steadily lost wickets throughout the last day. By lunchtime it was clear we weren't going to win and I started to pad away the ball for the first time in my life, as I bided my time in waiting for the right ball to hit. Ironically it was my first ambitious shot, a sweep of a ball on off-stump, that cost me my wicket, Azhar running back from first-slip to bag the top-edge and seal the win for India with me out for 93. It would have been good to have reached my first Test century on home soil but it would have been even better if my runs had counted towards saving the match. It was a thrill to swing Kumble, against the spin, over the midwicket boundary to get to that first home hundred in the first innings of the next Test. I can still taste that one. With six prior hundreds all scored away from home, people were starting to question my ability to handle the weight of the home fans' expectations, my appetite for performing in front of the home fans, even my affection for them!

In spite of our defeat to India we thought we were improving all round in terms of (spin)bowling, batting and fielding. Fitter ever than before (mentally, emotionally and physically), we could tangibly feel the improvement within ourselves. We walked taller on the field, were more positive, Arjuna more authoritative. There were smiles on our faces where before had been the smudges of worry. In the absence of having our own fast-bowlers, we were still the underdogs in almost every encounter but nevertheless a competent side. We felt that taking on South Africa would be a good Test of our progress. In the short time since they had re-emerged on the international scene, they had shown they were hardy fighters, a bit unsure of themselves tactically but nevertheless fine competitors. And they were superfit too. All the world's cricketers thought they were fit until they encountered Hansie Cronje. Seeing Jonty Rhodes in the field and Allan Donald so lithe that he could touch his forearms to the ground while loosening up to bowl, made us realise we had a way to go yet before we could really compete physically with the big boys.

We could have won our first ever Test against South Africa, should have won it. But needing to take the last eight South African wickets on the final day, we were denied by the soft hands, quick feet and broad pads of Jonty Rhodes who went on to an undefeated century. He broke Murali's heart and showed up the young bowler's limitations. Murali had taken a lot of wickets in his short career up to this point, including five in the first innings of this Test. But it was all done with the one type of delivery. All Murali had done since he was a schoolboy prior to being fast-tracked into the national team was bowl big turners from wide of the crease at a briskish pace. Flight, loop, change of pace, use of the crease, variations of line and length were yet beyond his capabilities; but in spite of all kinds of advice and encouragement from the rest of us, he couldn't get his head around the need to change.

The merits of a finger-spinner depend not only on turning the ball on pitching, they rest on being able to deceive the batsman in the air. Like a batsman who only knew one way to play, Murali only knew one way to bowl and the fear that in changing, he would lose the one thing that made him special was a big concern to him. He'd listen to the coaches who suggested he develop variations, he'd nod his head but all his thought processes and muscle memories would simply lead him to repeat the one kind of delivery that made him successful: big turners delivered from wide of the crease. Jonty Rhodes in his second innings wised up to Murali and simply took a big step forward and padded away the majority of his deliveries, confident in the knowledge that he couldn't be given out lbw to a ball that pitched outside off and was spinning sharply enough to beat another set of stumps. It was the same over after over: ball to pad to silly mid-off to bowler to batsman to short square-leg. Slip might just as well have gone home for the day. And whenever Murali dropped short or overpitched, Jonty was on to it in a flash. Being a predominantly on-side player Jonty actually welcomed playing Murali. Even one arm-ball would have gone a long way to undermining Jonty, who alone stood between us and victory in the final session of play. But that was a weapon not yet in Muri's armoury.

In the second Test of the series at the SSC, we were simply blown away by the South Africans' four-pronged pace attack. The local groundsmen in those days would prepare spinners' wickets, but the accuracy and hostility of the South African wasn't to be blunted. The length at which you played forward or back to them became quite different in comparison to other bowlers we had encountered on our wickets. Pinned to the crease and given no room to play our strokes, we made only 168 in our first innings, where the left-armer Brett Schultz was particularly impressive. We in turn used eight bowlers before eventually dismissing South Africa for 495. Hansie made a hundred, and Kepler Wessels made a patient 92 against the extravagant spin of Murali and Dharmasena. Murali actually dismissed Brian McMillan with one that pitched half a yard outside off-stump before it spun back to take leg. And that was our one highlight of the Test as we lost by an innings and plenty. Rain and an inability to force the pace when batting cost us any chance of levelling the series at the P. Sara a few days later. South Africa were always bowling tight and taking momentum-sapping wickets at vital times. We were beaten by a thoroughly professional team that simply played the game better than us. Themselves not too highly rated in comparison with Pakistan, West Indies and Australia, I think South Africa felt that they just had to beat us for their own self-worth. Losing to us would have really set them back on their quest for competitive legitimacy. Their attitude was the essential difference between the two sides. We thought we might win, they thought they just shouldn't lose.

Two further one-day tournaments in Sharjah and India, and we were back for what we all had thought as soon as the schedules were announced would be the ultimate test of our abilities: a Test against the West Indies, who if not quite the force they were in the 1980s were still great competitors. The contest really captured the public's imagination but unfortunately the whole tour was compromised by unseasonably damp weather and the Test at Moratuwa had barely two days of play in it. Funnily enough, after the South African pace battery the West Indies attack of Walsh, Ambrose, Kenny and Winston Benjamin seemed relatively tame. After Allan Donald bowling with what seemed like a golf ball, the following fast bowlers were all medium-pace. If taking a hammering from Donald and co. had that effect then maybe getting blasted by them wasn't so bad.

Our tour of India early in 1994 was a disaster. We lost all three Tests and won only the last one-dayer thanks largely to having to chase a reduced target because of rain. All the wickets were prepared for the express purpose of turning, and our spinners just weren't able to impose the same amount of pressure as the Indians or win as many decisions. Conscious of the fact that in preparing wickets that helped their own spinners, they'd be playing into the hands of Murali, the Indian batsmen made a conscious decision to belt Murali as soon as he came on to bowl, irrespective of the state of game. They messed with Murali's mind and he didn't bowl half as well as he should. The match pattern was that India would pile up a huge first innings score and we would try and match it over two innings of our own batting. It was the series where Kapil broke Sir Richard Hadlee's record of Test victims, and as a by-product it brought worldwide attention to our calamitous performance. Hashan was long remembered after that by cricket fans around the world for being the landmark 43-second wicket. On the field we were batting without any appetite for a fight. All our fighting was being done off the field. Management was at the throats of the players, the dressing-room was seething with anxiety; everyone seemed to be defeated before we even went out to play. Everyone spoke in whispers and nobody cared to laugh out loud. Plus, with such a strong security presence it was impossible to escape from the confines of the hotels, from the presence of chafing management.

Management complained bitterly about my attitude on tour, as what they called my 'undiscipline' was singled out as being the cause of all the team's troubles. By this was meant not my unfortunate knack of getting caught bat-pad in this series or anything to do with my cricket, but rather my tendency to regard the instructions of the manager as nothing less than objectionable. I had no respect for the man for the way he pushed his weight around, abused his position of authority and bullied the youngsters. People back home were most curious to know why we had performed so diabolically, it was one thing to allow Indian troops to part-police our island, another to have them as our dominant trading partners, but quite another to have them whip us at cricket. It made the country really look bad, and all the chips we habitually carry around on our shoulders just got weightier, skewing the equilibrium of a lot of people. Someone would have to pay for the national disgrace.

A high-level inquiry chaired by former Board secretary S. Skandakumar questioned the manager, Arjuna as captain, me as vice-captain, the physio and other senior players along with management about the goings-on behind the scenes in India. The net result was that the 'Skandakumar Report' advised the selectors to pick a new vice-captain for our forthcoming tour to Sharjah. Arjuna's scalp was demanded too but the selectors and the Minister of Youth Affairs and Sport, who is ultimately responsible for approving all national team selections, held firm and Arjuna and I were free to continue in our duties.

In our absence the Singer Inter-Provincial tournament had started back home and I joined my team Western Province (North) in the semi-final stages prior to our ultimately winning the tournament. The day after the final, and a week before the team were due to leave for Sharjah, a routine fitness test had been scheduled for national squad members. Considering we were going to Sharjah where we could play up to four games in the midday desert sun in little more than a week, these fitness tests made sense. They had initially been suggested by the Minister so that those with injuries could be spotted and not have to play, out of a sense of loyalty to the team, while carrying them. Not only were we short of adequate replacements but bringing in any other players would simply have been risking too much. Marvan Atapattu for example, had been brought in for the third Test at Ahmedabad only to make another pair, putting his international career back a few years.

My mistake was not to play the game that certain administrative elements were playing. A game of cunning and deviousness. Coming off a big game the night before, those of us who had taken part in the Inter-Provincial final turned up at the SSC to go through what we took to be a routine assessment of fitness and flexibility, having gone through them often before. It turned out that just gently going through the motions when in effect cardiovascular performance, speed and stamina were being tested wasn't enough. I, along with Ravindra Pushpakumara, Don Anurasiri, Sanjeeva Ranatunga and Ajith Ekanayake were found to have performed below requirements. We weren't going to Sharjah. When I heard the news I didn't know whether to laugh or cry. For sure I was a little more rotund than I am even today, and I did wobble slightly from side to side like a guy carrying too much weight when I chased the ball over the outfield, but I was nothing less than fit to play cricket as my performances in domestic cricket had shown. Like Arjuna I was an easy target when it came to looking less than Olympian-athletic, but it was just as well that Ian Botham, Merv Hughes and David Boon weren't Sri Lankan or they wouldn't have been picked to play either. Pushpa is nothing less than a shire-horse in terms of fitness, and Ajith Ekanayake had been the top domestic wicket-taker of the season. It was obvious, too, why Arjuna's brother was singled out. Certain factors other than physical fitness were at play: clearly I had to be stopped from playing for Sri Lanka.

Arjuna resigned from the team in protest at my exclusion, to be joined by Murali, Wicky, and Dulip Samaraweera and three other squad members. Five of the selectors, Duleep Mendis, Roy Dias, Ranjan Madugalle, Mr Daya Sahabandu and Mr K.M. Nelson resigned too. The team was split, the administration was split, the country was split. It became headline news. There were public demonstrations outside the Cricket Board offices at the SSC. Questions were raised in Parliament. The President, Mr D.B. Wijetunga, took an active interest and insisted that we players undergo a second fitness test. Which was duly retaken and duly passed. And I, along with half the team, sat back in Colombo while the rest went on to Sharjah. The second test was an expediency, like the first one had been.

The public, political and administrative support during this time was heartening, and taught Arjuna and myself in the revolving-door that is public opinion who our true and most abiding friends were. Such was the intense interest in the selection controversy in the Sinhalese press that it was a real eye-opener to all the brown sahibs who thought that cricket was only of deep appeal to the English-speaking community. While all this was going on, Brian Lara made his Test-best 375. In my heart of hearts I knew that I might never come close to emulating that feat, but the prospect being deprived of the chance to ever play Test cricket again was a real gut-wrencher. A lot of good Sri Lankan cricketers had been forced to retire before their time because of the Machiavellian machinations of certain administrators, I just might have joined them too.

People should be judged by their ability to play and I was being judged on other things. But I loved the game, loved my buddies, loved myself too much to turn my back on Sri Lankan cricket. The end was the classic holding-the-door-open-for-the-return-of-the-transgressor. Yes, the door was being held open for me to walk back into favour, except that, to judge by the attitude of those elements hostile to my presence in the team, I was expected to make that walk back on my knees and apologise for any perceived transgressions. That I was not going to do. Once you've kowtowed to somebody, the future of your vertebrae is set: you'll kowtow again. The team manager at the centre of all this, a former player, wanted to run the team with us all frightened, submissive and unquestioning. The assumption of human insecurity and cowardice on which he operated was so profoundly insulting as to be laughable if it weren't so sickening. A lot more could be written about the chicanery of these times and Arjuna in his own book, which he threatens to release after he retires, will uncover every malign and murky team-hampering episode that he and his team have suffered over the years at the hands of certain administrators. It'll make for explosive reading. You're probably wondering how all this conspiring against my and Arjuna's 'undiscipline' on our tour of India actually started. It all came about because, when the manager ordered me to, I wouldn't fetch him an ice-cream.

CHAPTER FIFTEEN

Ironically, amidst all the controversy over my selection for that Sharjah tournament, it was overlooked that fitness is the one aspect of cricket you can control, or at least control more easily than what goes on between your ears.

It might be hard to conceive now, but when I first started in the national team I was as skinny as a stringhopper. A regime of weight-training – and the appetite for nutrition it demanded – caused me to bulk up to a fighting weight of 62.5 kgs. Once I reached a certain physique (barrelly around the chest) I then found it hard to stay trim. More food was not only more fuel it was also more pleasure, with sponge cakes the most pleasurable of all. So I became a little barrelly around the midriff. Coupled with my slight wombling as I ran, I guess I didn't really look much like an athlete. Arjuna too has yo-yo'd in girth over the years, and it is a moot point whether a trimmer frame would have spared his hamstrings and back the painful stresses they have undergone. It's a difficult one: you can't train too intensely because of the risk of aggravating an injury and yet in not being able to ever maintain optimum fitness and physique, you risk making the injury worse. None of us in the team ever want to miss a game but there were many times when Arjuna and I felt we just had to play come what may.

Pain and all its tentacles has regularly had me in its grasp. One injury often compounds another and I have probably played 70 per cent of my cricket with an injury of one kind or another. I've always passed myself fit to play because there's a certain amount of discomfort you're going to have to overcome. My first two hundreds in Tests were made with the help of the long needles of muscle-freeing, tissue-rotting relief provided by my friend Mr Cortisone, for the groin I had severely strained after a slip at the crease. I think I had eighteen of those injections in the space of a couple of weeks and they were an awful experience but I desperately wanted to play, so I took them. It was at that time, as I stood in front of a full-length mirror in a Karachi hotel dressed in nothing more than a T-shirt as the hydro-cortisone was injected, that the team doctor pointed out to me that one of my legs was shorter than the other. No one had ever noticed it before, and if they had, they hadn't said. Even my repeated drills in front of mirrors with bat and gloves, hadn't revealed this to me. Self-admiring as I am, I was interested only in the way I batted, not the way I looked. It was a mystery as to how this unevenness in stance had developed or had gone unnoticed. Orthotic aids – heel and instep wedges – were soon developed to fit into my shoes to 'even me out' but it is this difference of an inch in the lengths of my left leg and right, that accounts for my slight side to side lurch when running.

Having one leg shorter than the other doesn't really affect me, though Freudians among you will probably point to my love of fast cars with willowy lines and pert carriages as evidence of a subconscious urge to compensate for not being able to run properly. Yeah, right. If I have anything in common with nifty sports cars it is an equivalent power-to-weight ratio; we might not be very big but we do pack a punch. Dr Dan Kiesel and Alex Kountouri, the most recent techno-boffin physio-therapists to the team, are somewhat amazed by this minor 'deformity' of mine because, apparently, a person's reflexes are quite likely to be affected by all the misalignment of nerves and vertebrae and whatever. Certainly I am often all the better for a deep-tissue massage but tiredness and non-motivation are my enemies, nothing else. Anyway, who can say that there haven't been other cricketers with the same physical impediment? Apparently Bruce Lee had one leg shorter than the other too, and it didn't seem to hamper him in any way; before he conquered the martial arts world Bruce Lee was even a dance champion back in Hong Kong. All players are pretty fit these days. It's mental skill that makes the difference between the good and the outstanding player. Common sense is a necessary quality for survival; as I've stated already, up to August 1992 I hadn't shown too much of it. What was under such ruthless examination in the days when we were so easily beaten wasn't our physiques, spindly or robust as they were, the examination was of our mental capabilities. With the proper mental discipline, we could have won and saved a lot more games. Every one can hold a bat once they're at Test level, what matters is whether they can play an innings. And to be able to do that you need focus and concentration. If a bowler can't do what he wants to do – keep the ball full on a length around off-stump – the problem has more to do with poise or concentration or proper thinking on, than with the physical act of bowling a ball. It's getting to be a cliché as more and more of us say it, but it's true: at the top, the game is all mental.

So having established to everyone's satisfaction that I was fit to play, as soon as I received the opportunity to play again for Sri Lanka I made a hundred in the first Test of the 1994–95 series against Pakistan, getting to three figures with a six over long-off. If the field's brought in, I see no harm in hitting the ball over the top. We lost the test, however, by a long way and lost the following by an innings as we were blown away at the

Asgiriya by Wasim and Waqar in our first innings: all out for 71. It was our fourth successive Test defeat in four days, and we had lost by an innings on four of the last five occasions. India had beaten us with our own weapons, Pakistan had destroyed us with bowling the like of which none of us in the team could hope to emulate. Pushpakumara might have modelled his run-up and slingy action on Waqar, but he hadn't quite developed Waqar's aggression, nor Waqar's clever use of the wrist and fingers at point of release. The left-arm swing and seam-bowler Chaminda Vaas was picked to play his first Test at Kandy, and though he showed plenty of potential it was clear that just being a lively left-armer wasn't going to generate a strike-rate comparable to Wasim's.

The slow, low pitches of Zimbabwe, where we drew three Tests later in 1994, caused us many headaches; the prospect of grinding out scores put paid to quite a few of us, me included. We came good in the limited-overs games, however. I think the seniors in the side were all very cautious; we were desperate not to lose and be seen at the bottom of the international ratings. It was unfair to instantly label Zimbabwe as a poor team because they themselves hadn't played many Tests. Since their first against India a couple of years earlier, they had only played six, losing three, two to Pakistan who could roll over anybody anytime. We were actually made to follow on in the second Test, after a big double hundred from David Houghton, and some distressingly accurate bowling from the seamers Heath Streak and Malcolm Jarvis. Towards the end of the game we had heard of the assassination in Colombo of Sri Lanka's Opposition Leader the Hon. Gamini Dissanayake, who had recently been reappointed president of the BCCSL. He had once famously said that 'doing politics is much easier than running the affairs of the Cricket Board'. Mr Dissanayake died after a suicide bomber had blasted him and more than fifty others during a political rally. As cricketers, the news was particularly shocking as the charismatic Mr Dissanayake had been our Board president during our inaugural Test. His efforts had been crucial in getting us Test status. We cricketers owe him a lot, as does anyone who loves the game in Sri Lanka. On the final two days of the second Test, batting to save the match, we didn't score many runs but we only lost four wickets. We were determined to save the game in Mr Dissanayake's honour. There was no way we were going to lose the third Test right after, and on winning the toss we racked up 402 on another baked blancmange of a wicket, which took up the best part of two days and thus ensured a draw at least.

We moved on to contest the limited-overs Mandela Trophy in South Africa at the end of 1994, where we were distinctly better than New Zealand but were always just a notch behind Pakistan and South Africa. So we didn't make it to the final. New Zealand on their own turf were always going to be tougher opposition, however. And the feeling was we would do well to emerge undefeated in the Test series. They were without Martin Crowe, but they had any number of seamers who could wreak havoc in their conditions. That we would win our first ever Test overseas, at Napier by 241 runs, was a terrific boost. All out for 183 in the first innings, our seamers then hit back to bowl out New Zealand for 109, Wickremasinghe and Chaminda Vaas and our debutant wicketkeeper Champaka Dunusinghe to the fore. After a stumble at the start of the innings, everyone else piled in to make runs and we set New Zealand a target of 427. Which they never looked like getting as Vaas and Murali had them in trouble from the start. Given the upper hand, Arjuna set about applying the screws and the young New Zealand side caved. Ours were the cooler heads out in the middle, and that's something we hitherto hadn't been able to say too often. In our 59th Test we had won our first ever away victory. Arjuna, who'd been there from the start and had played in almost all our Tests, was as happy as a man who sees his childhood dreams finally come true could be. In the middle of a small town half a world away from home, with only a few hundred or so Sri Lankan supporters cheering us on towards victory, we had done something we had almost forgotten was possible: win a Test match away from home.

The ambition to be a far better side than we were was prominent in the minds of a fresh new regime of administrators. The fear was, in the words of then Board President Ana Punchiwewa, of the 'real danger of Zimbabwe or Bangladesh becoming better than us'. Overtures were made to Allan Border to be the national coach, and then Ian Botham was strongly in the running. At the same time word had it that Bangladesh, themselves still not a fully-fledged cricketing nation though they were playing a few one-day internationals, were looking to Sir Richard Hadlee to coach them! And if they had landed him, their performances would have been boosted immeasurably. We had the beating of them quite easily when we played them in Asia Cup matches, but who was to say that it would always be so easy? At junior levels the difference between our two countries' performances was much smaller. Bangladesh were, at that stage, probably no better or worse than we had been a decade or so after our own independence. I remember the first time I saw myself on television, for the first time I had an objective view of my batting and it revealed all manner of things to myself as to how I could enhance my game. Televised cricket was spreading its net and the more that Bangladesh's, Zimbabwe's and Kenya's cricketers saw themselves in action, the better too they would become. The 'greenhouse effect' of television means that things observed by the cameras tend to grow abnormally fast and large. Obviously the imperatives for success were getting more and more urgent.

When you can see defeat from a long way off, I guess you can adjust to it. Out of these millennial worries, some far-sighted administrators came up with the 'Cricket 2000' campaign, geared to make us 'the best Test-playing nation in the world by the year 2000'. Winning the World Cup in 1996 and all the emphasis it put on the limited-overs game might have upset their calculations slightly! Obviously the slogan was more marketing than mantra, for who could get behind a campaign which aimed to make Sri Lanka realistically the 'third- or fourth-best team in the world by 2000' with the same amount of passion as one that aimed to get us all the way to the top? A lot of good was undoubtedly done by these people to concentrate the administrators', the public's, the players', the youngsters', the expatriates' and the sponsors' attention on the task of making us if not the best team in the world, certainly way better than we had been so far. A major policy thrust of the campaign was to send coaches and scouts to the innermost country corners to find promising colts. But the first most tangible benefit of this impetus for improvement was the appointment of Dav Whatmore as our coach from mid-1995. This man with a two-year contract helped to create a result that will last forever.

Dav's family had roots in Sri Lanka, but since childhood he'd been in Australia and had played seven Tests wearing the baggy green. I first met him when he toured Sri Lanka in the early 1980s with a semi-expats' team captained by Dr 'Bunny' Reid when, after an innings, he presented me with a set of batting gloves. And batting gloves, even more than cricket bats, were what I prized most as a youth. It was so hard to find a good pair in Sri Lanka in those days. We met later whenever Sri Lanka toured Australia, but my relationship with Dav really developed during my season at Prahran in 1988–89 where he was the senior player after his time in Shield cricket with Victoria. Pretty murderous of spinners, he was also a terrific slip-catcher. Not all slippers make good skippers but you can read the game pretty well from first slip and Dav grew to be a little more learned than most. I was already playing for Kent when Dav's appointment was announced and didn't catch up with him until I joined the team in Pakistan at the end of the English summer. It was immediately clear that the most basic elements of cricket had taken on new meaning once Dav had become our coach.

At this stage in my career I still considered myself to be a work in progress. I wasn't even close to where I wanted to be. A long county season at Kent would be a good test of my mental and physical stamina. Kent had chosen me to play for them in 1995 as a substitute for Carl Hooper who would be touring England with the West Indies. Plenty at committee level had faith in my ability and with that faith a certain adventurousness I'm sure, but to many, undoubtedly, I was a bit of an unknown quantity. Sri Lankans just weren't known in the way West

Indians, Pakistanis, Australians, South Africans, New Zealanders and Indians, even Zimbabweans, were known for their ability to be county cricketers. Dr Churchill Gunasekara for Middlesex in the 1930s, Gamini Goonesena for Notts in the 1950s, Clive Inman and Stanley Jayasinghe for Leicestershire in the 1960s and early 1970s were very distant memories, even for those counties' supporters. To the greater world the abilities of Sri Lankans had been rather overlooked. The general concern when it came to someone like me, who was known primarily on the circuit for his ability to play big shots, was whether I'd be able to cope in seaming conditions on lowish, slowish wickets. Hoops sets a Rolls-Royce standard with his performances for Kent: regularly well over 2,000 runs in all competitions, a bagful of wickets, some incredible slip-fielding and a great team presence. A pretty valuable all-round contribution to a team that relies on him greatly. I had a lot to live up to, and a lot to prove. I wanted to have an outstanding season for Kent. Ten centuries in all, two of them doubles, including one against the touring West Indies themselves, gave some satisfaction.

It's rare to see a dashing back-foot player thrive in England, yet Azharuddin had a great season for Derbyshire in 1992 and I turned to him for advice during our April 1995 encounter in Sharjah. I figured Azhar must have done something to temper his 'back-foot on the up' predilections on county pitches, otherwise he wouldn't have prospered. Which was true enough; Azhar told me he had only played fifteen square cuts in the whole of his time at Derby and gave as the foundation of his run-scoring all over England as simply getting on to the front-foot far more commonly than he would back home. He steered me to have a chat with Zaheer Abbas, then also in Sharjah, who in his time had made mountains of runs for Gloucestershire. Zaheer told me that in England, he'd always move onto the front foot as the bowler came to the point of release in his delivery stride: 'there's always time to move back'. Zaheer also suggested that I get a little more side-on in England. And he gave me a few tips on my grip too, like keeping the hands a little lower on the bat than I was doing on Sharjah's wickets, as I was likely to find many of the wickets in England playing slow and low. It was true in Zaheer's time, and it's true to this day, batting on good English pitches can be the easiest batting in the world. But they're not always batsman-friendly and the county season, as Peter Roebuck once so pithily put it, is 'a five-month fight to play only strokes that are intelligently calculated'. Forties and fifties would be all but worthless, hundreds were what mattered. It wasn't just a matter of just doing well for the fans and for my own sense of achievement, it was all to do with repaying the faith that Kent showed in me. I was their employee and I wanted to thank them by being the best I could be.

My first few innings for Kent were a disaster. Cocooned in a bundle of sweaters against the early-season winds whipping off the North Sea, it was all I could do to keep my hands out of my pockets when fielding and away from my dripping nose when batting. I was a little stiff and a little flat-footed, and didn't trouble the scorers for too long. So very early on, fed by some misguided comments about my ability in a pre-season report in one of England's cricket magazines, many Kent supporters were openly wondering whether I was going to be an asset or a liability to the team. In our first game of the season at Canterbury against Northants, one of the opposing players was even heard to remark that I must rank as the worst overseas signing in the history of the game. I always love it when I have something to prove. I love it when things get personal; it makes me try even harder. The Kent fans are among the most loyal and devoted in the land, attendances are good for all home championship games and there is a great tradition of stylish winning dating from the 1970s (the teams of Colin Cowdrey, Alan Ealham, Asif Iqbal, Allan Knott, Brian Luckhurst, Derek Underwood etc. etc.) which every team since has felt measured by. Kent hadn't won a trophy since 1978, however, and their best year in recent times had been 1992 when they were second in the championship (only losing the contest on the last day of the season) and runners-up in the Benson and Hedges Cup. The need to win something just got greater and greater each year.

In terms of playing staff, Kent had to have one of the most talented in England. The senior players had almost all represented England and the youngsters Dean Headley, Mark Ealham, Trevor Ward, Min Patel and Matthew Fleming (he'll like being called a youngster) were all strong potential England candidates. Undoubtedly, Kent were a team who were better than their results suggested. They had youth, experience and ambition: almost a perfect blend. But they were perhaps just a little short of self-confidence and terribly unfortunate with injuries. Bowling wins county championships and yet it had been so very rare for Kent fans to see bowlers of the quality of Alan Igglesden, Martin McCague and Dean Headley all bowling together. Even when we played on the proverbial 'Bunsens' (Bunsen burners = turners) in the last half of the season, Min Patel couldn't play on them because of a cheekbone fractured at the end of July. Mark Benson too, the opener/captain and a monster asset to the side, had to miss the heart of the 1995 season with injury. One-day cricket, where we had a team of hard-hitters, attacking swing-bowlers and accurate spinners, was where our strengths were probably most able to shine. And so it proved in a season that brought joy and heartbreak in just about equal measure. There were any number of parallels between Kent's and Sri Lanka's performances and manner up to then, but the greatest feature of my season at Kent was that I felt as if I were playing with Arjuna and the boys all over again. The joshing, easy-going familiarity of the Kent dressing-room, the warmth and camaraderie was a feature of the English game I hadn't fully experienced until I spent this season with Kent. The dressing-room atmosphere was probably the best I've ever experienced and I look back on those months as a particularly happy time.

Running between the wickets with new partners took a while to get used to, as did my colleagues' nicknames. Typical of the county scene, all sorts of ingenious variations and off-shoots from the original name could be coined. 'Jazzer' was short for Jazz Hat, which referred to Matthew Fleming's stripy school colours and his general misdemeanour, or so it was explained to me, and he was also known as Swan Vesta by the opposition. In the same convoluted fashion I became known as Arry. Go figure. As soon as the sun came out, I was rocking. A hundred at Hove in our second championship game and a bag of wickets from Dean Headley almost took us to our first win. The team's upswing led to a win at Canterbury against Leicestershire, and then another win at Southampton had us shooting up the championship table. Simultaneously, we were winning all our Benson and Hedges preliminaries by huge margins and were well up the AXA Sunday league table. A drawn arm-wrestle of a championship game at Tunbridge Wells could have produced any of three results, the ninth Glamorgan batsman being run-out by our wicketkeeper Marshy (alias Steve Marsh) off the last ball of the match as he ran for the bye that would have tied the scores. In our next four-day game we then beat Durham in a game of rain, contrived declarations and much lateral movement and were well set at the head of the Britannic Assurance County Championship table. It was all downhill after that. A combination of injuries, bad weather, more injuries, and the inability to take wickets quickly enough on good wickets all meant that we slid further and further down the table. We played well pretty much throughout, but the most we could do after that was draw games and draws are pretty worthless in the championship.

Our all-round form in the Benson and Hedges Cup was terrific. The openers Trevor Ward (alias Wardy) and Mark Benson tended to make good starts, early season I think they had a run of four consecutive century partnerships, and then the rest of us would all make capital from there. Martin McCague and Alan Igglesden (alias Norman or Iggy) and Dean Headley (alias Frog – though I never called him that of course) were actually all on the field at the same time in our group match against Sussex, something that hadn't happened for nearly a year apparently. The quarter-final at Canterbury against Middlesex was going to be a real tester though, and in a game in which we always had our noses just in front, was swung irrevocably in our favour once Mark Ealham (alias Ealy or Skate) bowled Ramprakash, and the victory sealed when Jazzer bowled Fraser. This was the first time I'd seen Canterbury full. It was midweek and the game was on television too. I can think of no other country where capacity crowds would gather for a domestic cricket quarter-final taking place during the working day. There is an appreciation of the game in England which is often undervalued; for sure some of the attendees were the guests of corporate hospitality but just looking at the men and women in the stands, and all the fans of all ages who gathered outside the pavilion to congratulate us after our victory, you could see how deep the affection was for the cricketers who had performed that day. The endearing thing about English cricket fans is that they are almost resigned to losing, wins are what they hope for but don't expect, seeing good cricket is enough to send them home happy. Any occasional win is treated like manna from heaven.

Ealy came to the fore in these cup matches; his brisk late-innings batting had revived us against Middlesex, as did his innings in the semi-final against Somerset. Their overseas star, Mushtaq Ahmed, bowled particularly well and I survived a stumping chance off him before he knocked me over with his top-spinner. Ealy and Steve Marsh then hit about them towards the end of the innings and we ended with a challenging total of 250 which was enough to see us home. Bowling as well as he batted and perhaps fielding even better than that, Ealy was proving himself to be the team's most valuable player. As a batsman he was inventive and bold, as a mediumish seam-bowler he was faster than a lot of batsman anticipated him to be, with great accuracy, excellent change of pace and a peach of an outswinger. He'd do me in the nets if I wasn't careful, and later to his utmost delight he did me for 1 in a big game in the 1998–99 World Series in Australia, prior to taking five Sri Lankan wickets in the match. Our opponents in the 1995 Benson and Hedges Cup final were going to be Lancashire, next to Warwickshire probably the best one-day team in the country. We were the underdogs, but we all felt that we could beat them at Lord's.

Summer's day, full house at Lord's: magical. It's part of the reason why you dream of being a cricketer. Lancashire's 274 gave them every chance of success; I had finger-tipped Atherton off a swirler at long leg early on when he was 4 and without ever looking totally dominant, he went on to make a big score. Crawley batted well too and Lancashire passed 200 for the loss of only one wicket with plenty of overs left and with Fairbrother, Lloyd, Akram, Watkinson and Austin to come, mighty hitters all. Ealy alone was able to tie the Lancashire batsmen down, but our fielding held up in the last overs, we took some good catches and effected a momentum-sapping run-out of Graham Lloyd. With Wasim run out off the last ball of the innings, we needed exactly 5 an over to win. My parents were in the audience, having made the trip from Sri Lanka to spend a couple of weeks in England. They had missed my double century and century against Derbyshire the week before and, with our fixtures so arranged that Kent were matchless for another two weeks, I fancied giving them some memories to carry home.

Mark Benson, our captain and leader in so many things, was unfortunately unable to play at Lord's. The week before the final he sustained a double fracture of a finger taking a catch in the last over of the Sunday league fixture. We were all keen to win the big one for him. He was the kind of batsman who could have carried his bat to the very end of our innings. His replacement, young David Fulton, strode to the wicket helmetless to open the innings against Wasim Akram, prefiguring Sultan Zarawani taking on Allan Donald without a helmet a few months later in the World Cup. Fresh from the Kent second XI, David figured that Wasim would have more respect for him if he didn't wear any protective headgear. I'm sure Wasim was too busy laughing to give it much thought. David was soon pinned on the shoulder by Wasim but he also hit Wasim for two boundaries before being beaten by one that kept low from Glen Chapple. When I came in with the score at 37 for 2 we were a little behind the required run-rate, with Lancashire tightening the screws. Ian Austin had been brought on first change from the pavilion end and had reeled off three maidens in his first four overs, but I was able to hit him twice into the Mound Stand, and the last two overs of his spell cost 21 runs. We were back in the game.

We were finding the flattish off-spin of Yates and Watkinson hard to get away; Neil Taylor was bowled by Yates trying to force the pace, which brought Graham Cowdrey to the wicket. He was going through a bit of a purple patch at this time, having finally realised that his destiny in life was not to try and play classically and with finesse but simply to belt the daylights out of every loose ball that came his way. It happens to talented batsmen sometimes, their strengths as young men don't quite fit in with the team and they go through a season or three of neither being one kind of batsman or another. It happened to Asanka Gurusinha in his first years in the Sri Lankan team too. Not feeling free to bat with his youthful flamboyance at No. 3, Asanka chose to cut out a lot of strokes from his game and predominantly play the anchor role, which he did with some success for some years, becoming the bass-line to the rest of our improvisations. Graham had originally come into the Kent team as a late-order one-day hitter, did pretty well, then realised that the longer game was a better measure of a man and tried to play like a top-handed classicist further up the order but found that with his ingrained bottom-handedness, he didn't quite come off. I think batting with me that season helped him to realise that if you have the ability to hit the ball then you should use it in whatever form of cricket you're playing, from any position in the order. Once Graham concentrated solely on his strengths and they were plenty, he revitalised his game. Together we started getting a handle on the game.

Rain during the tea interval held up play for half an hour, and the tension within many of us ratcheted up. Our dressing-room was normally on the rowdy side of decorous, but this time the atmosphere was just a little tight. Ealy was eating some fruit quietly in a corner, Jazzer strapped in his pads was buzzing like a bee trapped in a lightbulb, and none of the bowlers looked like they fancied having to bat. The occasion was just getting to them all, perhaps. I could see all the parallels between the way Sri Lanka had been and the way this young Kent side were at the time. Before, Sri Lanka would have been equally tight, not really relishing the battle ahead. But Sri Lanka had been through the mill and we had come to know ourselves and the game better. These kinds of lessons of composure are perhaps best learnt the hard way. The great thing about chasing runs in a one-day game is that the target is fixed. As are the amount of deliveries available in which to reach that target. One can always count on having to receive the necessary number of balls from which to score the necessary number of runs. The eye can always be on the prize. It concentrates the mind wonderfully. Every batsman knows what they have to do. Success simply becomes a matter of application. Winning with one ball to spare is the same as winning with one dozen deliveries remaining. Chasing a target allows you to work things out in the dressing-room and, more importantly, out in the middle.

At tea, Kent needed about a run a ball with 30 overs left. At this distance from the finishing-post, whether the required run-rate fluctuates upwards or downwards over the next twenty overs doesn't really matter – the target remains the same. A couple of big overs at any time, but particularly around the 45-over mark would do wonders for us mathematically and psychologically, and I was determined to be there to make it happen.

As soon as we restarted after the shower, I knew Wasim would come back on to bowl and I was ready for him. A four was flicked to square-leg and then one pitched a little wide of off-stump gave me a chance to find the cover boundary. Graham at the other end was doing the right thing: rotating the strike, taking every opportunity to score his own runs, forsaking big shots in the interests of not getting out. We had more than halved the target when Yates won the umpire's decision against Graham, lbw for 25, and then Jazzer was bowled soon after. Two big blows. The pressure was back on us now. Every time I have chased runs, I have told myself 'as long as I'm there, we're going to win the game' – basically, I look to bat through to the last four or five overs at least. We passed 200 in the 47th over: a six off Chapple taking me to 98 and then a four through cover took me past 100 and Kent past 200. Now we needed 9 runs an over off the last 8, three runs every two deliveries. Gettable, very gettable. I was seeing the ball so well, my timing so crisp, my hitting so clean that everyone on the field knew that the more deliveries I faced, the more chance Kent had of winning. Try as we might, however, Ealy and I couldn't manufacture enough of the strike for me. Lancashire were a jungle of Jontys, scrambling everywhere to cut off runs and threatening run-outs on every possible occasion. Ealy then fell leg before to Watkinson and we were needing 60 off the last 5 overs – two runs a ball. Pretty difficult but still gettable. The only way to get them was to play even bigger shots and more of them. Going for another six, I was caught by Graham Lloyd on the midwicket boundary. It was a difficult, droppable chance and nobody in the Lancashire team would have blamed him if he'd missed it. But he took the catch. Game over. I was so disappointed that I just took my helmet off and headed straight for the pavilion, hiding my feelings behind hooded eyes and a raised bat, not taking in much of what was going on around the ground. Everyone was on their feet, apparently, and several have said that they saw David Shepherd the umpire joining Lancashire in clapping me off too. The rest of the lads tried their hardest, but we ultimately fell short.

They say the innings – 112 off 95 deliveries – really was something special, which is gratifying. I was able to bat in the way I liked and stamp myself in the English consciousness as 'Aravinda de Silva the Sri Lankan batsman' but it would have been so much better if that innings had brought the trophy to Kent. It would have been so much better if I had made less runs and someone else had made more and we had won. The boys had done so well to get to the final, only to lose the campaign at the last. The English season with its two leagues and two cups is so hard to be 100 per cent for in every game, and a single loss early in the season in any of the competitions can cost you so much come August and September. Indeed, once the second round of the Nat West trophy is completed in the middle of July, the competitive season can be all but over for half the counties. Our championship position wasn't looking at all good, and we were knocked out in the second round of the Nat West by Warwickshire, the eventual winners, a few days before we went to Lord's. But we still had the Sunday League title to aim for.

Success in this competition depended on motivating ourselves. Throughout the rest of the season we all lived for our Sunday 'fixes', when a few breezy innings from Graham, Jazzer, Wardy, Ealy or myself would overcome the opposition before or after Jazzer, Ealy, Min, Iggy or Dean would peg them back. It's impossible for a human being to give 100 per cent day in day out and quite possibly a few of us would be a little under par during the week in between the physically and mentally demanding Sunday fixtures. It's easier for a batsman than a fast bowler to keep going physically between the middle of April and the middle of September, but it becomes hard mentally as well. Everyone in England feels they play too much cricket, and a solution needs to be found, especially for those who have to combine international duties with county cricket. I can quite easily see the international players accepting contracts from the ECB in the future which means they will have to rely less on the counties for their income. The American basketball and baseball seasons are long too, and players have huge transcontinental distances to travel week in, week out as they rack up 100-plus games a year. But these athletes play a stop-start game and are on the bench for long periods during play; cricketers are regularly in action for hours at a time, five/six days a week for five months.

Plus, in America ballplayers can lose almost half the time and still get to their World Series or championship finals. Our increased density of cricket is still way short of reaching the point when defeat is quite so meaningless, but it is heading towards the point of being just 'television product': runs and chases and runs and faces. The real drama of the game can get lost amidst so many mini-climaxes. But once in a while along comes an individual who you will specially tune in to see. The reason being that he makes you feel good about yourself and human nature. I came to appreciate basketball only recently and that was because during an empty hour in an Auckland hotel room with only satellite-television for company, I saw that man Michael Jordan play. I had heard so much about him that I wanted to know what made him special. It became apparent almost immediately. All the basketballers on display were amazing athletes, but it was obvious Michael Jordan did things no one else in his game could, or dared to do. I kept on watching him whenever I could after that and he just kept proving time and time again that he was the wholehearted best. Desire flooded out of him like the sweat from his head. Moreover, after his return from his first baseballing-retirement it was quite apparent that he made everyone else in the Chicago Bulls play better than they otherwise would without him. But the most remarkable aspect of the Michael Jordan legend is that as good a player as he was, they say he's ten times the person. Incredible!

So much of the real value of cricket is only apparent to those who recognise the game as being a test of character, not just of one's ability to beat cover-point on the fence. If cricket were as easy as some of the radio and television commentators make it sound there would have been twenty Bradmans by now. I have seen many of the modern greats and they have seen me. No one, it becomes clear, can conquer this impossible and unpredictable game. No one can meet all its demands. Yet we are all trying and those with the most ambition try the hardest. So much of the real value of cricket is only fully appreciated by those who have the patience to get inside the game. By those who read cricket books for example. This game is so hard. Only a small proportion of deliveries get hit for boundaries or take wickets. If that procedure were to become any easier, then the game would become devalued for those who play it and, in due course, for those who watch it. The game has to matter if it is to matter. Cricket's administrators are on the horns of a dilemma: they wish to broaden its appeal and they want to make each individual 'event' matter more to the viewing public, but they will have to ultimately cut down on the number of saccharine events that threaten to engulf us. There is a risk of the standard of cricket being reduced unless administrators are careful how they are taking the game forward. We cricketers all wish to be entertainers, but we also want to be far more than mere eye-candy.

Professional bowlers have to be mentally and physically tough, batsmen too. I was lucky during my time at Kent. Normally, I would have looked forward to spending as much time as possible behind the wheel of the sleek white Ford Probe coupé which was the car Kent gave me to drive during my time with them. But driving down the eccentrically signposted highways and byways of Kent and rural England which apparently link all the grounds with 'cricketers' shortcuts' (and which were once the scene of a car-crash involving a few of us after a game at Stone) would have been too problematic for a 'novice county cricketer' like me. So it was with considerable enthusiasm I accepted Ealy's offer to drive the Probe at every opportunity, and I spent the travel-time between games resting comfortably as his passenger. I'm sure it helped me to perform.

I would play in that team forever if I could. We were like a bunch of guys in our last year at school, we had a lot to prove every time we played and yet we also knew we could only get better the more we played. It was a team of friends, you'd play cricket with them just because they were great to be with. Graham and his racehorse-trainer wife Maxine found a filly which they wanted to have trained with a view to competition. A couple of the players bought shares in the horse as well, named Aravinda as it had rather short legs. Given the best possible training, they expected great things from the young filly. Unfortunately the horse lived up to its name rather too well as, like me, it soon revealed that it didn't much like running. Last seen grazing in some Kentish field, the horse is living out the remainder of its life as some young lady's pet. There are worse ways in which to retire. For a long time my friends thought I would never get married, but I will.

Jazzer blitzed a Sunday fifty at Worcester, Wardy and I broke a few county records as the team reached its highest ever Sunday score against

Surrey the following week and then we absolutely destroyed Somerset prior to beating Middlesex at home thanks to a hundred from Graham. At this stage, with three fixtures to go, the Sunday league title was going to go to either one of five teams, three of whom we would be playing in the run-in. Every game was a cup final. We struggled initially against Essex, and it took another rescue job by Ealy in partnership with Nigel Llong to bring us up to a score of 221. Mark Waugh and Nasser Hussain were cruising towards a century partnership when Martin McCague struck to dismiss Mark Waugh and then Graham Gooch. Nasser Hussain and Ronnie Irani then took them to within fifty runs of victory before Ealy and Dean got rid of them and we won a crucial victory. The fighting spirit of the side was evidenced by our big comeback in the championship game against Surrey when needing 409 to save the follow-on, and with us at one stage 5 for 3 (including me), Dean and Min then added 74 for the last wicket to get there. Eventually set a target of 400-plus in five hours on the last day, we fell only about twenty runs short. Our championship position didn't do our talents any justice at all.

We didn't have a fixture the following Sunday, but the other title contenders, Worcestershire, Warwickshire and Lancashire, all won. So the pressure was really on us the following week when we played Lancashire. Earlier in the season the dates for the Pakistan–Sri Lanka Test series had been announced with the first Test at Peshawar starting on 8 September, followed by Faisalabad from the 15th. The Sri Lankan Board expected me to be there from the onset and Wasim himself had to leave Lancashire before the English season was out, in order to make it to Pakistan in time for the Peshawar Test. I made it quite clear to the Board, and they were good enough not to raise a fuss, that I would have to miss the first Test. Our last Sunday fixture was on 17 September, by which time we all expected the title to be decided either way. I would leave Kent only after the 10th and not before. The AXA title was something we wanted very much.

Amazingly, it rained everywhere but Manchester on the 10th and everyone else's matches were washed out, making our victory against Lancashire all the more significant. My last scoring stroke for Kent was a boundary, as we won by seven wickets. I walked off the field with Jazzer, elated and depressed after overcoming this major hurdle. Heading the table by two points, it was still too soon to celebrate anything as, if we lost the following Sunday to Warwickshire and Worcester beat Glamorgan we would only be runners-up after all our efforts. I left for Pakistan directly from Old Trafford, and taking leave of the lads was heart-rending. I hugged them all individually in the traditional Sri Lankan mode of farewell. Four and a half months in England had not only straightened my bat it had stiffened my upper-lip, but if anyone else would have cried, and it looked as if half of them might, so would I have. It took a big effort to close the door behind me.

The last Saturday of the season dealt a body-blow to the lads as Durham, the other wooden-spoon candidates in the county championship, beat Hampshire, thus consigning us to the bottom of the table for the first time in 100 years. It was pretty obvious, once Warwickshire had Kent following on in their own quest for the county championship title, that a last redeeming win was out of the question. I heard all the news from Graham as we spoke over the phone; then at 9.30 p.m. in Peshawar on Sunday the 17th, I heard the news I had been hoping for: Kent had won the Sunday League. Even though the loss to Dermot Reeve's men and the abandonment of Worcester's game meant that the top three teams all finished level on points, Kent won the title by virtue of their superior run-rate.

You have got to believe, if you believe in work at all, that a good work ethic, a good moral fibre running through the club, will bring success and not failure. Kent had extreme highs and lows during 1995 but the long-term foundations of success had been set. Team spirit was high, team performance was getting better and better as all the young players registered career-bests in one competition or another. And the results since then have reflected that. 1996 saw the team going into the last week of the county championship with a chance of winning the title, and in 1997 they were runners-up in three of the competitions. Sometimes you do your best and you don't win, but if you keep performing with the right attitude you're bound to win more than you lose.

CHAPTER SIXTEEN

Before boarding the plane at Manchester I knew that Sri Lanka were following on in the first Test, and I landed at Karachi nine hours later on the afternoon of 11 September to learn that we were poised for yet another innings defeat. Waiting in the airport terminal to continue my journey on to Faisalabad, the venue of the second Test, like almost everybody else there I was engrossed in watching a television set that was tuned to the cricket. Naturally the crowd were pro-Pakistan to a man and heartily cheered every falling Lankan wicket. I felt uncomfortably powerless, like a racing-driver without the keys to his car, and almost wished that I could get hold of a bat right there and then to show Pakistan's supporters that Sri Lanka had some fight left in them yet.

I couldn't join the team fast enough and I couldn't wait to set upon the Pakistan bowling. My first ball in the series was from the teenage off-spinner Saqlain Mushtaq playing in his second Test. He tossed it up high, which I'd heard he liked to do. When playing against guys making their debut or in their first series you want to make them realise just what a big leap they're making, and apart from imposing your game on them you want to play a little with their heads. Just to let them know they're in a different game now. Also as Pakistan's only genuine front-line spinner in this match, Saqlain was an important part of their attack and I didn't want to let him settle. Taking him out would put a tremendous amount of pressure on the remaining bowlers. So having taken guard, I came down the wicket to Saqlain's first delivery to what looked like a ball that could be made into a half-volley. It might well have been if it hadn't suddenly dipped and pitched a little ahead of my onrushing bat. The net result: caught and bowled for a golden duck. All those revs at the starting-gate and I'd stalled the engine. Next man in Arjuna was laughing his thigh-pad off as we crossed and once the red mist had cleared out of my head, I had to laugh too. None of us was laughing when Saqlain had Arjuna caught at short square-leg, three balls later. The kid was starting to play with our heads!

And 33 for 4 and the kind of situation that brings out the best in Hashan. With Chandika Hathurusinghe he steadied the ship and then, on Hathurusinghe's departure at 117 followed by a run-out of Kumara

Dharmasena at the same score, Hashan marshalled the tail to score a century, take us past 200 and give our score some respectability. Hashan's a simple uncomplicated batsman: he defends good deliveries, taking singles whenever he can, and the relatively poorer deliveries he hits to the boundary. He thrives on responsibility, the bigger the challenge the better he performs. And really for a long time he has been one of the team's unsung heroes. He can bat aggressively and defend indomitably, he can field anywhere, keep wicket competently and has even taken wickets in internationals with his seamy-spinners. He's the kind of all-purpose utility player that every team does well to have. Sometimes his all-round talents have been sacrificed in the interests of bringing in a specialist batsman/bowler/'keeper but he is practically a fixture in the side and is valued highly for his contributions. Using a soccer analogy, he's the kind of midfielder who might not score the most goals during a season but he is the one who scores the vital last-minute winners.

In their own first innings Pakistan then cruised to 333 without ever really being able to dominate the bowling. We lost two wickets before being in credit in our second innings and were pretty far away from the prospect of victory. When you tour and winning seems as far away as home, it can be most dispiriting. Wasim was out of the Pakistan attack with a shoulder injury, but nevertheless the century I scored that innings hasn't been my easiest in Tests. Hathurusinghe (he of the French Foreign Legion headgear) fell a little short of a deserved century and though Arjuna didn't notch too many, the tail all chipped in and we managed to set a demanding target of 252 to win the match. The wicket was taking spin, there was something in it for the fast bowlers; we thought we were in with a good chance of winning. Every day of the series so far, we had been behind. Now for the first time we were in front and it troubled Pakistan. Generally, it can sometimes be easier to play with the Pakistani cricketers' heads than it can be to play against their skills. They like to be on top and when they're not able to be so they fret and lose concentration and can be quite surprisingly lackadaisical in their efforts. Similarly, it can only take just one small incident to remotivate them and they can switch from neutral to overdrive in an instant. Certainly our cause was helped while we were batting by a number of dropped catches which you'd expect Pakistan, if they had been attuned to victory, to have taken.

With such a small target and with so much time to get them in there were only two possible results: a win for Pakistan or a win for us. Vaas struck at the start to have the dangerous Sohail lbw, and then Ramiz fell in the last over of the day. Saeed Anwar and Inzamam were the big guns remaining, but it was Shoaib Mohammad's wicket we wanted most of all. Apart from being beaten by good deliveries, the other Pakistani batsmen might self-destruct through impetuosity or boredom but Shoaib was a Test batsman content to simply occupy the crease and cussed enough to play at his own pace and simply nurdle and push runs forever. The man was a crab on two legs, and could be a bugger to prise out. Most uncharacteristically he had been run out in the first innings (batting with Inzamam you always run that risk) but here in the second innings Wickremasinghe produced a beauty to have Shoaib lbw. 119 for 5 and the game now well in our favour. Wasim and Moin Khan threatened for a while to wrest the initiative away from us but Dharmasena bowled Wasim with one that went away from him as he came forward, clipping the top of off-stump, and then Murali took a terrific catch at cover to get rid of Moin. The last two wickets fell straightaway and we'd won by 42 runs. Our first win against the mighty Pakistan who had so often humbled us in their own land.

Pakistan were now the team on the run and, unusual for a home side, injury-stricken; Waqar had to miss the whole series and Wasim, Saqlain and Saeed Anwar all had to pull out of the deciding Test at Sialkot. On a slow, low pitch batting first, the gutsy Dharmasena rescued us from 158 for 6 with 62*, my contribution to the innings being a blistering 0. In my experience, the majority of games are effectively decided by the teams' comparative performance in the first innings. What we had done in the last two Tests was extremely unusual. Second innings are mostly about grinding the opposition down, stopping them from winning, that kind of thing. Many of the runs (and the speed with which they are scored) don't count half as much as the ones scored in the first innings. Our spinners were to the fore in Pakistan's first innings as even I took two wickets. Pakistan were all out for 214, giving us the luxury of a first innings lead. We now really believed we could win the match and the series. All the other batsmen apart from me made runs in the second innings as we were all out for 338, setting Pakistan a victory target of 357. Vaas and Wicky, inspired by the thought of another series victory, really made each ball count and soon Pakistan were 15 for 5. Only Moin Khan held us up on his way to a gritty century, and Pakistan were all out a little after lunch on the final day. We had won the series 1–2.

For so long Pakistan had been a wreckers' yard for our hopes and now we had won two Tests back to back. It's hard to win a Test in Pakistan let alone a series, and coming from behind while away from home was practically unheard of for any team to do in the history of the game. But international cricket was levelling out; there was far greater knowledge of foreign conditions and opponents than there had been even ten years previously; coaching was informed and innovative; for the first time players needs' were being understood and all teams had developed their own match-winners for most of the existing playing conditions. Sri

Lanka had certainly become much better. Not world-beaters in Test cricket yet by any means, but no longer the easy opponents we had been thought of previously. It's a constant battle for supremacy in a game that has so many variables, but it tends to follow one constant truth, the better you think the better you play.

We won our first ever triangular one-day tournament, the Singer Champions Trophy, the following month in Sharjah against Pakistan and the West Indies and the talk was starting to build of our chances in the World Cup. Few expected us to win the World Cup, of course, but our cards were being marked as greatly improved opponents. 1995 saw us with two overseas Test series victories and one-day tournament winners: our prospects were looking good. We were playing with confidence, we were happy. We might lose a few games every now and then, but we'd win plenty along the way too. A tour of Australia was going to close the year for us and it proved to be our biggest test yet.

The tour is famous, or rather infamous, for what happened to Muralitharan as he was called for 'throwing' for the first time in his career. Up till then the world had thought we weren't good enough to compete at the highest at level, now they were led to believe that our main bowler, Sri Lanka's highest wicket-taker, couldn't even bowl properly.

There is no doubt that Murali's action is unorthodox. It does look unusual. There is no one else like him in the world. But he does not 'throw' the ball. The Laws of Cricket as enshrined in *Wisden*, clearly state that :

'A ball shall be deemed to have been thrown if, in the opinion of either umpire, the process of straightening the bowling arm, whether it be partial or complete, takes place during that part of the delivery swing which directly precedes the ball leaving the hand. This definition shall not debar a bowler from the use of the wrist in the delivery swing.' Law 24.11(a) Definition of a Throw.

'Throwing' is an intensely emotive and contentious issue and at the time we all let our emotions run away with us initially. Me, especially. I thought the umpires were wrong about Murali at the time, and I still think the umpire was wrong about Murali when he called him for 'throwing' three years later. But distance has given me the chance to be objective, and in as much as one can be in such a subjective recollection as an autobiography I will be.

Let's break Law 24.11(a) down into its constituent parts and apply them to Murali and the umpires in the proper context. First, the clause 'If, in the opinion of either umpire . . .' Umpiring can be an immensely subjective authority: lbws, catches, bouncers, wides, etc. etc. are all often subjective decisions, decisions based on a careful and rapid interpretation of the evidence before them. In Murali's case as with another former national bowler of ours, Jayananda Warnaweera, as soon as they appeared on the international scene eyebrows and voices were raised by the opposition. Warnaweera's jerky twitchiness in delivery actually made Murali look orthodox in comparison. Ostensibly a spinner, Warnaweera was practically a medium-pacer, bowling with a blurringly bizarre wrist-action. He was rather boorishly called 'spear-chucker' by the England B tourists in 1986; Martin Crowe never took to him either when he captained a side against us, and Pakistan raised objections against him prior to our August 1994 home series against them. Warnie would now readily admit that he had developed certain varieties of delivery, initially unchecked by local authorities, which were suspect. Those were the deliveries where the arm, bent throughout his delivery stride, did straighten at the point of release. Hence, a throw. But on being pointed out these discrepancies at international level (and the pressures of international cricket accentuated these quirks), Warnie eliminated them from his game.

Simultaneously, Murali was being looked at very closely by the authorities too. He was a more consistent threat to the opposition than Warnaweera and thus attracted more attention. Bruce Yardley the one-time leading Australian off-spinner, later our national coach, in a bowling clinic he conducted in Sri Lanka in 1991 spotted Murali's potential for getting into trouble and had ironed out some kinks in his action, nothing more. From his debut in 1992, Murali took his first 50 Test wickets in only 18 innings bowled, a rate faster than Shane Warne and Anil Kumble. During our Test win against England early in 1993, when Murali featured prominently, Dermot Reeve was filming Murali with a camcorder and apparently that videotape landed on the ICC's desks at Lord's soon after. Murali can spin a billiard ball on a sheet of glass; he is an off-spinner with a leg-spinner's wristiness, he's like those magicians who can flick playing cards a hundred feet with their fast hands. His arm comes over pretty quickly, his wrists are super-supple and his fingers incredibly strong. With his grip of the ball between his first two fingers, when Murali delivers the ball it's like he's unscrewing a lightbulb at high speed.

These are my 'opinions', made not as the result of video inquiry but just from having watched Murali bowl over the years. To say that I or Arjuna, or anyone else with nous in Sri Lankan cricket, wouldn't know a 'throw' when we saw one is almost insulting. But there, I'm getting emotional and I promised I wouldn't. So there's this amateur videotape, then there is all the television footage of his action between debut and December 1995, slow motion replays, side-on views, bowler's end cameras, front-on cameras. Umpire Hair along with Umpire Steve Dunne officiated the Singer Champions Trophy matches directly before they stood in some of the games of our Australian tour, and perhaps they raised the issue of Murali's action with the tournament referee Mr Raman Subba Row. Mr Subba Row certainly did ask the television company broadcasting the event to provide Lord's with all-round slow-motion coverage of the bowling actions of Murali, Dharmasena and even Hathurusinghe. A lot of videotape was looked at by any number of people for what must have been some considerable time. Enough time surely for the spontaneous subjectivity of 'opinion' to go out of the window and the clear precise objectivity of fact to enter the equation.

Dharmasena and Hathurusinghe may have looked suspect on the field of play, but videotape evidence obviously cleared them of 'throwing' at the time. In the Boxing Day Melbourne Test of 1995 Umpire Hair, having not noticed Murali 'throwing' anything in a limited-overs game at Sydney in which he was standing a few days earlier, and surely not being able to see much from where he was standing when he called Murali from the bowler's end, intermittently found several of Murali's deliveries to be 'thrown'. The umpire at the other end/square-leg who had the best possible view of Murali and who didn't call him? Umpire Dunne. He had the best chance of forming an 'opinion' and in his view Muralitharan's action wasn't worthy of being called illegitimate. Murali continued bowling in that Test and even played another limited-overs international with no further alarms until Umpire Emerson (making his international debut) called Murali for 'throwing' at Brisbane, again from the bowler's end. The fact of the matter remains however, that for the almost metronomic bowler Murali was then, with as yet little variation (only off-spinner and top-spinner), all his deliveries were pretty much identical to each other: big spinners, pitched outside of off-stump, given plenty of air. Either all his deliveries were legitimate or none were, because his action was the same for each and every one. There was no possible way for anyone to conclusively differentiate between the action involved in delivering one ball or another. Either it was obvious that Murali throws or it isn't. And if it isn't, then every possible means of evaluation should surely be used before a young professional is barred from practising his trade when so much expert 'opinion' is apparently contradictory. Like the batsmen, the umpires 'picked' Murali on the evidence of the ball after it pitched. If it didn't turn to leg it was called as a 'throw', because Murali's top-spinner was the delivery singled out as being the result of a suspect action. No doubt it was the one because of its extreme wrist rotation that had looked easiest to query after having studied the broadcast videos of his action.

Now to address the issue of 'the process of straightening the bowling arm, whether it be partial or complete'. According to the laws of cricket, a 'throw' occurs when, during delivery, the bowler's bent arm straightens, well Murali can't straighten his arms, for the simple reason that they are naturally and permanently bent in their connection to his elbows. Whereas you and I can place our arms in front of, and either side of us, parallel to a flat surface, Murali can't. His arms are set at an angle, and his forearms curve upwards slightly when he extends his arms. The bend is not really noticeable, he doesn't carry himself like Popeye, but nevertheless it is there. Dav was well aware when he took over the job as Sri Lanka's coach that Murali's action came under considerable scrutiny, and he had made his own video studies to ascertain for himself what grounds he had to defend Murali. After Brisbane Murali took no further part in the tour and he was sent for a battery of tests to establish once and for all the nature of his action. Murali was filmed in 'lab-conditions' at the University of Western Australia from six angles, bowling four deliveries each time (three off-spinners and a leg-break – nothing was left to chance). Filmed from behind the bowler's arm or from square-leg it does look like Murali's arm straightens late – but it's an optical illusion, the product of a fast arm, swivelling wrists, and a torquing shoulder. The case of Murali reminds me of nothing more than the fable of the examination of an elephant by three blind men each of whom, in 'seeing' only one part in isolation to the rest, miss the complete picture. The only position from which one is able to view the arm in its full rotation is to stand where mid-on would be if Murali was bowling to a right-handed batsman. From that view-point it is clear he doesn't 'throw' according to the rule-book. And that is what the comprehensive video examination proved.

To the naked eye Murali's action is hard to define, so all the more reason that the most thorough of photographic evidence should be used. Certainly in one particular widely circulated stills photo of the time, it did look as if with wrist cocked prior to delivery, and much of his arm draped diagonally within his shirt-sleeve, that Murali's arm was bent dramatically. But these pictures were not taken 'during that part of the delivery swing which directly precedes the ball leaving the hand'. Take a still picture of any number of bowlers as they approach the crease, and their arms will look bent too. Nobody carries the ball stiff-armed, but Murali's arms looked particularly bent in these photos, thus further fuelling the controversy. These were then placed side-by-side with photos of Murali with his 'straight' arm at point of release. A picture is worth a thousand words and millions were influenced by an optical illusion. These pictures resonated in everybody's consciousness; the implication was that the arm within its flapping sleeve looked so outlandishly bent, it would have had to be straightened prior to release, or the ball would end up at third-man. So in the University of Western Australia tests Murali bowled in a sleeveless vest and was filmed from run-up to release at normal speed and super slo-mo, the camera recording at 200 frames per second (normal speed in a cine-camera is 24 frames per second). The tests conclusively showed that Murali had an unconventional bowling arm, a 'deformity', an 'abnormality', call it what you will. Doctors reports confirmed that Murali's arm was naturally bent and therefore impossible to straighten. Murali bowls with a slightly bent arm throughout. There is no 'partial or complete' straightening directly preceding 'the ball leaving the hand'. The obvious is not necessarily untrue.

Suspicion is one thing, conviction another. Murali is unique. He does what no one else has done before who has played at the highest level. Such is the unusual nature of his action that he leaves many observers bemused by his unorthodoxy. I dare anyone else to try and bowl with that action and achieve the same accuracy and movement. Some have dared call him 'freakish'; Murali does what no one can or dares to do. Surely it would be impossible to arrive at a conclusive 'opinion' about Murali without some element of premeditation. And yet all the evidence points the other way. Either these umpires who reckoned Murali was guilty of 'throwing' were extremely confident men in being able to rise above the laws of the game or they were extremely mistaken.

Some commentators have insinuated that the powers that be, eager not to unduly capsize the boat of 'poor little Sri Lanka, struggling so hard to make their way in the fast-bowling infested waters of world cricket' granted the benefit of the doubt regarding Murali for as long as they were able to, until their patience finally ran out. After all, it wasn't as if Murali or Sri Lanka were consistently winning Tests or tournaments until 1995. But such a patronising attitude does the administrators of the game and Sri Lanka a disservice. Of course there is always a game played by administrators just as there is a game that is played out in the middle, but Sri Lanka has never asked for or received favours from anyone who runs the game. All our playing days we have wanted to be treated as no more and no less than equals. And that is an attitude shared by every Sri Lankan cricketer and administrator.

A young man's career was at stake during these bitterly disputed days. And this was where things got emotional. During the first Test at Perth, and even in the warm-up games, Murali and Dharmasena came under much media scrutiny, apparently some pundits had gotten wind of something brewing. Murali had a pretty undistinguished game at Perth (most of us did) but none of us had any fear or any idea of what Umpire Hair would eventually do at Melbourne. Certainly, as I've stated already, a few days before the Melbourne Test during a World Series game against Australia in which Umpire Hair officiated, Murali wasn't called for 'throwing' from either end. So what happened to Murali at the MCG came like a bolt from the blue. The MCG is an awe-inspiring ground; so big, with its panorama of towering stands looming so grandly, that when you're out in the middle looking up, you can see nothing but seats and sky. When Umpire Hair called Murali on the opening day of the Melbourne Test in front of 55,000 people, it looked as if the whole visible world was looking down on Murali. His was a peculiarly public humiliation. To be said to be a 'chucker' is tantamount to saying that you're either too stupid to know any better or you're a cheat.

This accusation came fast on the heels of us being mistakenly branded as 'ball-tamperers' during the first Test when the umpires at the time thought that we were guilty of 'sharp' practice. Naturally this is another contentious issue, but it was a charge of which we were completely exonerated following an official ICC enquiry right before the start of the next Test match. We were making headlines for more than our cricket and that is never a pleasant sensation. When a team is on tour it can be so easy for a kind of siege mentality to develop. You're hemmed in by a constantly circling press, the pleasures of life outside the hotel (home cooking, movies, shopping, sightseeing) can't be properly savoured and you can get to be in a constantly defensive mood. Naturally this kind of mentality is only the privilege of a team that is struggling on the cricket field. Our ploy of getting after Shane Warne had backfired in Perth during the first Test. I, to whom that job had been majorly entrusted (or rather I who asked for the job), twice found myself coming down the wicket and playing a fraction too early to balls heavy with spin, and was out both times to Shane for low scores. Kalu and Arjuna both had their minor victories against Shane but he or Glenn McGrath got them both in the end. Up against an Australian first-innings score of 600-plus we were second best by a long way. The Murali controversy was brewing obviously, but we were also suffering off the field with injuries. The pace-bowling and extra bounce afforded by the Perth wicket accounted for both Roshan and Arjuna being hit on the hands while batting. As soon as Brendon Julian (the same bowler on the same wicket who later broke Sanath's forearm in 1999) got one to rise sharply and hit Roshan, Roshan knew that he was in trouble. Over the years, Roshan's fingers and knuckles had been fractured and dislocated several times, to the point where his fingers have become arthritic and have to be strapped whenever he bats. Right after Perth just touching Roshan's hand made him wince. At this stage, with Sanath still regarded as predominantly a one-day performer, we had no comparable batsmen with Roshan's abilities, certainly none able to fulfil the job of opening the innings in a Test match. Roshan knew he had to play on for the team's sake. The knuckles on his right hand were so painful that he couldn't sleep for the three nights before our opening World Series game against the West Indies in between the first and second Tests. Roshan even swore off painkillers or sleeping pills in case they slowed his reactions out in the middle. Arjuna was struggling too, and another blow to his bottom hand at the MCG mid-way through the tour, led to a hairline fracture and his sidelining for three of our hitherto most intense weeks of cricket. And as soon as Arjuna came back, I was hit on the tip of the thumb during a game and was reliant on cortisone injections to the nail bed during the World Series finals to be able to wrap my inflamed bottom hand round a bat. I needed injections just to put my batting glove on. Pain's a peculiar thing, when you're in its grip you think things cannot possibly be worse than they are (though they often become so), but as soon as the pain stops you have no physical memory of it. It's like the pain never happened. Yet the feelings of joy can be recalled at any time and they can flood your mind and body with the physical sensations of pain relief. Some rely on adrenaline to get them through the pain barrier, but such relief is generally short-lived. Once one has realised how deeply the mind influences the body, it makes sense to use this relationship in a positive way. Whenever I'm in pain I try to manufacture as much of my own mental painkillers as possible by concentrating on feelings of success and well-being. It definitely helps me to play through my perennial bouts of soreness.

We were fighting against so much on that tour. After Melbourne, Murali had a trouble-free World Series match but was called for 'throwing' during our next game against the West Indies. I was captaining during this game and when Umpire Emerson called Murali, I was determined to keep him bowling. It might have looked as if I was subjecting poor Murali to further torment but I simply wanted the watching world to know that Murali was being subjected to inconsistent treatment. Umpire Emerson even called Murali for 'throwing' when Murali bowled a leg-break with a leg-spinner's action. It is physically impossible to 'throw' a leg-break. Even Abdul Qadir's grandfather couldn't do it. Only when our twelfth man brought out a message from the management that it was in Murali's and the team's best interest that Murali not bowl anymore, did I think of taking Murali off. So after his third over at Brisbane on 5 January 1996, Murali didn't bowl another ball in international cricket until the ICC cleared him of all taint of being a 'chucker' in time for the World Cup in February. Murali wasn't asked to change anything and was thus fully vindicated in his unconventionality. Just because he has been cleared once in 1996 and ever after by the ICC Technical Committee, though Umpire Emerson called him yet again in 1999, doesn't mean that Murali will never fall under suspicion again. His action will always be seen to be unusual. Murali knows it, we all know it. Let me assure you, Murali will be the first to know when he 'throws' a delivery because it will be different to anything he has done before. The authorities can and will continue to monitor him, but he has never so far been a 'thrower' according to the laws of the game.

Throughout all this huge, raging controversy in which he was a focal point there was something about Murali that remained profoundly unabashed. Sure he had tears of rage and frustration and a set to his smouldering eyes that suggested that until you were proven to be his friend you were his enemy, but during that time when he was unable to play and was scorned by so many, he formed an opinion of good behaviour and bad behaviour that will stand him in good stead for all of his life. He brings that black and white quality onto the field with him and it's vivid and hot. It's the raw material of where he's coming from. He's still very much a kid at heart, eager to please and hungry to learn, but that traumatic experience in Australia made him into the match-winner of today. Before he was good and took wickets, now he's great and takes even more. He would often come to my or Arjuna's or Dav's hotel rooms in those days to unburden himself and in those emotion-filled meetings he made me, and all of us in the team, understand more of what we fight against and what we fight for and what we have come to mean to those who truly support us. Murali's grin and bright eyes have kept their sparkle, because he knows that being the best you can be is reward in itself. Actual results, a win here, a loss there, don't matter as much as being Sri Lankan and being like no other nation of cricketers. Murali's trials bonded all his team-mates into a common unit. Before we had been Sri Lankan cricketers now we were the cricketers of Sri Lanka. Now we were really emotional.

Out of adversity came triumph. Our first World Series game, after Murali had been left hanging in the wind in Brisbane, saw us beat Australia and we dedicated the win to Murali. Effectively we won the game for him and our national pride. Our young paceman Nishanta Munasinghe gave himself what turned out to be a stress fracture of the back in taking the wickets of Michael Slater, Mark Taylor and Mark Waugh in Brisbane to finish with 3 for 30 off his ten overs. And when we came to bat Kalu comfortably outscored me in racing to a run-a-ball 77. It had been the first time that Sanath and Kalu had been paired as openers. Sanath was the established one-day opener if not yet fully reckoned to be capable of filling a Test opener's role. Kalu, already with a Test century against Australia to his credit, had been doing enough to the second new ball down the order to suggest that taking on the new ball in a one-day game could work very well. Kalu is an incredibly sweet hitter, he's got shots on both sides of the wicket and he can play off the front and back foot with equal ease. We didn't give him and Sanath any special instructions: we just gave them their head and asked them to play their natural game.

Openers using up a lot of overs at the start of an innings used to be a problem for everyone (with the exception of the West Indies with Greenidge and Haynes), us in particular. Pairing Kalu and Sanath was an experiment, a ploy arrived at by the manager Duleep Mendis, the coach Dav Whatmore, Arjuna and myself. With Arjuna out with a broken finger, and Roshan with his hands needing to be protected from the new ball, Kalu and Sanath might be just the men to blitzkrieg the maximum number of boundaries while the fielders were all mostly inside the 30-yard circle. It worked a treat. Every 4 they drove and cut and pulled and plundered rocked the opposition fastmen, who took to bowling faster and faster at them. Kalu and Sanath ate lightning and belched thunder. Kalu went on to hit two more robust half-centuries in the remaining matches, his big innings at the MCG in our must-win World Series game against Australia doing much to get us to the finals. At this point he was even outscoring Sanath and had the self-belief to hit through, and over the heads of, fielders placed specially for his favourite square-cut. Kalu's is the uncomplicated spirit of adventure, he likes nothing more than to be given the licence to hit the ball as well as he possibly can. And his wicketkeeping was improving mightily too.

But then the whole team was outperforming expectations. Our fast-bowlers were bowling with fire and accuracy. Pushpakumara, who for so long had threatened great things, now actually did come good. If Pushy is pointed in the right direction and then given just one thing to think of – pitch the ball on off-stump/bowl outswingers/bowl inswingers etc etc – he is capable of knocking anyone over. Vaas and Wickremasinghe chipped in with big wickets, Dharmasena was proving himself invaluable with his off-spinners/off-cutters and was a useful bat too in the middle order. All our batsmen were making valuable runs at one time or another. For the first time in our lives Sri Lanka were making partnerships under pressure and when in the field, to a man stopping the opposition from asserting themselves. We'd be dealt body-blows and we'd shrug them off, gather our thoughts and come right back at our opponents. We came good at critical times. We were playing the game as hard as the Australians, the very same Australians who had already won one of their World Series qualifiers off the last ball, and another off the penultimate delivery. Of course, one couldn't at this time compare Murali with the force that Shane Warne had become, but could you imagine Australia having to compete without Shane or without Mark Taylor? With half of the rest of their team injured? To get to the World Series finals we had to win our last two qualifying games against all the odds, and we did, winning a thriller against Australia at the MCG by three wickets with two balls to spare to book our place in the finals.

So rather than the expected showdown between Australia and the West

Indies, the 'plucky little Sri Lankans' were contesting the finals. We had masses of public support in Australia because the Aussies love an underdog and they love a fighting spirit; it was clear to them that there was more to Murali's 'blackballing' than met the eye, they responded to our emotional public crusade to clear his name and even looked askance at reports of all the racial slurs being tossed our way on the field. What few bad umpiring decisions there were seemed to be all coming our way too, as the television replays made clear to everyone watching. Glenn McGrath shoved Sanath in the chest during the first final, no doubt in the heat of the moment, but like all the other boorishness totally unnecessary and seen as such by the crowd. We had even cleared the rather 'prickly' air that had developed between us and Umpire Hair. While I was captaining during a World Series game in place of Arjuna, and we had twelfth and thirteenth men running on and off the field, filling holes in our injury-afflicted line-up, I thought Umpire Hair had said to me 'get on with it you blacks' when Umpire Hair had actually said 'you blokes' merely added a little gunpowder to the plot. In public, Arjuna kept smiling and saying nothing overtly negative about anyone or anything and was winning friends and influencing all kinds of people. More importantly, he communicated to the team that would hear his interviews on radio and television and would see them in the newspapers that he was upbeat and positive in spite of all the hardships. Sometimes what a captain says and does off the field is just as important as what he says and does on it. A captain can do an important job by fine-tuning his team's mood by his choice of public and private words. He can't completely control how each individual in the team will perform, but he can shape performance, lead it, help it to arrive at a useful pitch. Language, as well as strategy, is a captain's medium. Picking the right tone of voice, the proper gut response to events, is an art. And Arjuna is a maestro.

In the midst of all the hostility to anything Australian being stirred up by fanatics back home, at the start of 1996 the Australian Cricket Board top-brass visited Colombo on a mission to gauge whether a visiting Australian team during the World Cup would be safe from all cranks and vengeful patriots (i.e. bomb-throwers). A World Cup was at stake in more ways than one. Travelling the world and meeting people from different cultures, I tend to be surprised by their impression that because Sri Lankans are thought to be great respecters of authority, fun loving and generally well mannered, that we should also have another side to us where we are fiery, stormy tempered and quick to vent our anger. The semi-official word came through that Australia would tour if Sri Lanka, and in particular Arjuna, promised them a warm welcome, and if also the third Test at Adelaide after the World Series finals would be a pleasant affair(?!). Arjuna duly promised the best in Lankan hospitality, adding the rider, 'I'm playing gentlemanly cricket because that's what the Australian public want'. Diplomat, populist, media-savvy guru, spokesman for a nation: there's not much Arjuna can't do from his position as Sri Lanka's cricket captain.

Public support for us in Australia just grew and grew, but the Aussie crowds turned against us once Arjuna started calling for drinks, fresh gloves and a runner during his innings in the second and ultimately decisive World Series final. The Sydney skies were stormy and we were chasing a reduced target at a higher run-rate than would have been the case had conditions stayed fair. It looked to some as if Arjuna might well have been aiming for a postponement. Arjuna, who was playing in these do-or-die games with a broken hand and a general lack of match-fitness, was just trying to keep himself and his team alive at the crease. He had done it before, in roughly the same circumstances, during Australia's 1992 tour of Sri Lanka in a day-night game at the P. Sara. Ian Healy was the keeper on these occasions; Arjuna and Healy had run-ins about the conflicting ways they felt the game should be played going back to 1989. It got vocal between those two, it got vocal between those two and the umpires, in fact the confrontation almost became physical. Arjuna really lost his rag. Being called fat didn't really bother Arjuna, but being called a 'cheating son (of parents who weren't married)' upset him mightily, and having all the close-in Australian fielders bend the umpires' ears with their views upset him too. As far as he saw it, he was within his rights to ask for a runner for a disability sustained during play. The umpires, perhaps unduly prompted by Ian Healy, felt that if Arjuna hadn't brought a niggly hamstring with him into the game, he'd certainly brought his belly and lack of puff was no reason for a runner. They were right, of course, in what they said. If Arjuna really admitted it, he too would now say the umpires were right. If only because you always know how right your opponents are by your reaction to the times they hit the bullseye: you react with the righteous rage of someone trapped and wounded. So Arjuna didn't get his way, the runner didn't come on to the field and the final was over soon after.

During the presentations only Arjuna and one other Sri Lankan player shook Mark Taylor's hand. My reflex reaction was not to accept the outstretched offering. A captain might not effect every single action of his men, or even condone them, but ultimately he is responsible for the performance and conduct of his men. As far as I was concerned, while I was captaining Sri Lanka, I had seen and heard nothing in Mark Taylor that suggested he was even in one little way sorry for his team's rampant boorishness. It might all be heat of the moment, but surely athletes of considerable mental and physical discipline can channel their will to win in ways that don't refer to the colour of a man's skin. A lot of onfield argy-bargy can be resolved over a drink after a game and when the Australian team came to our dressing-room after the second final, we were perfectly polite to them. I made it a point to go over to Mark Taylor and shake his hand after the World Cup final. It must be said that since that World Series Cup of 1995–96 Mark Taylor's team have stopped the race-oriented sledging which did them no credit.

Sanath opened for the first time in Tests at Adelaide and scored his maiden Test century in the second innings, a real barnstorming affair. An innings that, viewed in retrospect, was the making of him. Had just two more batsmen along with Sanjeeva Ranatunga (65) been able to play a decent innings we may even have won the Test. We lost the Tests in Australia because we kept dropping catches and our batsmen didn't concentrate on building innings and partnerships. However, in a World Cup season winning is important and we had won a significant number of one-day games against tough opposition and, even more importantly, had proved our competitiveness time and time again. We were battle hardened, confident and capable of beating anybody. Next to the World Cup itself, the World Series Cup in Australia is the toughest tournament there is and winning so many big games confirmed us as dangerous warriors. In one-day matches things happen so quickly that you have to think on your feet and be intelligent and aware all the time. They are a quick way to mature a cricketer. And the youngsters Arjuna had at his command came on leaps and bounds in the space of a couple of months.

We thought we would do well in the World Cup that was going to start three weeks after our tour of Australia ended. Ian Chappell used to say, in the days we promised so much but delivered so little, that what Sri Lanka lacked was self-belief, but we had that now. Few, apart from Sir Richard Hadlee most notably, thought we could win the World Cup but everyone in the team felt that we were in with a good chance. At this time Australia were walking into Test matches thinking they could win. We were doing the same in relation to one-day games and that kind of attitude's worth a win or two by itself.

CHAPTER SEVENTEEN

Dav Whatmore would be the first to say that Sri Lanka won the 1996 World Cup because of its players, but the players will never forget quite how much help Dav was to them. There wasn't much that he could teach Arjuna or myself, his influence was most pronounced on the youngsters, but he did teach us all how to win. Part of wanting to win is wanting to make other people lose and that we hadn't understood before his arrival in our midst. Dav had come to us from his post as Head of Cricket at the Victoria Institute of Sport where he worked with a batch of young cricketers on all aspects of their game: technique, physique, psychology, bio-mechanics, fitness and nutrition. Dav knew how hard the Australians played the game, he knew what had taken Australia to the top in recent years and what was promising to keep doing so in the future. Dav knew what was needed to succeed. Coaches at the highest level can only build on the foundations laid down by players in their formative years, at most theirs is, if one is to put a figure on it, an addition of no more than 10 per cent to a player's ability. But it is a vital 10 per cent and it is often the difference between a player fulfilling his talent or underachieving. Talent just by itself is never enough.

And with his Sri Lankan roots and contacts, and the avuncular eye he had turned our way during our previous tours of Australia, Dav knew the Sri Lankan ways well too. He knew we could play shots all round the wicket and that we tended to play them a little too early in the context of a Test match. He knew batting was our strength and felt that it had to be more disciplined if we were to succeed. Attention to detail, efficiency and sheer tactical and technical competence was needed too. The point he kept drumming into us during our tours of Pakistan and Australia was that there were no short-cuts to be taken in our mental and physical approach to the game. Dav's was more than a professorial interest in the game, he passionately cared about Sri Lanka doing well, he wanted us to be the best we could be for our sakes. He could often be heard explaining to various pressmen and his cricketing mates in Australia that Sri Lanka didn't have the resources or the financial backing to provide everything that it was felt a player should be provided with. But he and the Board did try to provide the players with the most important things for greater performance. Undeniably, Dav felt that Sri Lanka were now starting to match Australia for talent. But he knew that wasn't enough to win. What he felt we lacked were the fully firing engines of mind and heart. 'You've got to have the stamina, the power, and the responsibility to guide the destiny of the team,' he said to no one in particular during one team-talk, though I think he was looking at me. 'It is quite amazing what an experienced cricketer can contribute with the bat, once his mind is made up.' And that is where I came in. Arjuna, Asanka and Roshan too.

Before Dav we had plenty of well-meaning advisers but virtually no individual coaching and teaching. I, Arjuna, Asanka, Roshan ('the seniors') and all those before us: we have had to work things out on our own. We helped each other as much as we could because we were the only ones who had experienced what we had, but when it came to coping with all the difficult questions asked of us by the world's best bowlers we all chose our own ways of going about things. I, because I risked more than anyone else, perhaps had to think hardest of all. Because my game was played mostly on the thin line that separates flamboyance from fallibility, mid-career I had to really think about how to maximise my boundary hitting ability. Youngsters coming into the team once we started playing cricket all the year round after 1992 would find the schedule too demanding or our resources too stretched to receive the full attention and guidance they needed. There is always an assumption that a player arrives in international cricket in full possession of all the basic skills. It is a mistaken one. For even if a young player makes a big splash initially, he will start to sink once he reaches the limit of his original capabilities. Too many Sri Lankan cricketers were sinking through not being buoyed up by someone. A captain's job is so demanding that he can't be mother and father to everybody, but someone needs to be. And next to the captain a full-time coach is the best alternative.

From technical advice to fitness advice to psychological advice, the whole regimented set-up was brought in by Dav. We had proved to our first official team physio Dr Dan Kiesel that we had the appetite for hard physical work and the desire to improve, and in the mid 1980s the team had benefited from the advice of the sports psychologist Dr Rudi Webster. But until Dav came on board the all-round training structure was a little haphazard. After Dr Dan was recruited (poached!) by the Pakistan team a new physio, the young Greek-Cypriot Australian Alex Kountouri who had worked with Dav at the Victoria Institute of Sport, became part of our team. More dedicated than a fax machine, he has been the team's twelfth man ever since. Alex has patched me up so often that he has practically been my most important batting partner. He has kept many a sore and aching bowler going in the middle of a hectic tournament schedule or Test match, when even the bowler didn't think it possible he would be able to take the field. Not quite a mystic masseur, more of a totally rigorous technician, it still somehow seems that Alex has the ability to 'heal' through touch alone. His surplus energy radiating through his brightness and optimism seems to actually help the curative process of those whom he treats. We have been essentially the same squad of players for the past seven years. Whereas that has been our undeniable strength in so many ways, it has also meant that our constantly active bodies have been tested to the full and have suffered their fair share of fatigue-induced injuries. Nor are some of us now as sprightly as we have been formerly. Alex keeps us all going with his uncanny ability to assess the optimal course of treatment for each of us. A measure of Alex's contribution to our cause can be seen by the Cricket Board's establishment of a lavish new fitness and treatment centre in March 1999, named the 'Kountouri Gym'.

Naturally any player and coach and physio would prefer that fitness training alone would prevent the need for any cure. Dav was only just in his 40s and had even played against a few of us during his career; yet he could never ever play at the highest level again. His playing days had run their course. Careers such as Imran's, Gooch's, Viv's and Javed's spanning three decades are all too rare in the modern era; five to ten years at the top is the norm and any one of our careers could be over at any time through injury or enduring loss of form. Dav knew how vital it was to live and play each day as if it were our last. 'Guys, in this game you never play as long as you want to, or as well as you want to. It's a short road we run in this game, so run hard,' he said. He had us running getting dressed, he had us practising with intent. Every action, exercise and drill had a purpose. The aim was strength, stamina, flexibility and concentration. Training programmes based upon (a) an in-depth physiological assessment, and (b) analysis of the performance function of each individual were prepared for all of us. Whenever I am even a few weeks away from the team I, like all the others, am expected to adhere to a whole cycle of exercises and diets and on my return to the fold I am expected to present myself for examination. Alex misses nothing. Not even the curses I throw at him as he sees just how lax I have been in my freewheeling ways.

Fat, skinfold, weight, aerobic and anaerobic capacity, speed, standing jump and flexibility are all measured, calculated and recorded. I am always happy when the ball comes out! Alex has the great ability to read us all as individuals and suggest the ideal workouts for us. Training privately, I particularly need to follow something that fits my energy and enthusiasm level or I simply get bored with the procedure. Contrary to popular rumour I do put in an enormous amount of effort into my physical training nowadays. I work hard, very hard, to come back from injury. Nobody's there for you during the most agonising times in the pain-house when you push yourself to the limit in the gym. There are no short-cuts. The work has to be done. It all comes down to how much you want to play. When practising with the team I do my exercises religiously. I have my usual inhibitions (i.e. I don't want to appear bested by anything), but I work through them, because I want so much to play as well as I can, for as long as I can. As I've said already, footwork is the first thing to go in a batsman. I'll work like a soldier ant to stop that happening. The prize at the end of the struggle makes me worry less about making an ass of myself as I do these burpees, squat-thrusts and gut-baring activities, as I sweat like I've never sweated before. Maybe I always wasn't as fit as I could have been, yet now in Alex's squad tests only Murali and Ruwan Kalpage are consistently rated higher than me. I am as hungry to succeed in practice as I am out in the middle. I want everyone, especially the youngsters in the squad, to know that there is no substitute for hard work.

Being fit is such a good feeling. Energy glows out of you, there is a spring to word, thought and deed. Getting to that state is worth all the effort. Fitness is only the platform from which to launch yourself, however. What determines how high you will fly is what goes on inside your head. Talented Sri Lankan youngsters had the habit of underperforming through fear of failure. There was only so much Arjuna or I or the other seniors could do to bring out the best in youngsters out in the middle who were perhaps a little too much in awe of us on and off the field. Our first generation of internationals may have felt the same when Sir Garry Sobers was the Sri Lanka coach. Dav drilled into the minds of each individual the necessity to exude composure even in the face of adversity. He did his best to give the players plenty of confidence. He didn't talk to them about technique in great detail, but he made them mentally attuned to match-situations. He had us recognise what we couldn't do anything about and stopped us feeling frustrated about that and had us recognise what we could do something about and had us doing it. Dav's criteria for judging a cricketer had less to do with a person's figures than with their work ethic and their willingness to take criticism on the chin. He wasn't interested in what they'd done before, but what they promised to do.

Anybody taking the field in international cricket can run, throw, catch and hit pretty much on a par with his opposite number in the line-up. Cumulatively, the teams must be equal in physical ability. What sets an individual apart is his response to any given situation. The individual battles are very significant. These are what every team member should look to win. Win enough of those in a match and the team usually wins too. Our young guys, who had the habit of saving their best for the nets, now came out to do their best when it really counted. And it worked.

They surprised themselves and the opposition with their new-found drive and determination. Players like Vaas, Dharmasena, Chandana and Pushpakumara particularly benefited, we all benefited from Dav focusing his efforts on the youngsters in the squad. He turned them into players who might do well into players who wanted to do well. Australia, for example, used to beat us half the time simply by imposing their mental strength on us. We weren't up to the challenge. We were passive, more acted upon than acting. Out in the middle too many of us would wait for things to happen, hoping they were going to go our way. Not enough took responsibility for themselves and the team, fewer still played to a plan. Maybe some of our guys felt inferior. That's something I've never felt. Never understood. Nothing is easier than to play with a batting partner who is finding it easy or to play in a team where you have faith in the bowling. Dav took a hell of a weight off Arjuna's and my shoulders. Suddenly, for the first time since we ourselves had been youngsters, Arjuna and I could play without having to worry about having to compensate for the fallibilities of our team-mates who were on a learning curve, a learning curve that we ourselves were only just coming off. The best coaches empower the players in their care to simply go out and do what the players have always wanted to do from the day they first picked up a bat and ball: be as good as they could possibly be. Dav is one of these kinds of coaches.

When you have confidence you can relax. Previously, our reactions to danger and pressure would have been gabbled and inarticulate: we'd throw our bats harder or bowl faster or spin the ball more. We'd run ourselves out. Calm and unfussed minds are required to win big matches. And what you're prepared for, you're best able to do. Big games are decided on mind strength, mental fitness, the ability to absorb pressure and keep the brain operating at high speed in tandem with hands and feet. From knowing all about losing we were starting to know all about winning. The perceived difference between winning and losing was getting noticeably smaller. The difference isn't just measured in runs and wickets. The difference is fractional, like the split-seconds of difference in qualifying times between race-cars which translate to being at the front or out of contention near the back of the grid. It has to do with skill. Skill and raw ambition.

We used to think that the deciding factors between winning and losing were that we couldn't play like the other teams, that we didn't have fast bowlers, that we didn't have batsmen who were comfortable on seaming wickets. We'd often go into games when just one opposition batsman had more centuries than the rest of us put together, an opposition bowler more wickets. We did ourselves a disservice, subconsciously we'd bought into the ethos that said there was only one way to play and that was the way developed by others. We didn't know that any team could win as long as it had developed a particular style and played in a certain consistent way. Australia for example were so good at focusing all their competitive forces on a particular player, so that in targeting the opposition's most important batsman or bowler, they would ensure that the rest would be made to capitulate too. All the Australians have an inner licence to kill. They want to play hard and they want to beat your brains out, and that's the way you have to be. Pakistan, as demonstrated by Imran, Wasim, Waqar, Qadir and Javed, were the same. The West Indies had it for the longest time; South Africa are starting to have that killer instinct too. That's the way to play winning cricket, the way to win at any sport. Look at Tiger Woods, Pete Sampras, Michael Jordan: it's not necessarily an ugly thing, you try to be a gentleman about it but you have to be very, very focused. You have to be hard. We used to care too much about what people thought of us. Now we don't. We still love to be crowd-pleasers, but just being entertaining is now no longer any consolation should we lose. And for too long we took comfort in our ability to be extraordinarily flamboyant when we should have focused on the ends and not the means. But you will understand that it is hard to step back and be clinically objective when so much of you is engaged in simply trying to get by.

Our problem used to be that our extraordinary talent was never given any sort of direction or framework in which to operate. Arjuna was undoubtedly the leader calling the shots on the field and knew the players and opposition best of all, but Dav came along at just the right time. With his technical and strategic knowledge and his almost unique insight into Aussie and Lankan culture he was able to provide that vital overview. He was the bridge between our past and our future. There's a basic problem all coaches face and it is that when you tell people something, you keep them from ever knowing. If they find things out on their own, they'll know it in a way they never will if you tell them. When Dav communicated to the youngsters what he wanted it was very specific and involving. It went way beyond little things like 'don't give the batsman room to play shots' and 'use yorkers at the end of the innings', 'don't fall into bowlers' traps', 'keep the ball on the ground'. Dav would paint pictures of match scenarios we were likely to go through. What he typically did was illuminate a particular situation, then he would sketch each player's role brilliantly, defining their place in helping to achieve the best possible outcome. So to Chaminda Vaas for example he would suggest bowling a particular line and length to Mark Waugh, another to Ricky Ponting; to the fielder in the covers, he would suggest exactly what angle to run in for balls hit on the off-side, to Asanka he would suggest the best way to keep the momentum going after Kalu's and Sanath's opening partnership had ended and so on. By making them think about their roles in a team-wide effort, he made each player feel just that little more in control of their destinies on the field. Dav had us searching for the heroes inside ourselves way before any of us had even heard the song by M People.

In such small ways does a team gain a sense of composure and mutual trust. We created amongst ourselves a culture of improvement. Practice became the glue that held the team together. As I've stated earlier, we started thinking only about our strengths and gave up thinking about compensating for our weaknesses. Strengths that could be magnified to an overwhelming intensity within the parameters of a game that lasted a maximum of only 100 overs. Sure we might lose a wicket every five overs but we had ten batsmen who could hit the ball to all parts of the ground from their very first ball. We might not have bowlers who took wickets every five overs but we didn't need to, if they bowled to one side of the wicket and were backed up by good fielding. Before 1996 we had won only three games in five previous World Cups, because we weren't sufficiently like the other teams. Then in 1996 we steam-rollered every other team in the world because they couldn't play like us. Even when we won the World Cup we weren't as good as we could be; we're still improving to this day. But for a very long time we were undoubtedly the best in the world at limited-overs cricket, the team that consistently had the beating of anybody in any conditions. We won a great many matches between the 1995 and 1999 World Cups, in fact we were probably at our peak the year after the 1996 World Cup when we won a bundle of tournaments and threatened to win all our Test matches. But we won our first World Cup by being fearless and fresh and a lot of that has to do with the attitude Sanath embodied as the first batsman the opposition would encounter each and every game. He didn't always have to hit fifties or bat for long. The manner of his attack is what counted.

After Australia the squad had ten days off, giving us all invaluable mental and physical refreshment. My flaringly painful thumb calmed down and by the time we all regrouped at the SSC I was ready and raring to go. I concentrated on tuning up my physical fitness before I even picked up a bat. A bomb went off in Colombo in the meantime, devastating the business area and killing and maiming so many unfortunate people. The West Indies and Australian teams pulled out of their scheduled World Cup group matches because of concerns for their players' safety. The Australian players had been receiving death threats from cranks as well. It was a big blow to the island's cricket fans who regard international matches to be an extravagant assault on the grind of daily life and a compensation for all the inconveniences they have to endure. And our administrators lost a lot of money. But missing the West

Indies and Australia games was a blessing in disguise because we had more time to relax and refresh ourselves and we ran less risk of picking up strains and injuries. Anyway the way the group system worked, Australia and West Indies could forfeit points to us and still qualify. Assuming they both beat Kenya and Zimbabwe . . .

A fit Arjuna back in the side made the team much more balanced and as a captain he has no peer in the side. We wanted to play our best XI through the World Cup and go out and win every possible game. We were not expecting to lose during the World Cup. The World Cup was so important for us. We had just started to develop a proper domestic infrastructure for the development of the game, a process that might have been still-born had we done badly. I felt we really needed to make clear that we could be the best in the world, that we could triumph by playing our distinctively Lankan game. A consolation 'Friendship' match for the fans at the SSC, where Sri Lanka played a combined India/Pakistan team showed me I was batting well, and my form just carried on from there. It looked like being a long tournament for us and I just wanted to ease myself into it. Pakistan's 1992 World Cup win had taught me that it's not how well you start, but how well you finish that matters.

In our first group game, against Zimbabwe at the SSC, Kalu was out to the first ball he faced, Sanath played on and I, trying out a lighter bat than normal, played a little early at one away from my body, the ball catching the edge and luckily flying just wide of the keeper before I'd got going. Asanka played a very good innings; I made 91, having found a heavier bat more suited to the conditions. I felt on the slow home wickets I was getting less deliveries to pull and cut so I started using a heavy bat to give my shots enough force to reach the boundary. I didn't really feel the need to hit the ball hard. I just concentrated on getting my placement right. In our next group match against India at Delhi under a flinty sky and a bony wicket, we got off to a brilliant start chasing a Sachin and Azhar dominated 271. After I came in, I tried to keep the runs ticking at the same sort of rate – eight an over after 15 overs (Sanath and Kalu had hit 50 in the first three). The field was up. Sighting a well-pitched-up off-side delivery from Anil Kumble, I thought of going over the top. Having reverted to using a light bat, to generate the necessary power I really had to swing it hard. I lost control of the shot and was stumped. Every time we get off to a brilliant start I tend not to perform well! A bit of a blunder, but at least I learned my lesson. It has always seemed to take me two mistakes before I realise the error of my ways. With a heavy bat, I find that I don't have to try to hit too hard; I always have the stroke under control. A light bat for me is 2lbs 6oz, a heavy one 3lbs 3oz. A 'normal' bat for Wasim Akram is 4lbs! 'Pick-up' is important in all my bats, and unlike the bulk of batsmen I actually like my bats not to feel heavy towards the bottom of the blade. I like them as evenly balanced as possible, and you will see that my bats are actually a little curved from toe to splice as the 'middle' is shifted just that little higher than the norm.

I'm as sensitive to the weight of my bats as a goldsmith is to the ore in his care. A heavy bat stops me playing too early and getting into airy-fairy trouble, but I find that prolonged use numbs my adroitness and limits my range of stroke from innings to innings. You can't be quite so responsive with a heavy bat, and in Test matches and tournaments when I'm playing a lot of games in a short period of time I always like to use a midweight (2lbs 14 oz) bat. When you're repeatedly playing the same set of bowlers in a short space of time as we often do nowadays, you don't want to let them realise you're only inclined to play certain shots. With a heavy bat I am less able to improvise at the last instant and thus my range of scoring area is reduced. And thus a pattern of scoring can emerge over a period of time and opposition fields and bowling plans can be formulated. The crucial factor in my calculations for despatching a cricket ball to the boundary is the impact force (weight times velocity) of the bat as it hits the ball. As I read the wicket, so I'll choose the weight of the bat. A quick wicket means that I use a light bat. I have plenty of bats, but I'm not sentimental about them, they're there to have a bash with. When I was younger I had my own 'bat-cave' in an annex to my bedroom at my parents' house, but now most of my cricket gear is kept in a 'museum' a cricket-enthusiast friend has set up in Colombo.

The qualifying-round games were where Sanath made his name as one of the world's most dangerous batsmen. He had been in and out of the team ever since his international debut late in 1989, mostly as a one-day batsman and all-rounder. He had first won his place in the side on the back of hitting two undefeated double hundreds and a not-out century in the seven matches of a 'B' team tour of Pakistan. He had played no first-class cricket before that tour and was chosen for it more out of curiosity than expectation. He played for an unfancied domestic team and was from an outstation, Matara, at a time when Colombo cricketers still largely held sway. But reports came to selectors' ears of a young lad who could simply stand and swat with a cleanness of stroke and precision of timing that was wondrous to behold. Of course international bowlers make a living out of exposing weakness and in the hundred or so limited-overs internationals he had played until February 1996, mostly at No. 7, he had a career that bumbled along inconsistently. Only the year and a half before the 1996 World Cup had he been playing as an opener. Since then he has never looked back. As with Sachin Tendulkar, one is surprised that people didn't see earlier how much more useful it is for batsmen with such incredible strike-rates have the chance to face as many deliveries as possible in an innings. Both Sachin's and Sanath's one-day careers took off once they started opening.

Possessed of the most amazing eye and incredible reflexes, Sanath could overcome his deficiencies in technique. For a long time he wasn't good with the ball that darted back into him and he would often find it a struggle at the highest level. If Sanath's career had not progressed and he was assessed on the performance of his first few years he would be considered mediocre. But to him hitting is a gift requiring no effort, and sometimes just on the evidence of one stroke played out in the middle you realised that his was a talent worth persevering with in a squad that had any number of batsmen all-rounders. Sanath could do what no one else could. You picked him on potential. Many's the time when the selectors would, unbeknownst to Sanath, give him just one last chance to keep his place in the side. He might not do well with the bat in that make-or-break game (lower-middle order is a very difficult position in a one-day game) but to redeem himself he would hold a breathtaking catch or bowl a brilliant spell and thus gain another stay of execution.

He was, at best, inconsistent until the start of 1996 but his greatest attribute still came to the fore: his ability to be amazing. He would often show a sudden improvisation of supreme audacity and play strokes with an unexpectedness which was exhilarating. He hit a terrific rearguard hundred the first time he opened in Test matches and was a big thorn in Glenn McGrath's side in the 1995–96 World Series matches with his ability to hit identical balls past point or past square leg! You always felt with Sanath that success was not far away. He only has to be told something once to take it on board. Once he felt in himself that he knew enough he became a world-beater. He is not a graceful player but there is something exuberantly athletic about him, like a boxer in training. Every moment in the field Sanath is always looking for the ball, always wanting to make things happen. It is Sanath's voice you always hear calling 'catch it' before anyone else's whenever the ball is in the air. Of all the promising youngsters in Sri Lanka, Sanath seemed the hungriest and he had an instinct for scoring if not a complete understanding of it in the context of a game. Every time you observed Sanath you saw a little more to his game than before and were more impressed.

Regarding his range of stroke, his bat speed, his hand-eye co-ordination, Sanath is a phenomenon. He sees the ball so early he can get himself into position very quickly; sometimes he doesn't even bother, he has so much time to play the ball. Sanath – and to some extent Saeed Anwar – go against the grain of opening batsmen because they tend to play away from their body, scoring runs in a wide arc from cover-point to midwicket. Sanath must be a nightmare to field to because his typical slash of a bottom-handed stroke, with the face closed until the very last instant, means that it is very hard for a fielder to anticipate the flight of ball off bat. Sanath's style is unorthodoxy wisely applied. He hits the ball in the air a hell of a lot for a man entrusted with the responsibility of opening in Test matches, but if you hit the ball as hard as he does you have to feel that you're less likely to get caught. Like me, Sanath is particularly fond of them fast and short. They go that much quicker to the boundary.

Sanath is only really ever in trouble when he checks his natural instincts. He doesn't have much in the way of footwork so he can sometimes be caught in no-man's land, but he is so sure and quick with hand and eye that he is able to attempt strokes other batsmen would still be thinking about as the ball is on to them. Basically he's so fast with his bat and so well co-ordinated that's it's very hard for a bowler to beat him. A lot of the things he does would be very difficult to duplicate by anybody else. Observe him closely and you will see that Sanath literally climbs into each of his attacking strokes; his long arms reach so far for the ball, his spring-loaded thighs are able to lever so much power, his balance is so good, his swing so quick with such amazing bottom-hand acceleration and his timing so sharp, that he can look for balls to hit from anywhere to anywhere. A bowler can't really set a field for him, because there's no delivery of any length or line that he can't loft in any direction out of the park. So many times when he's batting you hear the rifle-crack of bat immediately followed by a silence as everyone wonders where the ball's gone, until it's broken by an explosive roar from an unlikely side of the stadium. The name Alvin Kallicharan doesn't get heard too often nowadays (he wasn't on television enough) but those who saw Kallicharan play think that Sanath has many of the same qualities. Let's not forget, Sanath is still a young man and is still on an upward trajectory.

Nowadays Sanath sets such high expectations for himself in the public's consciousness that as soon as he goes through a poorish run, the idiosyncrasies of his technique become remarked upon, and he is found to be wanting in so many aspects. His low scores are often blamed on unorthodox technique, whereas his high-scoring innings are greeted with praise. If you score runs then everyone says your form and style is good. If you don't, every minute flaw becomes evidence of a deep-seated fault. And if a player gets to hear about his so-called problems (who else have we to talk to at grounds apart from well-meaning pundits?) such knowledge can really play havoc inside his head. Sanath struggled for longer than necessary in the past because he hadn't worked out what just what made him special. Because his is literally a hit and miss talent, so finely calibrated is his strokeplay, he either wins big or he fails big. Whenever he fails it's the result of just one little thing being out of sync; invariably its because he's thinking too much about his game. I have never come across any other batsman who so explicitly embodies the simple truth of cricket, that it's a 'see ball hit ball' game. None of us want him to be anything other than Sanath Jayasuriya, it's when he tries to be 'responsible opening batsman/blunter of opposition attacks' that he lets himself – and us – down. He's at his best when he simply recognises situations and reacts. First Test century, Most Valuable Player of the 1996 World Cup, then the fastest one-day hundred, the fastest one-day fifty, a share of the highest ever Test partnership, a Test innings of 340; fame, wealth, success, respect, the good life beyond his wildest dreams: all these happened for him in a very short space of time because he simply hit cricket balls that were thrown at him as well as he possibly could. Ask yourself, if you had the chance to play international cricket would it scare you or would it excite you? Sri Lankans are generally an excitable race and Sanath's a cricketing genius not because he reinvented the opener's role but because he can see the obvious and then act on it, no matter if it had never been done before in the history of the game. His intuitive shot-making to fast and slow-bowlers on wickets of all kinds, to redefine and announce in a flash of the bat a new way to attack a bowler, has inspired a generation of opening batsmen to cast away their inhibitions.

Plus he's a terrific bloke. Modest, humble, a completely devoted team man. In his gestures, his way of speaking and holding himself, he is so bursting with charm and simplicity that it is impossible to know him without liking him at once. His sense of humour is exuberant and contagious. Sanath's openness and naturalness are so total that he becomes, conversely, enigmatic to all those who want a piece of him. They can't believe a guy who does such incredible things on the field can be so down to earth off it. He feels deep roots of responsibility to his friends and family and never tries anything less than to be a credit to the people he represents. The fact that since our 1995–96 Australia tour the dressing-room atmosphere has particularly been like that of a family has helped him to relax and give of his best.

Hitting a cricket ball (once you've practised for a very long time) is really very easy. You can't force it. You can't overpower it. You let the bat do the work. Its all rhythm and flow. Successful batting depends on knowing your scoring shots, visualising the gaps, hitting the ball hard, hitting the ball true. Sanath just takes that process a little bit further than the rest of us. Sanath's more or less the same as I was when I was a kid just going out to hit the ball around; we have high hopes but moderate expectations for him, as others did of me. That he should have come quite so far has really surprised us, as no doubt my career has surprised so many too. Sanath's glory in the 1996 World Cup reflected on all of us because he was one of us out there standing for all that was remarkable about Sri Lanka and he'd suddenly lifted the game to a higher plane. We were all larger and better during his periodic assaults on opposition bowlers.

Our final group match was against Kenya at Kandy. It will show you how relatively unfancied we still were at this stage because some people envisaged that Kenya might just beat us. They had beaten the West Indies in their previous match, bowling them out for 93, and if they had beaten us would have progressed to the quarter-finals at the West Indies' expense. But really, Kenya didn't have a chance against us as we batted first and made the world record limited-overs international score of 398 off 50 overs. I kind of felt sorry for them as they gamely did nothing more than try their very best. It wasn't so very long ago that we had been in their position. The Asgirya stadium, hemmed in by ancient forest in practically every direction, can feel awfully small to a fielding side and every time the ball is hit in the air it can easily be lost in the tree-line. Sanath and Kalu were particularly merciless and raced to an 80-run partnership in no time. Asanka too came in and indulged in some awesome power-hitting. He hit some of the biggest sixes I've ever seen. At the other end, I was just relying on punchy timing for my runs and I was timing them sweetly. When told after reaching my hundred on the way to Sri Lanka's highest ever one-day score that it was Sri Lanka's first ever World Cup century, I didn't know whether to be proud or chastened. At one level it showed how far we had come, at another it showed how much we had struggled earlier. Our aggression looked rather tame compared to Arjuna's, after he came in following Asanka's dismissal and smashed his way to 75 off just 40 deliveries.

The Kenyans were always likely to be beaten but we beat them by a far bigger margin than their more fancied opponents in the World Cup, Australia and India, and that stood us in good stead at the end of the qualifying rounds. Kenya have talent, particularly as batsmen; they could match Sri Lanka's progress in due course. If they fully work towards a certain goal and have the support of enlightened administrators, then they could be like us. One thing's for sure, the Kenyan cricketers play because they love the game and that shines through in everything they do.

The quarter-finals were the only game I was worried about as, having qualified head of our group, we were drawn against England, the lowest-qualifiers in the other group. I told Arjuna that if we got through the quarter-finals we had a good chance of getting through to the final. More than anything else it was the first knock-out game and we hadn't played England for a long time. Most of the guys didn't know what they'd be like. The English didn't have anyone who could be outlandishly extraordinary but they usually play a solid game. All of us tend to contribute in a team-meeting but, as I'd played against most of the English, I was asked to bring my knowledge to the fore. Basically I said we shouldn't bowl short and wide to Robin Smith, Graeme Hick, Graham Thorpe or Alec Stewart and that we shouldn't bowl at their pads either, particularly Atherton's. And that we could rely on their seamers (of whom Gough was the fastest and Reeve the funkiest) to bowl consistently on or around off-stump. As you can see, cricket tactics aren't rocket science. The point I wanted to make was that these guys were just like any others. Anyway I was sure England would be even more concerned about us than we were about them.

It must surprise any eager, aspiring cricketer who would like nothing better than to play for his country at the highest level that the attractions of interminable international cricket can pall. England had come to the World Cup straight from suffering a 6–1 hammering against South Africa in seven consecutive one-dayers after a hard-fought Test series, and you just knew they had to be hurting. If we hadn't had our mini-break after Australia we'd have been in exactly their condition too. When we saw them in the morning warm-up, we had the feeling that the English players were a little jaded. Bleary-eyed and unshaven, they acted like men who would rather be playing on another day in another country during another lifetime. Call me a traditionalist but unless a player is an accredited beard-grower or really likes the look of himself with designer stubble, being unshaven matters. It shows the world that you don't care what people think of you. And if you don't care, you don't perform to the best of your ability. It didn't even look like England would be in the mood to celebrate a win should they pull one off. I knew we had a good chance of overcoming anything they could raise themselves to throw at us. This was a World Cup quarter-final, the first one we'd ever been in. The last one any one of us might ever play in. We were going to treat the eight hours of the game as if someone had said to us, 'You've got eight hours left on Earth. What are you going to do with them?'

England opened the bowling with Richard Illingworth which was surprising because Kalu and Sanath are both good players of spin but perhaps after our performance against India at Delhi, England felt they had to try something different and take the pace off the ball. Fortunately the target we were chasing wasn't difficult on the Faisalabad pitch which played hard and true throughout. England's 235, which owed much to some late-order hitting by DeFreitas, Reeve and Gough, was a decent total, but we were to pass it with some ease. Although we had a bit of a hiccup at the end, Hashan and Roshan saw us home. The way England were behaving when I was batting was surprising: even with about a hundred runs left for us to score they'd given the game up as a foregone conclusion. Sanath, with his opening barrage of 4s and 6s (82 off 44 balls), had knocked the fight out of them. Kalu had played a typically Kalu-vian innings in getting out for 8, third ball. England had played so much cricket I can sympathise with them. Still, they were professional enough not to give the match to us on a platter, we definitely earned our victory.

We left Faisalabad for Lahore where, after training at the Gaddafi stadium, we saw the ending to the epic India–Pakistan quarter-final on television in our hotel. India played very well in a pressure game. It looked like Pakistan's openers thought they could win the game on their own. Their team, with the probable exception of the wily Javed Miandad padded up back in the pavilion, probably thought so too. The openers fell on their own swords, the remaining batsmen took their foot off the gas, and Javed's nudging and pushing game which was so successful a tactic in the 1992 World Cup proved futile in this innings. He had no firing strokeplayer opposite him. And if Javed really admits it, he wasn't the same player in 1996 he had been in 1992. The difference was marginal but his opponents could sense his limitations, and at this level, once that happens you're seriously handicapped. Javed had been feared like no other Pakistani batsman in the past; not any more.

We learnt quite a bit about India's tactics having seen them under pressure in this game, and as we headed for the semi-final in Calcutta, we were confident that we would prevail against them.

CHAPTER EIGHTEEN

Playing India on their home turf in front of 100,000 partisan fans was obviously going to be a big challenge. For us and for India. You never know with Indian cricket fans: they love the game and love to see good cricket irrespective of who's playing it, but they are even quicker than fast bowlers to vent their frustrations. What they want most of all is not to feel cheated of a contest. They will even turn against their own beloved players if they feel that India aren't performing.

A potentially fractious crowd and a heavily armed paramilitary guard that shadowed us everywhere we went in India were the least of our worries. The state of the Calcutta wicket posed the biggest problem. So much can depend on the toss of a coin let alone the state of a wicket; what any team wants to do is to be prepared for any eventuality. The World Cup's opening ceremony had taken place at Eden Gardens and while the actual square itself had been protected by being under the central stage, none of the teams had a chance to get an impression of the playing surface. You'd have thought that local knowledge would have provided some clue but no cricket had been played there for months before the tournament and India themselves hadn't played any cricket there for eighteen months prior to the semi-final. How the wicket would play was anybody's guess. The day before the semi-final as we practised in the stadium under lights, the wicket was slightly damp to the touch because of the evening dew and was just a little crusty on top. Crustiness means bounce first, then turn. It was obviously going to be at its best for batting under the baking sun during the day before giving the spinners progressively more assistance as the game went on. I say obviously, but as the next day's action demonstrated it wasn't obvious to all in the Indian camp.

For on winning the toss Azhar put us in to bat. Perhaps the feeling was that irrespective of the inevitable worsening of the wicket and the difficulties the team batting second would have, Sri Lanka as the most dangerous chasing side in the game were best controlled by insertion. It's true we had absolutely annihilated them in Delhi when they would have expected their 271 to have beaten any other team but batting first on this occasion we thought that 220 would be enough to win. That score perhaps looked a little far away when we were 1 for 2 at the end of the first over, with Sanath and Kalu both back in the pavilion.

When Sanath's and Kalu's adventurous no-holds-barred strokeplay first proved successful in Australia no one thought we'd have the nerve to persist with such an unorthodox policy in the World Cup. But we did and in a very short space of time these two had captured the public's imagination and struck fear into opposition ranks. Opening bowlers had to think of things they never had to think of before, like 'how do I stop feeling like Goliath taking on David?' and 'how do I get the ball back from the tenth row of the grandstand when there aren't any fielders near the boundary?'. Sanath and Kalu rewrote the rules of the game. They demoralised the opposition and enlivened audiences. They were bold and fearless and their threat was even stronger than their reality. In full flow they made it look as if they could win matches by themselves, or at least make it so that after blasting 80 to 100 runs in 15 overs all the following batsmen would find the going very easy. But what no one realised was that we ourselves didn't put all our faith in our openers. They were only opening together so as to maximise their talents on the principle that early runs are psychologically more valuable. As outrageous strokeplayers we thought they might just as easily make a score as not. To the opposition, the commentators and the spectators, they might have been the most dangerous opening pair in world cricket but to us they were just a couple of guys having a go.

So when Kalu was out to his first delivery, caught on the fence at wide third-man, we weren't disheartened. The bunker-like dressing-rooms at Eden Gardens are not in direct view of the play and the dressing-room television wasn't working so I who prefer to just sit quietly while waiting to bat, saving my mental energy, was reliant on the crowd noise to guide me as to the state of play. The roar that greeted Kalu's dismissal was pretty loud, the way it had started promisingly before catching in people's throats prior to exploding into ecstasy suggested that a catch had been taken off a big hit. A couple of balls later, another massive roar and prolonged applause. Sanath had become so popular in recent weeks that I thought the crowd were responding to another big one. Therefore it was a big surprise to me to see Sanath in the dressing-room. He had hit a big one. Into wide third man's hands. Azhar had done his homework. We had lost two wickets four deliveries into the opening over. 1 for 2 in a World Cup semi-final. The only people in the world who were still convinced we could win were the guys in the team.

I walked out to bat a little faster than normal to make up for lost time and joined Asanka at the crease. There are two qualities an international cricketer respects most of all: mental toughness and the ability to chat up women. We don't go around comparing averages but when we look at each other we pay heed to a player's ability to make runs when it matters. Everyone knew I had all the shots in the world and had a very special talent but, and it was a big but, there were doubts about my temperament and an ability to play at my best under the most intense pressure. Cricket-writers would sometimes refer to me as being 'touched by genius', meaning I wasn't the fully-fledged variety . . .

1 for 2 and with it all to do would seem pretty pressurised. But it didn't bother me. Mentally I was ready to go in early. A couple of months earlier in Australia, the times I had the opportunity to I hadn't set the world on fire, thus before the World Cup there were whispers that I was on the way down as a batsman. This innings would be a chance to show the world what I was made of. I had started my career to find out how good I was, I had found out I was pretty good, but I just hadn't irrefutably proved it. Having turned 30, time was running out. This was the biggest stage I had yet played on. It would be overstating the case to say that I played with anger in my heart but there was a well-stoked fury simmering in there. I wanted what everyone wants. Respect from one's peers. If I hadn't played as I did in the semi-final and the final then I probably wouldn't be writing this book now. I put all doubts to rest. As for relationships with the ladies . . .

You live for those moments, moments when an innings that you play is of such overwhelming significance that it leads to the biggest triumphs imaginable. You give a piece of your lives in those innings and are defined by them forever. My fans love to watch me bat I know, but they also tell me that I fill them with fear. A fear similar to the one felt by those who watch someone performing aerial acrobatics without a safety-net. They love to see the spectacular move succeed but hate to witness a guy over-reaching and falling splat from a great height. Risk and reward may have held equal sway in my soul before, but now I was playing a much more reliable percentage game. I used to bat the way I liked and that way brought me a lot of success. But batting is not only batting. It is understanding what it takes to be successful. You don't just look for runs. You look to be effective.

If my perspectives had sharpened in recent times, so too had they narrowed. I felt I knew enough about the game to not have to rely on nets for my sole batting practice. The morning before a game I might just have a few hits to loosen up, but really the main practice goes on in my head. I just need a mirror and a bat and a few minutes to myself. I check my stance, picture the ball coming to me at different lengths and speeds and simply play the appropriate stroke each time. It need only take two minutes. It's just a way to set myself and get comfortable, remind my body and self that I am a batsman. My match rehearsals really developed in this fashion when I actually started thinking my way through innings before

I'd even played them. Not by means of premeditated shot-making, which is a sure step to disaster, but through just preparing myself to give of my best. I never set myself numerical targets. I just set my state of mind, a state of mind where I simply let the game come to me, I don't go out to chase it. It's like driving at 150 m.p.h. with a clear view of the road ahead: it's not about the destination, it's about the journey. Before it would kill me when we lost matches. I would hate it when I had underperformed. And this tension and underlying seething rage to prove myself in competition didn't make for the most consistent returns. In recent years I'd adopted a more mature attitude to my own performance. I became less concerned about the outcome of games, and focused more on simply being the best I could be. Because when I'm at my best I'm pretty good. And the team tends to win too. It's like if I were a Grand Prix driver, before I would have been good for the occasional spectacular victory but now I know I'm consistent enough to win a championship. I've got a great team supporting me and I have a sound engine – my head.

Thinking your way to success is all well and good but you've still got to go out there and score some runs. If the Indian bowlers had got me out straightaway we would have been in trouble. The whole psychological weight of the situation would have shifted against us and not even the combined weight of Asanka and Arjuna may have rebalanced matters. There was no way I was going to get out early on. There was no earthly reason why I should. I felt good. I was seeing the ball very early, playing the ball late. Nothing could surprise me. This kind of arrogance is necessary in a batsman. You just have to feel master of the situation. Sometimes I feel so good I have no idea why I get out. Everyone else in the opposition thinking they're the king of the world too, and the fact that the game and the people who play it will always find ways to surprise you, is quite enough explanation for the fact that you don't score a century every time you feel you ought to. This game is so humbling that you don't really want to make a big noise when you have done well. Anyway, if cricket were easy it wouldn't be so fulfilling.

I went out to bat in Eden Gardens wearing what people have come to recognise as my 'game face'. Few words, no smiles, no worries. No eyes and ears for anything but the task ahead. All I was interested in was seeing ball on to bat. Anil Kumble opened the bowling from the other end as we expected, and his first delivery bounced chest-high and with the finest of off-glances for four I was on my way. You play that kind of shot first ball and you know and the bowler knows you're in tip-top form. It soon became apparent that Azhar had instructed his bowlers to bowl a distinctly off-side line, challenging me to either attempt to beat the bulk of the fielders on the off-side or to play against Kumble's spin and Srinath's outswing in looking for the wide-open spaces on the leg-side.

It doesn't matter where the fielders are if you hit the ball between them. The bulk of my early runs came between cover and point off-side as I simply made sure that when I did play an attacking stroke, I played it in the best way I could: elbow high, bat angled down at point of impact and wrists cocked to control the direction of the ball leaving the bat. I was hitting everything with power, punch and purpose. As soon as Azhar moved square-leg to short extra-cover for Kumble I made it a point to hit the ball through square-leg. The only time I misplayed anything like an attacking stroke was when in wanting to stretch the field and Azhar's thinking a little bit more, I pulled a ball on off-stump intending it to fly over midwicket's head. It did, but not by much.

Asanka unfortunately fell soon after to Srinath for 1 which brought Roshan to the wicket. Normally it would have been Arjuna's turn but Arjuna had two reasons for putting Roshan ahead of him. First, Roshan is lightning between the wickets and he would be adept at feeding me the strike. Secondly, and perhaps more importantly, with an eye to being in the final when an innings from Roshan could be needed, this was a great opportunity to let Roshan get some time in the middle under his belt. So dominant had been our upper order in the competition, Roshan at No. 7 had hardly had a chance to bat.

In a team as well balanced as ours with six bowlers and batsmen all the way down the order, even if a player isn't seeing much of the action or not taking many wickets or making volumes of runs, the times when they are called upon to be special are the times when their contribution really makes a difference. It's really all for one and one for all. You have faith in each other because everyone has faith in themselves. Roshan has always been a fine batsman, a brilliant fielder, smart tactician and a very popular cricketer. But don't let all that fool you; he is a very good guy to have on a team. We've been friends since we were boys and he has always been the same Roshan: immaculate in his whole attitude to life and the game. Even though he himself is never one to make a chest-beating fuss about it, he lives to bat and play cricket. Nothing gives him greater satisfaction than doing well for Sri Lanka.

By being so different in outward style of play and behaviour, Roshan and I have been compared and contrasted throughout our careers and set up as polar opposites by people who like nothing more than to stir up trouble. People often said 'why can't Aravinda be more like Roshan, Roshan is so less headstrong and impetuous?'. People often unfairly disparaged Roshan in the light of his relative lack of flamboyance. All these people have agendas of their own which are totally at variance with the needs of the team. Yes, Roshan scores runs in a different style to Sanath, Arjuna and myself. But it doesn't bother any of us. For a long time Roshan was our 'Larry Gomes/Gus Logie', the anchor-man (with strokes of his own) who allows the other stroke-makers the freedom to play their game. Asanka and Roshan alternated this anchor-man responsibility over the years and they played an invaluable role in developing our playing strategy. Asanka himself re-emerged as a big hitter in his later years, but let anyone who thinks of Roshan as just an accumulator of runs not forget the brilliant cameo he played in the Calcutta semi-final when he did everything he could in lifting us after the loss of three quick wickets in partnerships with myself and Arjuna. And when Roshan eventually retired hurt mid-innings, with us approaching 200, he had scored a 50 of his own at a fair clip. He's scored plenty of Test and one-day centuries by simply being judicious and clever. For sure, he would have scored even more runs if he hadn't been quite so vulnerable to the ball that moves away, but then wouldn't we all?

Roshan and I countered everything the Indian bowlers threw at us and I reached a 32-ball fifty, the bulk of my runs having come in boundaries. I was so focused on the task at hand that I felt I could have gone to 150. Hence it was a big surprise to find myself inside-edging a ball from Anil Kumble onto leg-stump. A bit of a walking stroke to a rare googly from the master-flipper, but out for 66 with the score at 85 I realised we had some work left to do. The fifteen-over mark had barely been reached and we had lost four batsmen. But the psychological initiative meant more than the state of the score-line. We had judo-flipped the onrushing Indians and the game was now ours for the taking. Roshan went on till he had to be carried off the field with cramp. Arjuna, Hashan and Vaas hit about them sprightly and pretty soon it became apparent that we were going to sail past 220. We ended with 251 off our 50 overs, this on a wicket that was already showing signs of misbehaving as the night drew in. It had to be a winning score.

However, against a batting line-up that included Sachin, Sidhu, Azhar, Kambli and Jadeja you could never be sure. Any one of them could go absolutely berserk and inspire the rest to victory. It was asking a lot but while Sachin and Sanjay Manjrekar were together with the runs flowing and the Indian score approaching 100 with more than half the overs to go, there was just a small chance that they might make it. There was an even smaller window of opportunity for the stumping that Kalu made of Sachin. Sachin had scored the bulk of his team's runs and looked set for more until a missed drive, as he came down the wicket to Sanath, gave Kalu the chance to whip off the bails. It was a brilliant piece of work. Kalu had gone way down the leg-side to gather and could only have beaten Sachin's lunge back by an inch. The third umpire signalled red. Sachin was on his way. That had to be it. Sachin is such a genius that he might just have survived against the spinners even though he'd have had to go after them. But his wicket was all Kalu's. Kalu had come in for much criticism over the years for his keeping, because he had often made some glaring errors. He can be so outstanding at times, by far the best wicketkeeper-batsman on the island, but he's also capable of letting his mind wander out to sea. Yet he's always forgiven, for how couldn't you forgive a guy who has the smile of the Artful Dodger and a laugh as deeply sweet as warm molasses?

Sanath then bowled a ball which turned a yard from the rough outside Manjrekar's leg-stump to castle him, a delivery which put the frighteners on India's remaining batsmen. The ball was starting to dig bits out of the wicket on pitching and was either popping up or practically turning square. India's batsmen fell all in a heap and seven wickets went in a very short space of time and with it all chance of their winning the game. A couple of water-bottles and the like came flying over the barbed wire and concrete walkway separating the crowd from the field of play near to where I was fielding. Arjuna (captain, my captain) swapped me over with Upul Chandana (youngster, expendable), the sub who was on in place of Roshan. Fires were being lit all over the stadium. The next missile to come over the fence just missed Upul and the umpires brought us off with India still needing 132 with 16 overs left. With no let-up to the crowd's activity, a short period later the match referee Clive Lloyd awarded the game to us by default. We were through to the World Cup final.

If we had thought our comeback had been spectacular it was outdone by Australia's against the West Indies in the other semi-final at Chandigarh the next day. Batting first, after ten overs they had been reduced to 15 for 4 and had managed to recover to 207 thanks to Michael Bevan (who generally did wonders for Australia that season), Stuart Law and Ian Healy. And then they rescued themselves again in the closing stages of the match when the last eight West Indian wickets fell for 37, three of them to Shane Warne, as Australia won by five runs.

So Australia were going to be our opponents in the final. Ironic, because of all the bad blood that had been spilled between us and Australians on and off the field. A lot of it was overblown by the media, but undoubtedly if there was one team we wanted to beat to become World Cup champions it would be Australia. No one really gave us a chance against them. Our few wins in the World Series against them were seen as aberrations, man for man they were considered as better than us in all departments. Bobby Simpson, their coach, said they'd beat us seven times out of ten, and in a one-off game with all at stake Australia would undoubtedly simply show their class and demolish us. We were so much the underdogs it was like we were mongrels compared to the pedigree of the Aussies. When you are up against it, and in my career I have been with Sri Lankan teams that have been up against it, you just get used to people patronising you. But you get fed up of not being rated. You feed on this need to prove your worth and you start devoting your mind to the thought of winning. Everyone starts achieving. Team-mates take chances and they always seem to work. That kind of play just takes over and amazing things start happening. Boldness has genius, power and magic in it, I once heard someone say. And they were right.

Australia and the rest of the world might think Australia were overwhelming favourites for the Cup but the rest of the world and Australia still didn't really know what we were capable of. The night before the final there was a big storm in Lahore but luckily the final was able to start on time. The outfield was a little heavy, but the wicket firm and true if a little on the slow side. It was going to be Lahore's first floodlit international and what with the particularly heavy moisture content in the air, there were prospects for the white ball to swing prodigiously in the evening session. And had it rained during the innings of the side batting second, they would almost certainly find themselves compromised by the revised required run-rates. In any event, all the five previous World Cups had been won by the team batting first.

Everyone predicted that the side winning the toss would bat first but Arjuna confounded them by inserting Australia. And when Australia were 136/1 after 26 overs, it might have looked as if we were going to have to chase 300. It's very hard to kill a team's momentum in the middle of an innings but thanks to a terrific catch by Sanath, over his shoulder at square-leg to dismiss Mark Taylor, and some brilliant teamwork all round, we slowed the Australians' rate of progress. Murali and Dharmasena were the most responsible for halting the run-rate and I was able to bag a few wickets and take a couple of catches. We were playing very smart cricket, giving away nothing in the field and giving the batsmen no room to play big shots. Whenever they tried to hit over the top, they almost always found a fielder. Arjuna used his four spinners in rotation, never letting any of the batsmen get comfortable with any bowler's line. He had the fielders move a yard to two here and there, constantly regulating the run-routes. There was a collective smothering of the Aussies in the manner of placing a heavy blanket on a puppy. Until the penultimate over, the Australian batsmen hit only one boundary following Mark Taylor's dismissal. This was a lesson to all watching who thought our game was founded purely on attack; we could also play top-notch defence. We were truly an all-round team.

We were eventually set a total of 242. At stake was the chance to be world champions. It was the chance to be ranked among other champions of the past, to set a standard for the future. What we were playing for was recognition of being the best in the world by playing our own distinctive way. The World Cup is incontrovertibly the biggest prize in world cricket, the most tangible benchmark for performance. Could we be the few good men who achieve the goal that every other team had been planning for months to achieve? We had great confidence in our ability to prevail. We had come through so many pressure situations that we all knew exactly how to respond. All our roles were clearly defined, we knew exactly what we had to do. We had a workman-like attitude to matches, yet there was deep feeling invested in all our performances. Before each game is about to start the team gathers together in the dressing-room, and takes a couple of minutes to do what we call a 'worship'. Just about every team in every sport has their pre-match huddles where minds are composed for the encounter ahead. Ours is distinctive in its own way. We don't ask the Lord for victory as such, only the chance to play as well as we can. But only if we deserve to. We always pray with that 'if'. And having played well enough to win, we come back to the dressing-room and give thanks for the privilege of prevailing.

Sanath was in the mood to get the runs all by himself but was run out by a whisker following a Glenn McGrath throw from third-man and then Kalu was a little late on a pull off Damien Fleming to be caught at midwicket. Asanka was mighty determined and together we set about building up the innings. We knew we needed to be nothing other than positive. We had to challenge the opposition with our bats: play cuts, pulls, hooks and drives. In particular, I knew exactly how the bowlers would come at me. They knew I had the shots: what they were going to test was whether I had the mind to play them. Only three of the Australians had toured Australia in 1992 but that innings of 37 against them was still something I had to live down in their collective conscious. And that of the watching world's. But I was mentally harder and physically stronger now and the only person I was really competing with was myself. It's almost an aspect of Buddhism in application. Playing an innings is like living a life. Self-transcendence is all; you want to keep yourself going, you seek fulfilment every single moment of your life, you never quite know how long you'll last.

I was expecting a slower ball early on to test my predilections and Damien Fleming duly obliged, with one aimed at leg-stump. I drew the ball to me rather than plunged out to it and smoothly clipped it to the boundary in front of square. A short one had to come too, and next ball it did, smack off the meat of the bat to the vacant midwicket boundary for a one-bounce four. The Australians now knew that I was completely uncowed by the situation. And really the rest was up to me. The Australians could do nothing to stop us; the run-rate was always maintained; the boundary regularly found. Asanka and I even managed to take some quick singles. When a team believes it can win, luck also seems to favour it. Asanka was dropped badly by Stuart Law just after he passed

50, and a couple of other half-chances didn't go to hand. Every delivery just seemed to confirm to us that we were going to triumph. Asanka brutalised Shane Warne with one screaming straight six and when he departed for 65, Arjuna came in and immediately started playing some outrageous shots. The Australians relied mightily on Shane to make it happen for them, but the combination of slow wicket, dew-doused ball and discomfited spinning-finger neutralised his threat. Plus, we were in no mood to fall for his wiles.

As in Calcutta, I played with a straight bat where most appropriate and halfway through the innings there could now be no doubt that I am at my best when the stakes are high. If I'd scored a hundred and we had lost, my innings would have been worthless. As it was, the Australian total gave me the opportunity to make a big score and I have to say that getting to a 100 in a World Cup final as we were on the verge of victory, has to be rated as one of the highlights of my life. Arjuna's and my career have been intertwined ever since we were teenagers and now, in the closing minutes of this game, our victory was to be sealed by our batting partnership. The general feeling in the team is that no one wants to let Arjuna down, for no one has tried harder than he has to make us world-beaters. Being trusted by him, I learnt to trust myself. Once my runs really started to matter to the team, I scored more of them. It was left to Arjuna, he of the mythically heroic name in Sri Lankan culture, to stroke the winning runs for Sri Lanka.

The win had actually happened in my heart before the last ball was bowled, and once we'd won, we'd won. The past was over. We had more cricket to play in the future. More challenges left to face. But the sheer triumphal joy amongst my countrymen for the next few days and weeks was wondrous to behold. When we won, the country had won. A country had invented a new set of heroes. For the people of Sri Lanka this victory in the national game was a vivid tangible thing that gave their country a greater significance. Sri Lanka now signified more than wars and terrorists and tea and tourism to the outside world. It was the fact that we had lost so many games before that made our victory so significant to us, the country and the world. Victory for the underdog, victory for the human spirit. The cricketers had won by being distinctively Lankan, embodying the iconic values of an iconoclastic nation. Cricket had comprehensively revealed our national character. Now Sri Lankans the world over started looking good and feeling better. We're very conscious of our fans whenever we go out onto the field. We are so apart from them and yet we are so much a part of them. Their love is very potent. It is demanding, but it also makes us strong. In the stadium at Lahore in a sea of Sri Lankan flags, having flown over specially with a contingent of the island's most devoted cricket fans, was my father.

CHAPTER NINETEEN

Suddenly the public eye was on us in a way it had never been before, our life became a spiralling whirl of invitations and events on and off the field. I must have been the world's most travelled cricketer in 1996. First, almost immediately after the World Cup, Sanath and I flew to Australia to play in Dean Jones's benefit game at the MCG. Then the team had a week-long tournament in Singapore, against India and Pakistan, our first performance as World Cup champions. The team was in no mood to play any sort of cricket especially in a place like Singapore where the festival atmosphere and rampant opportunities for shopping meant that our minds weren't totally on the job. Plus, we hadn't slept properly for two weeks since winning at Lahore. After we arrived home after the World Cup, during the day we were busy with our religious duties (perspective, it's all about keeping things in perspective) and during the night we were the victims of a series of boisterous attacks by loud music. Sanath alone roused himself for Singapore, I could barely lift my bat. We reached the tournament final and might even have won it, but we couldn't summon up enough power down the final stretch. There was literally nothing in the tank. Going to a tournament like that and losing immediately after winning the World Cup when as World Cup champions we felt we should beat everybody, really hurt the boys a lot. I decided that once we came back home we would prove a point by winning the Singer World Series scheduled to take place back home in August. Australia had promised to attend.

From Singapore we flew straightaway to Trinidad for a one-day game against the West Indies. We had beaten them several times before the World Cup, but we hadn't actually played them in that tournament, and until you beat everyone in the world I guess you can't fully call yourself 'world champions'. So we beat them. On the way back we went to Los Angeles for another couple of charity matches and took in all the sights of this world entertainment capital too. I don't care whether we were World champions (and frankly 99.99 per cent of the Americans didn't either), we were wide-eyed tourists in the midst of these temples of boom.

Back to Colombo, we then went to England to do some Cricket 2000

225

fund-raising and play some charity matches, prior to my passport getting stamped a couple more times when I went to Malaysia for a Super8s event and then zigged back to England for Dermot Reeve's benefit game at Edgbaston in early August before zagging home to take on India and Australia in the Singer World Series. It was the first chance our island fans had to see us in action since the World Cup and the crowds were fabulous at all the venues, as we were too. Unbeaten throughout, we won the event at a canter. Out of respect for the Australian coach Bobby Simpson, who had famously said we'd only win three out of ten games against Australia, we beat Australia the last three times he was in charge of them against us. Then, in Kenya, we took on Pakistan and South Africa in yet another one-day showcase. Brian Lara's innings in the World Cup quarter-final had knocked out South Africa so we hadn't had the chance to play them earlier in the year. South Africa were rated pretty high in the world and their lack of progress in the World Cup had surprised many. But that's knock-out cricket for you. So, our game against South Africa in Nairobi had a lot more riding on it than circumstances would suggest. We beat them, with everyone chipping in, by two wickets.

Amidst all this one-day cricket we actually had a chance to play some Tests (our first in nine months) when we took on Zimbabwe, winning both encounters. I was often asked during this time what with the Cricket 2000 campaign in full swing, would I rather we were the best in the world at one-day cricket or Tests, and I would say that I'd like us to be the best in the world at both. Batting was our strength, and the one-day game favours batsmen above bowlers so we could win far more easily in limited-overs cricket. Short of being considered as best in the world at Tests (and we do have some way to go yet), I'd settle for being one-day world champions. I'm all for a World Cup of Tests, of which the Asian Test Championship inaugurated in 1999 is an interesting exploration of the concept. We cricketers all know amongst ourselves who are the best, but it's nice for the public to have the instant mental short-cut to thinking of 'world champions'. And it's nice for the guys that are world champions too. The year ended with the team in Sharjah for another triangular, and with me flying off to New Zealand to play for Auckland.

For sure, our performance in Tests could be better. To win Test matches a team must score runs quickly and take wickets quickly; our batting is still generally stronger than our bowling. The good batting wickets at home nullify our bowlers' efforts and the promising bowlers who emerge from youth cricket really have their work cut out to make an impression on Test batsmen. The left-arm seamer Nuwan Zoysa who came in to the side fresh from school is one of the most promising prospects we have. He's capable of generating considerable pace off a short run and has that very useful ability to bend deliveries back into the right-hander from over the wicket. Suresh Perera impressed mightily on our 1998 tour of England too, but all these youngsters' bodies give way on them sooner or later. Zoysa had to pull out midway through the 1998–99 tour of Australia with a stress fracture of the back, a condition which Chaminda Vaas is all too familiar with. Whenever a whippety kid breaks into the team the rest of us watch them a mixture of pride and apprehension. They need the exposure, we need their talents, but their bodies let them down time and time again. It's enough to make you want to turn to being a nation of spin-bowlers in an effort to spare the fast-bowling youth of the nation. Almost, but not quite. Michael Holding says that as a bowler you only become strong enough to bowl fast in your mid-twenties. But until then what is a guy bursting with the desire to play for Sri Lanka going to do? We want them as much as they want to be with us. Alex Kountouri's input as well as Dennis Lillee's have been invaluable in this respect, and if in between the World Cups of 1996 and 1999 we haven't yet developed any fast-bowling champions, we certainly will have between now and the first World Cup of the next century.

From everyone thinking they could beat us now they wanted to beat the world champions. People have adopted our tactics and wised up to the methods we've been using and that has made it less easy to win, but no victory is ever easily achieved and every victory is highly valued. By us and our followers. Some victories are extremely hard won and ask a great deal of you. So many times our opponents put us under real pressure. But we covered for one another, we worked hard for one another, we were all dedicated to the cause of victory. We kept going and showed that necessary ruthless streak, sometimes we won only because we wanted it more. Commitment, dedication, passion. You have to have the talent, the team has to be put together in the right way, but we created a tradition of winning in this period which came down to us taking great pride in what we did. The personal commitment of each of us to our talent, the mental/physical/emotional commitment of a united team has raised us to this level of competitiveness. My feelings have always been that one side has to win, and it might as well be mine. You walk out on to the pitch and there are thousands of people watching you and they are looking to you and you've got to do it, you've got to pull it off every time; that's your job. There is something very exciting about that. You think to yourself I want to make this innings count and then somehow you do and it's just a great feeling.

I scored seven Test centuries in 1997 but I would have exchanged any one of them (apart from the undefeated innings at Chandigarh which helped to save a Test against India) for the privilege of scoring a hundred against the West Indies, or at least for being able to make a contribution to a victory against them. We played two Tests against them in June of

1997, losing the first Test in Antigua by six wickets, but the second Test in St Vincent ended in a draw due to rain and bad light with us pressing for victory.

The West Indies bowling may not have been quite as awesome as it was in the triumphant pomp of Ambrose, Walsh and Bishop, nevertheless they were a handful. Courtney Walsh, at 34, wasn't noticeably slower than the bowler who had taken 5 for 1 against us in a one-day game back in 1986. He definitely still had the ability to be at your throat all day with his accuracy, searching yorker and a bouncer that cut back in to the right-hander. Ambrose, with his height and bounce and rib-pinning line, was always difficult to drive, even on the slowish pitch we encountered at Arnos Vale. These two bowlers hardly waste a ball. Ian Bishop had certainly lost a bit of fire since his career threatening back injury and was more of a third seamer, but he still had pace and the ability to swing the ball. The West Indies were well keen to assert themselves against us challenging newcomers. We hadn't played them out there in the past and had only played one previous Test series against them (on wickets prepared for spinners). It hadn't seemed worth while to schedule a thrashing on Caribbean wickets. Sure, the West Indies weren't quite as formidable as they had been but these fixtures showed how greatly we had come up in the rankings.

As I suggested earlier, the essential spirit which the West Indies first brought to the international arena is shared by Sri Lanka too. Both nations fans like to see batsmen go out and play positive cricket. Both countries are packed with blazing stroke-makers. The crowds are very much a part of the occasion and they are so incredibly noisy! You have to think that their passion has helped the West Indies to win so often at home. It was evident how much they love the game, especially the sight of batsmen playing high-speed bouncers. Actually the crowds are pretty even-handed. When it came to bouncers they didn't mind if we bounced the West Indians or vice-versa, just as long as someone got hit! Hashan in this case was the unfortunate batsman, his arm being broken by Walsh in the first innings of the first Test. The Antigua crowd certainly took to Sanath, for his first innings of 85 was brimful of not-a-man-move strokes. If there had been any doubts about Sanath's ability to play Test cricket they were laid to rest on this tour because he followed up this innings at Antigua with a 90 in the next Test. The 340 against India two months later, so near and yet so far from Brian Lara's Test record 375, merely cemented his position as a master batsman in all forms of the game.

Brian himself came good with 115 in the second innings at St Vincent, the highest score of the game, helping to set us a target of 269 to win. 97 for 2 overnight going into the final day, we lost only one wicket in the morning session and at 179 for 3 at lunch were poised for victory. Then the rains came and we lost the whole of the afternoon session and then, first ball back after another interruption, Courtney Walsh beat me with a yorker – out for 78. I was so disappointed. If I'd been there till the end, I really thought we'd have won. Five more wickets fell as both sides pressed for victory, and when play was called off with sixteen overs remaining we were 36 runs short with two wickets left, Arjuna 72*. A win there would have crowned our year and would have marked a major advance in our Test aspirations. For try as we might, and we certainly dominated practically all of our drawn encounters against Pakistan and India home and away in the rest of 1997, our bowling just lacked that crucial cutting edge on these wickets.

Roshan and Sanath's phenomenal second-wicket partnership at the Premadasa stadium in August of that year, which started with the score at 39 with us looking to reach the follow-on saving target of 338 and ended 576 runs later, was defining evidence of how far we had come as a batting nation. It was good to have smashed the previous all-wicket record of 467 set by Crowe and Andrew Hudson against us six and a half years earlier, a game in which Sanath had been twelfth man. A full-house crowd of 30,000 came to cheer on Sanath, 326 overnight, to the next 50 runs that would take him to the biggest record in Test batting. Unfortunately Roshan, himself well past 200, fell lbw to Kumble early on and then two balls later Rajesh Chauhan popped one up for Saurav Ganguly to catch Sanath at silly point. It was a great gesture for the Indian players to all immediately offer their commiserations to Sanath. There were tears in his eyes as he walked off to huge, prolonged applause. Sanath felt he'd let the country down.

The highest Test total, England's 'timeless' 903 for 7 in 1938 was the next target as Arjuna reminded us and the rest of us went for it with a vengeance. Sanath and Roshan had kept me off the field for over two days and I was in the mood to make India pay. As next man in, I had actually kept my pads on for the duration of their innings, because saving the follow-on was important and with debutant Mahela Jayawardene following Arjuna in the order we were not necessarily in the strongest position if either Sanath or Roshan was out with work left to do. Once the follow-on was saved, if a wicket fell somebody would have to bat and it might as well be me. It looked like a total of 1,000 was on the cards, but once there was technically no possibility of a result according to the rules of the game, the match was called off with seven of the last twenty overs bowled with us at 952 for 6. Only 14 wickets had fallen in five days, yes, which meant that on such a wicket such a feat as ours was possible, but there have been plenty of shirt-front wickets in the history of the game and nobody else but we had ever capitalised on them. For generations nobody could have thought that the 1938 record would ever be broken, especially considering that 90 overs a day is the maximum a bowling side delivers nowadays. I'm very proud of our achievement.

If the year after the 1996 World Cup we had been playing a little too much one-off one-day cricket in comparison to Test matches, then the year before the 1999 World Cup we struck a better balance with tours of South Africa and England both incorporating Tests and limited-overs. We had toured neither nation for some time and these matches were quite important to our sense of worth. South Africa for some years now have been rated very highly in all forms of cricket. They play to win and have a tremendous desire to prove themselves. They think the game as well as they play it, and it was their sheer concentrated effort that took them to victory over us in the final of the 1997 Pakistan Independence Cup. In Allan Donald and Jonty Rhodes they have modern-day phenomena; in a vastly talented batting line-up they have seasoned performers with the ability to adjust to any match situation. In fact, what really makes them stand out is there rank of youngsters, people like Shaun Pollock, Jacques Kallis, Mark Boucher, Derek Crookes and Paul Adams, players all capable of the extraordinary. They all try so very hard. As do the senior players, whose attitude is best exemplified by their captain Hansie Cronje. I have never seen him give of anything less than his best. Indeed, in two very closely fought Tests against them at Cape Town and Port Elizabeth in 1998, it was Hansie's bold counter-attacking against a threatening Murali that effectively turned the two Test matches in South Africa's favour. Both teams got a good look at each other that year and should we meet in the 1999 World Cup with so much more to play for, it promises to be a great game. Certainly of all the world's batsmen Murali claims to play Allan Donald best of all. Pleasuring himself in self-defence, Murali likes to get fully behind the stump-high straight deliveries and whenever the ball's dropped short, Murali's agile footwork ensures that Allan Donald's threatening throat-ball passes over the stumps well away from bat or body. For Allan to find Murali's outside edge he'd have to bowl way down the leg-side for that's where Murali mostly plays him from.

As much as we don't want the excessive attention there is going to be a huge sense of expectation for us to win the World Cup again. We surprised many when we won it the first time, we want to show people we can do it again. We have every faith in our ability to perform like winners. Whatever we did in 1996 in response to the way the limited-overs game was played then is history. What will succeed in the 1999 World Cup and set the template for cricket for the following years will be different. We have all known for a long time that Sanath and Kalu can win a game on their own, that Marvan can play a big innings when it matters, and that Arjuna and I can make a contribution, we all know that Murali can turn a match in our favour in the space of a few overs, but what will be the real test of Sri Lanka in the 1999 World Cup will be whether we can counter the threat of all our opponents. The competition will undoubtedly be a very open one, and each team will have its own particular strengths. Being in England in early summer, it might be more of a bowler's tournament but at the end of the day it's still about scoring more runs than the opposition. And we're as capable as any.

There is a phenomenal amount of cricket played nowadays. Around a hundred limited-overs internationals worldwide every year – not all of them involving India – and a score or so of Test series. Anyone could be forgiven for thinking, from a distance, that with so much cricket being played, a lot of these games are meaningless beyond their statistics. But they'd be wrong. Each game, has its relevance to the individuals involved in that particular match, and in the next few matches between the sides. Each game has its unique characteristics, its particular match-ups that reveal something new and relevant to team and individual performances, reveal something to be stored in the players' and coaches' memories. Individual match-ups, bowler against batsman, batsman against bowler are what the statistics don't reveal, and these are what give each game their resonance. We all might be around for years, but really we might only meet a few times and you want to make every occasion count. Prior to meeting up with the team in Leicester for a game in our tour of England in 1998, it was a privilege to be invited to play along with Sanath, as Sri Lanka's representatives in the Diana, Princess of Wales Memorial Match arranged by the MCC at Lord's. I am so competitive, so keen to bat at every opportunity, that I even take benefit games seriously. I figure people want to see some big-hitting and I try to oblige. I have yet to meet the bowler who likes to be smashed all around the ground and even in these 'fun' games, I know and the bowler knows that our actions matter. Not more than they would in a full international, but nevertheless even on a village green it is a one-against-one confrontation and our competitive natures never like coming off second best. We all took it seriously at Lord's and I wanted to make the most of it. Sachin played particularly well and together we did much to entertain the public. How I love being an international cricketer.

Winning the Emirates Triangular against England and South Africa was pretty much what we expected but the real aim of the tour was to win our one Test at the Oval, our first in England since 1991. Tests were really what we were starting to value most. Again Arjuna confounded everyone by winning the toss and inserting England. People thought he was crazy, especially when England ended the first day only three wickets down. Certainly Arjuna would have wanted us to have taken more wickets but from the day before the match, having seen the wicket and assessed England's squad, he was thinking ahead to the final day. The game would be won then and not before. His insertion was an aggressive move in as much as given England's potential frailty with Atherton and Hussain out injured and a longish tail that started at No. 7 with Ben Hollioake, he wanted to be sure of having the chance to bowl at them twice. He was banking on us batting just the once, making a big score quickly, and then letting Murali loose to take advantage of a wearing pitch when all England could fight for at best would be a draw. England had to be made to bat on the last couple of days.

It all went amazingly to plan. England scored plenty but did it pretty slowly given the state of the wicket. By the time we equalled England's 445 just before close of play on the Saturday, it had taken us 308 balls fewer, and Sanath and I both had made comfortable hundreds. In a stand of 243 with Sanath, of the first 200 my contribution was only 69. It isn't often that I play second fiddle during a partnership but Sanath was hitting the ball so cleanly that it seemed churlish not to feed him the strike as much as possible. Not that he wasn't grabbing it for himself and taking full advantage! Prior to this game Sanath had actually had a pretty poorish run in the county games and the Emirates Triangular; he'd been getting out an awful lot to catches in the gully, a sure sign that his game was just a fraction off, for the very deliveries to which he was finding the fielder would normally be smashed through to the fence. In his desire to be of service to the team he had taken on board the thinking that on English wickets he'd have to be careful about playing away from his body, and thus he wasn't fully launching himself in his normal fashion at the ball. Normally this would be the prudent course for many a batsman but Sanath is a law unto himself and in paying service to conventional theories he was doing himself a disservice. He was opening himself up and playing a little too late instead of taking the ball early, hence his frailty. But at the Oval he went back to being his simple straightforward self and just played each ball for what it was: a chance to score some runs. Sanath's rapid 213 came in mighty useful as we took a decent lead and gave ourselves over a day and a half in which to defend it. And attack England.

And attack we did. Arjuna boxed the English in with incredibly astute field placings and Murali, so greatly improved a bowler since he had his action questioned, exploited all the weapons he now had at his disposal: change of pace, change of line, length, loop, turn, speed and angle, repeatedly varying his grip on the ball, his point of release and even the angle of his run-up. From the beginning of his career Murali has had the remarkable ability to bowl huge amounts of overs without getting noticeably tired. More balls are made to count now than ever before. His single greatest improvement has been his cutting down on the number of 'four balls' that he bowls. As well as keeping things tight he's also learned how to weave webs and set traps. Saqlain Mushtaq and Murali have to be the world's two best off-spinners at present, there is always a freshness and intelligence to their bowling. Saqlain maybe has just that little more variation and always seems to come up with something new each time you face him: 'Dayvilles' we call him. I really enjoy taking him on. We can expect him and Murali to take bags of wickets for many years to come. England did well to go into the final day with only two wickets down, but we knew that the match was going to be decided by Alec Stewart's performance. He was capable of scoring enough runs quickly and/or defending capably enough to take England to safety. In fact he was the one batsman whom Murali couldn't dismiss. Soon after he'd settled in, Alec went for a sharp single and was beaten by a sideways-on-the-run-pin-point throw that would have threaded the eye of a needle by our substitute fielder Upul Chandana, perhaps the only man in the team whom Alec should not have taken on. The player Upul was on for? Me — I'd gone off for treatment to a wrenched ankle, the result of running into the back of Dominic Cork as I had been eyeing a stroke to the cover boundary the previous day. You just had to believe that the gods were smiling on us.

For the remainder of the game Arjuna had Murali bowl at all the batsmen in short spells, around and over the wicket, always changing the angles, changing ends, never letting a batsman settle into a defensive groove against him. Murali kept plugging away and one by one the English batsmen fell. First ball after lunch John Crawley was bowled by a big offie — when that kind of thing happens it's such a big affirmation of a team's winning prospects — and then Ben Hollioake was out straight after. Nobody seemed to have a handle on how to play Murali and only Mark Ramprakash with a big front pad and Darren Gough, with an even bigger grin, managed to keep Murali out for a length of time. But they all had to fall to him sooner or later and when the last English batsman was out with the score at 217, Murali had taken nine wickets in the innings. We needed just 36 to win, with an hour or so remaining. Sanath set the tone with a stunning flat-batted six over cover (hit with both feet off the ground) and we won by ten wickets with plenty of time to spare.

As I've said, it's always nice to beat England.

I have so much more faith in the rest of the side now. I just try to do my job without worrying too much or putting too much pressure on myself. The team has come a long way since the time we first joined the ranks of first-class cricketers and that is all through giving our strengths their head. We developed a system for winning and we tried to use it whenever possible. In limited-overs matches we'd go on prolonged streaks of wins, especially at home. Matches stand out of course, and if I had to pick a match which summed up just how complete a side Sri

Lanka had become I'd nominate the one at Mumbai in May 1997 during the India Independence Cup where we beat India (225 for 7) by five wickets with almost ten overs to spare. My contribution being a first ball duck, lbw to Anil Kumble. My excuse – apart from it being a vicious top-spinner of a delivery that would have had even Bradman in trouble? Just before I went out to bat a pretty girl had been waving energetically in my direction trying to communicate her intentions (to invite me to some party of her boss's) the following night. So many times we've gone into the lion's den and come out victorious.

Our line-up remained mostly the same in all this time not because of continuity for continuity's sake but because these players were proven to be the most capable of implementing our game plans. We all had interlinked skills and complemented each other wonderfully. There were a number of players constantly on the fringes, of which Marvan Atapattu was the most notable. He came back into the side after a run of no-scores in his first three Tests that could conceivably have crippled him, but he was always the outstanding batsman in domestic cricket during all this time and you just knew he had to come good eventually. No longer does he come to the wicket like a batsman weighed down by knowledge of all the ways he can get out. He now knows his worth, is aware of his abilities, and is keen to show them off for the team's benefit. Marvan is greatly respected by the rest of the players because we see him as a very gifted player who has been determined to work hard and improve on any of his weaknesses. He has made a bundle of runs since his comeback in 1997, big hundreds as an opener in Tests and at No. 3 in our limited-overs line-up, all with timing more impeccable than Jeeves. He initially replaced Asanka Gurusinha in our line-up but he is the direct heir to Roy Dias. Marvan would be an even greater force if he had a greater hunger to assert himself. As it is, he just goes rolling along at his own pace and picks up runs with ease. He has to have one of the most exquisite cover drives you could ever hope to see. And our young middle-order batsman Mahela Jayawardene is a terrific prospect too. Not only does he have all the shots and the desire to play them, he has grit and the pride you like to see. You can only comprehensively judge a player over ten years, not ten innings. But I think Mahela, already one of the youngest batsmen in the game to have hit a Test double-hundred, will stand the test of time.

The bowlers who have come in to the side since 1996 haven't yet set the world on fire for they have been picked not so much for their ability to bowl quick or turn the ball a Murali-mile but for their ability to consistently bowl wicket-to-wicket with just a little bit of movement. Which normally should be enough. I am confident that they will come good but it has just so happened that, be it home or away, in Tests or one-dayers, Murali has the most impact of all our bowlers. In the absence of a bowling attack of distinct threat it has to be said that we still remain a team more capable of winning limited-overs contests than Tests. We in Sri Lanka don't have the luxury of being able to field specialist one-day and Test teams. It should be unnecessary anyway. One-day cricket heralds the debut of many an international cricketer but the important thing is to get the youngsters to adjust to Test cricket, for they are almost starting the wrong way round. A good Test player will succeed in the one-day game, but a limited-overs player will not necessarily make it in the longer, deeper, broader game. Not for any technical reasons but for temperamental reasons. Because a limited-overs 'specialist' is not thought of as good enough for the longer game, he doesn't think he's good enough and the myth becomes self-perpetuating. What should we look for when we pick a youngster? Big shots, fast balls, accuracy, broad shoulders, a face that fits, an eagerness to please? No. We should look for their ability to be mentally tough come what may. The will must be stronger than the skill. What I look for in a youngster is evidence of an overwhelming desire to succeed, as if they were to be grass cracking through concrete.

Any bowler can bowl the occasional delivery where everything comes together and the ball sent down the pitch is potent with destruction; the very best are simply capable of doing it with more regularity than anyone else. All the best bowlers' deliveries within an over, even within a spell, are in relation to each other. Bowling is actually a lot harder than batting to get right. Batsmen with imperfect technique can progress far in this game, even make it to Test level by having their strengths overcome their weaknesses; as long they're in form. When out of form, technique can shore you up, with no technique you'll break against the waves soon enough. Technique, once learned is ingrained in a batsman. The feet move properly back or forward, the head comes into line automatically. But a bowler relies on rhythm and physical and mental poise for his success. I have little sympathy for bowlers at the best of times, unless they're team-mates and bowling at our opponents, but I want the bowling standard of my opponents to be the best it can be so as to feel more satisfied with my runs against them. And because I bowl a little too, I know that there are at least half a dozen external factors (pitch conditions, temperature, wind, footholds, run-ups, ball condition, fielders) let alone internal factors like attitude and fitness that can affect a bowler's performance. Any batsman or bowler can lose their 'technique' by being forced into a series of improvisations and modifications in order to combat a particular problem or situation, and then habit and mental tiredness, a demanding schedule, poor training and an unexamined life, can hurt one's innate ability. Bowling is hard, but batting's harder, if only because bad balls get wickets whereas bad shots get outs. There's more to it than that of course, but that's the crux. Batsmen don't get second chances, bowlers have overs full of them.

Even when the West Indies were the best team in the world for so very long, they only won two-thirds of their one-day games, yet it came as a big shock for us to lose eight one-day games in a row after our Emirates Trophy triumph. The gala ICC knock-out tournament in Dhaka quickly followed by a tournament in Sharjah, during which we performed as tired men, meant we didn't do ourselves justice. So much of performance is to do with being tuned to the proper pitch; you have to trust yourself in the way a pianist trusts his fingers. But we had started to look at the score-book and had become a little hesitant. We who had for so long played like champs were starting to play like apparent chumps for no other reason than that, with less than nine months to go before the next World Cup, we were starting to think about our mantle as world champions. For the first time we were starting to feel the title weigh heavily upon us. We played a little too defensively when our attacks didn't immediately come off, doubts crept in, and we weren't the cavaliers we had been formerly. A few of us fell into a trough of bad form together and we were just not winning tournaments like we used to. We found ourselves looking at each other hoping that, as with so many times in the past, one of our team-mates would collectively rescue us. Arjuna did once, in the ICC knock-out against New Zealand, but the rest of us were unable to do quite enough at other times. Plus, I ripped a thigh muscle in Sharjah, Murali jarred his shoulder in Dhaka and every perceived weakness of ours – 'Sri Lanka is too reliant on its veterans', 'Sri Lanka is slow in the field', 'Sri Lanka doesn't have enough pace-bowling' – was exposed under the unforgiving glare of international floodlit cricket. The very same factors that had taken us to victory in the past were now seen as our weaknesses. And then we went to Australia for another pre-World Cup World Series triangular against Australia and England which should have set us up nicely in terms of developing the match-hardness that comes with playing big games back to back. Instead, I suffered a recurrence of my thigh problem in a warm-up game, and Sanath broke his arm mid-tournament. Biggest shock of all? Murali being called for 'throwing' yet again by Umpire Emerson.

From the start of the tour of Australia, Murali was the subject of much attention. His 9 for 65 at the Oval had made him prominent in the world's consciousness, which had again started to marvel at his ability to do what he did in the way that he did. Umpire Hair had released a book prior to our arrival in Australia where he had some disparaging things to say in his forthright way about Murali, comments which received much attention. Australian crowds (a witty bunch at the best of times) took to mostly screaming 'No Ball!' every time Murali ran up to bowl, semi-confidential comments were uttered by certain officials as to the prevailing doubts held about Murali's action and it just seemed to all the media that his encounter with Umpire Emerson at Adelaide mid-tour would be highly significant. Murali was indeed called for 'throwing' there. Arjuna had his response ready and marched the lads off. He wasn't going to subject his players to what he felt were rules arbitrarily arrived at. All of us who play the game are human, we all make mistakes. None more palpably so than the players. And none of us could function unless we knew that even when the umpires are occasionally mistaken, their decisions have to be honoured. But, as in 1996, Arjuna felt that calling Murali for 'throwing' was a decision not originated on the field of play. He strongly felt that the way Umpire Emerson was viewing Murali was greatly mistaken and on retaking the field after fifteen minutes of heated debate with umpires, the match referee, tour management and our Cricket Board by satellite phone-link, Arjuna made it very clear to Umpire Emerson exactly where he should stand, right above the stumps, so that he couldn't risk making a mistaken judgement about Murali as Murali ran up behind him.

That anyone should ever doubt our fighting spirit, will to win and ability to triumph even without me, never let them forget how we chased 302 to win on such a testing occasion. It was obvious England wanted to win as much as us we did, maybe as much to assert their own sense of how things should be done as for the points. That it fell to Murali to hit the winning run was just and fitting.

Clause No. 1 in the ICC Code of Conduct is: 'The captains are responsible at all times for ensuring that play is conducted within the spirit of the game as well as within the Laws.' Only Arjuna would have had the nerve to take on the whole establishment and do something that hadn't been done before. Teams have gone off when they were subjected to missiles from the crowd, batsmen have even stayed on when umpires have walked off thinking the light too bad to play in (e.g. Azharuddin and Ganguly, January 1998, Dhaka) but this was the first time a captain had deigned to take matters so greatly into his own hands. Perhaps even the first time a player had literally raised a wagging finger (à la Dickie Bird) to an umpire. And his boldness and daring largely paid off in the eyes of the watching world for he had risked so much on a matter of principle, as a captain and a man. It was interesting to note the general reaction to Arjuna in Australia and the rest of the world. On the day of the walk-off people were first shocked then full of praise for Arjuna's principled action. Our thrilling chase was a real crowd-pleaser too. The cricket world was buzzing. In fact, Arjuna only lost sympathy a few days later once he called the lawyers in to defend him against the charges he incurred from the ICC match referee Mr Peter van der Merwe, for his actions in leading the team off the field of play. For by calling in the lawyers Arjuna had struck at the very heart of what is thought to separate cricket from the outside world, what makes it a 'game' rather than a profession. It was then that it dawned upon everyone that cricket was being played by modern-day professionals and that even Sri Lanka, the country with the most cavalier spirit, had succumbed to professionalism.

As soon as the red mist had cleared, Arjuna realised he had overreacted and that his actions created an unfortunate atmosphere of confrontation. He really had risked plenty. In going into that meeting with Mr van der Merwe, Arjuna felt his and Murali's and the team's professional livelihoods and careers and future performances were at stake in a 'courtroom' where the ICC match referee would be both prosecutor and judge. But for the ICC to instantly impose a lengthy ban on Arjuna for doing what he thought right and just, his lawyers would argue, went against all universally acknowledged 'human rights' for an individual to practise their trade in conditions of fairness and equity. And the whole sentiment that has infused the game since it was first played: that in cricket the cares and concerns of the outside world are somehow set aside for a few hours of man-to-man combat with bat and ball were, in these arguments put before cricket's governing body by Arjuna's 'defence team', unequivocally disavowed. Arjuna had brought in the forces of the outside world to arbitrate a matter that happened on the field of play and this was something that jarred with the sentimentalists. He had lifted the veil that separates cricketers from everyone else and made a cricketer a citizen of the world capable of being judged by the statutes of civil society. Cricket should be governed from within, it is only a game. But it is also so much more.

CHAPTER TWENTY

Arthur Ashe in his moving memoir *Days of Grace*, written in full knowledge that he was dying, addresses the infant daughter he is to leave behind: 'We are being watched by our ancestors as I am watching you. We possess more than they ever dreamed of having, so we must never let them down.' That kind of feeling permeates my consciousness too. I feel inextricably linked to all those who have made me what I am. My parents made it easy for me to indulge all my childhood passions and for as long as I was under their roof they gave me everything I ever wanted – enough to eat, my first bat, my first motorbike, my first car. Then I started being self-supporting. If you're feeling on top of the world off the pitch, then you'll be a champion on it. But my parents' greatest gift to me, a pure present of their own generous spirit, has been their faith. I was brought up as a Buddhist. I am a long way short of being holier than thou, but Buddhism does ask me whether I live fully and honestly enough. Asks me these searching questions in a way I feel I have to respond positively to. I've been a cricketer for twenty years, but I'll be a Buddhist all my life. I'll be the son of my parents all my life too. My mother would say when she first heard others bring news of my cricketing successes: 'These things would not give me one moment's happiness if he were not loving and good and true.' Buddhism, essentially the following of the Eight-Fold Path (right attention to one's understanding, intentions, speech and actions; right livelihood, effort, mindfulness; right concentration), affects my whole life both on and off the pitch. It has given me the ability to look into myself and look outside of myself. It has made me who I am.

You don't have to be a Buddhist to be a successful cricketer; you don't even have to be a Buddhist to be a Sri Lankan. But in my case, where there is a passion for fast cars, pretty girls and soaring boundaries, my faith with its precepts and practices has instilled in me the mental strength to look beyond my hedonism. Call the essence of this capability what you will – focus, pride, professionalism, guts, smarts, attitude, confidence, drive, determination, desire – no successful sportsman or human being has ever achieved anything without the mental strength to overcome the indulgences of the moment. There are so many ways to fail. I know them all. And I have managed to overcome them all – for a time, until the next time, until I am sent back into myself to fail again but fail better. Buddhism has made it easier for me to attain the serenity necessary to give of my best. I am not a body with a soul but a soul with a body. The lives of sportsmen extend beyond the playing field and what kind of people we are off the field is replicated in our performance on the field. I would say that cricket, because of its succession of life-or-death moments, more than any other sport reveals the essential character of those who play it.

No one can compete at this level without having a big ego. And mine is pretty big. A bowler beats me once, I'm going to devote time and energy to make sure it doesn't happen again. I say to all the youngsters in the squad that they have to be 'arrogant' to the extent that every time they walk out to bat they have think they're superior to the opposition. They have to feel equal to any situation. Of course, egotism is totally at odds with the selflessness of Buddhism and yet this dialectic is what lies at the heart of my character. I am the kind of guy who could so easily have not made the most of his talents. If I didn't have others spurring me on, challenging me to make a defining contribution I may well have given up cricket. When I was younger I really only played just to see how good I could be. I heard about all the greats and I wanted them to hear about me. My thirst for personal gratification did famously come at the expense of the team that afternoon in August 1992 against Allan Border's men. It would have been exposed sooner or later. I am just so glad that it happened in time enough for me to resurrect my career. I think in order to be successful you have to be selfish, or else you never achieve. And once you reach your peak, then you have to be unselfish. The team sometimes loses if I lose nowadays, but I always lose if the team loses. That's the solution to any problems of egotism. I have now struck the right balance between what I give to myself and what I give to others. It has made me the player I am today.

I am without specific personal ambitions any more, my ambitions have to do with the team. Those around me know what to expect. They have confidence that I'll come through, that my performance will be pretty much the same from game to game, particularly when things get tight. I enjoy being the match-winner but I am just as happy when someone else brings a victory home for us. What does drive me nowadays is the realisation that in spite of being a batsman with over 250 limited-overs innings and over a 100 Test innings under my belt, effectively I have had only about 400 days of work in a fifteen-year career. If there's been one determining factor in my emergence as a top batsman it has been my realisation that I won't be a cricketer forever. I want to make every day count. If my batting now is a form of controlled euphoria it is because I have realised as Buddhist teaching would have it that 'self-realisation is the greatest contribution one can make to one's fellow-man ... when a man tries, with the gifts bestowed on him by nature, to fulfil himself, he is doing the highest thing he can do, the only thing that has any meaning'.

I'd like to think that this book is more than the life-story of a short, occasionally overweight, uneven-legged big-hitter. If this book has been about anything, it is about how playing cricket makes you feel intimately linked to team-mate and opponent, spectator and participant, home and away. The dramas of my life have taken place on just a few patches of grass, but they are dramas that go to the heart of the human condition. We all struggle against the odds to make a name for ourselves, to feel we have some meaning in life. We live not only with those we know but also with all of those who have ever meant anything in our lives. Because we all need it, the sense of connection, the feeling that we can be better than we are, even if we are better only through someone else, a colleague, a friend, the Lord Buddha, a priest, a doctor, a novelist, a musician, a parent, a relation, whoever. All I do is hit some leather-bound ball of cork with a stick of polished willow and it doesn't mean much in the grand scheme of things. But it was what I enjoyed doing most in my youth and in pushing myself to carry on being good enough to play at the highest level, I guess I stand for something aspirational in all of us. If I can get to the top then you have to think anyone can!

Who knows for sure whether those household gods ever came near my cricket-bat-filled crib but what has incontrovertibly been true is that ever since I was a child, I have been blessed with optimism. A lot of that is due to having the support of those closest to me, who have liberally encouraged me to feel that anything is possible for those who follow the rightfold path. I have always thought myself capable of achieving anything. Either side of this optimism lie strong will and whimsicality and they are always fighting for the upper hand within me. I live for today, trusting in myself to overcome tomorrow. So far, cricket has offered the greatest delights and the greatest challenges and thus demanded my greatest attention. I live to play cricket because nothing else in my life has asked so much of me. I have to give cricket 100 per cent. It's my duty.

As a young man I wanted to be a winning batsman on a winning team and until I did that, all the joyrides of my social life were unsatisfying. I enjoyed my life and my cricket but I wasn't completely satisfied. When I was a kid I wanted to be like Gavaskar, Richards, Mendis, Dias etc. etc., then when I was older and my horizons broadened I simply wanted to be respected by them as a great competitor. And all my focusing was on that. It was only when I finally decided to be me to the max, for better or for worse, that I reached a level of contentment and self-assurance that has made me feel like a real winner on and off the field. By winning, I don't mean the prizes and medals, coupés and convertibles that have come my way in recent years, for I could live without all my material possessions. I mean that I am now able to live a life where I don't care what others think of me. What matters is what I think of myself according to the values of my beliefs and my principles. It just so happens that I am a professional cricketer and that I do represent the hopes and dreams of so very many of my countrymen, but all I am in reality is just another guy trying to be the best he can be. The longer my career – life – has lasted, the greater my need to make something of it. Some tell me that many youngsters want 'to be like Aravinda'. Well, so do I.

Borg had McEnroe, Prost had Senna, Border had Hadlee, contemporary Sri Lankan batsmen have Shane Warne, Wasim Akram and Glenn McGrath as our most significant opponents. The contest between batsmen and these particular bowlers define batsmen in the world's eyes. If you can best them, then you can think of yourself at the top of the game. Averages and aggregates can be boosted by performances against everyone else, but these two bowlers are the ones that have dominated the 1990s. They have set new standards for their type of bowling. They have raised the profile of the game. Irrespective of the number of wickets they take by the end of their careers, they stand to be ranked among the all-time greats of the game.

Can you imagine any legendary batsman, from Ranjitsinhji, Bradman, Headley, Sobers, Chappell, Border, Gavaskar, or Barry and Viv Richards, not having to be at anything less than their very best against Wasim and Shane? How would Sunil play Shane? Would he play him from the crease? Would he ever trust himself to drive against the spin and play his trademark on-drives and leg-glances on a turning wicket? What would he do to try and upset Shane's line and length? Would Viv take up the challenge of the ball Shane tosses up a little higher, the one that floats in towards the pads before scooting away, and smack it towards midwicket? How many angles off the face of the bat would Javed exploit? And even bearing in mind what these legends would do, what would we lesser mortals do?

How do I play Shane and Wasim? With immense difficulty. Nothing less than total concentration will do. These guys are at your throat all the time. You just know that they are capable of making things happen. If you give them an inch, they'll take a mile. Show any weakness, from slow reactions to sluggish footwork and they'll have you out in no time. Show any chink in your mental armour and they'll be through it in a flash. Batting against them is a pleasure. I look forward to every encounter. 'Concentrate. Relax. Be positive in defence and attack,' is what I say to myself. What else can one do?

All people in cricket are trustees of a great game. When Arjuna first started playing Tests there was absolutely no legacy of Sri Lankan performance in Tests and limited-overs internationals to look back on and take as a standard. No records, no traditions, no legendary performances which to inspire. Our opponents had years and years of them, every country had given birth to all-time greats of the game. Arjuna and everyone else who played in that inaugural Test were standard-bearers for Sri Lanka from the start. Playing on a world stage and prominently carrying the flag of Mother Lanka and her children in newspapers, television, books, magazines, the Internet and in the conversations of cricket fans, our cricketers have always been aware that the hearts of many millions of Sri Lankans all around the world look to their cricket team as a source of national and personal pride and fulfilment. We really don't do much, many Sri Lankan medics and scientists and statesmen do more for the good of the country and the world than we do. There are plenty of sportspeople in the world, let alone in Sri Lanka, who sacrifice themselves to achieve success for only a fraction of the acclaim that international cricketers enjoy. We cricketers aren't too significant in the grand scheme of things but we are uplifting to all those who love the game, which is not unimportant.

I've been blessed but I work hard. I love playing cricket so much. I lay no claim to greatness but it is a great game. When you do something your whole life it's hard to walk away from it. I figure I'm good for a few more innings yet and I want to maximise my contribution to Sri Lanka. The life I lead is a little complicated and it's a little much at times but I try to keep it simple. The work I am able to do for various charities at home gives me great satisfaction, but it is not as if I see any real difference between myself and the people who aren't as fortunate as I am, and I think that all my childhood friends would say that I remain the same guy they have always known. Recently I have taken on some extra-curricular interests which are demanding much attention, namely a fiancée, a golf course development, a cricket academy for future internationals and so much more besides. And I want to do as well for them as I have done for my team-mates.

Sri Lanka's cricketers may not always have been very good, but they have always tried to represent their country with honour. In the cricket history of an emerging nation, individual highlights first stand out in fans' memories – a particular stroke maybe – then individual innings become memorable – a brilliant score in a losing cause – then an actual victory. It has been my pleasure and privilege to have written a few pages in the book of Sri Lankan cricket, and I look forward to seeing the performance of other Sri Lankans in the years to come doing the same. My generation of cricketers will never be forgotten, but there is every reason to think that our performances can be surpassed.

Appendices

Appendix I

ONE-DAY INTERNATIONAL CRICKET CAREER RECORD

P.A. de Silva

up to 30/03/1999

Batting

Match type	M	I	NO	Runs	HS	Avge	100	50	Ct	Ê
World Cup	20	19	3	724	145	45.25	2	3	7	-
Texaco Trophy	4	4	0	95	34	23.75	-	-	1	-
World Series Cup	35	35	2	941	81★	28.51	-	6	9	-
Other One-Day	195	189	20	6260	134	37.04	9	46	62	-
All One-Day	254	247	25	8020	145	36.12	11	55	79	81.79

Record Against Specific Opponents

Opponent	M	I	NO	Runs	HS	Avge	100	50	Ct	St
England	12	12	3	392	80	43.55	-	3	7	-
Australia	30	30	5	1289	107★	51.56	2	9	6	-
West Indies	25	25	0	436	68	17.44	-	3	8	-
New Zealand	31	31	3	748	66	26.71	-	7	13	-
Pakistan	67	65	5	2155	134	35.92	12	19	-	-
India	53	50	5	1662	105	36.91	3	12	15	-
Bangladesh	5	3	0	140	89	46.66	-	1	3	-
Zimbabwe	14	14	3	766	127★	69.63	2	5	3	-
South Africa	15	15	1	232	73	16.57	-	2	5	-
Kenya	2	2	0	200	145	100.00		1	-	-

Record In Each Calendar Year

Year	M	I	NO	Runs	HS	Avge	100	50	Ct	St
1984	6	6	2	105	50★	26.25	–	1	5	–
1985	16	16	2	384	86	27.42	–	3	3	–
1986	12	10	0	147	52	14.70	–	1	4	–
1987	8	8	2	155	51	25.83	–	1	2	–
1988	16	15	0	520	88	34.66	–	5	6	–
1989	10	10	0	441	96	44.10	–	4	5	–
1990	15	15	1	470	104	33.57	1	2	4	–
1991	4	4	0	53	26	13.25	–	–	1	–
1992	19	18	2	538	105	33.62	1	2	3	–
1993	22	22	2	699	75★	34.95	–	7	1	–
1994	22	21	3	712	107★	39.55	1	5	7	–
1995	17	17	1	481	75	30.06	–	3	6	–
1996	30	29	5	1188	145	49.50	4	5	11	–
1997	28	27	4	1212	134	52.69	3	8	11	–
1998	22	22	0	694	105	31.54	1	5	7	–
1999	7	7	1	221	52★	36.83	–	3	3	–

Bowling

Match type	Balls	R	W	Avge	Best	5w	Econ
World Cup	360	311	7	44.42	3-42	–	5.18
Texaco Trophy	24	29	0	–	–	–	7.2
World Series Cup	648	523	11	47.54	3-43	–	4.84
Other One-Day	2921	2378	65	36.58	4-45	–	4.88
All One-Day	3953	3241	83	39.04	4-45	–	4.92

Record Against Specific Opponents

Opponent	Balls	R	W	Avge	Best	5w	Econ
England	252	208	1	208.00	1-22	–	4.95
Australia	624	503	10	50.30	3-42	–	4.83
West Indies	498	426	10	42.60	3-43	–	5.13
New Zealand	386	282	8	35.25	2-22	–	4.38
Pakistan	1124	921	28	32.89	4-45	–	4.91
India	564	477	14	34.07	3-55	–	5.07
Bangladesh	132	101	3	33.66	1-25	–	4.59
Zimbabwe	139	117	0	–	–	–	5.05
South Africa	234	206	9	22.88	2-23	–	5.28

ONE-DAY INTERNATIONAL CRICKET STATISTICS

All Players All One-Day Most Runs Scored

(Based on all matches played up to 30/03/1999)

Name	Runs	Scored	Matches
M. Azharuddin	8869	310	37.90
D.L. Haynes	8648	238	41.37
P.A. de Silva	8020	254	36.12
S.R. Tendulkar	7801	211	42.39
Javed Miandad	7381	233	41.70
A. Ranatunga	7250	260	36.43
Salim Malik	7055	276	33.12
I.V.A. Richards	6721	187	47.00
A.R. Border	6524	273	30.62
R.B. Richardson	6248	224	33.41
D.M. Jones	6068	164	44.61
M.E. Waugh	6044	174	38.74
D.C. Boon	5964	181	37.04
Saeed Anwar	5852	161	40.35
Ramiz Raja	5841	198	32.09
S.R. Waugh	5706	251	31.01
B.C. Lara	5579	137	45.72
Ijaz Ahmed, sen	5575	215	32.41
Inzamam-ul-Haq	5369	171	38.35
C.G. Greenidge	5134	128	45.03
R.S. Mahanam	5026	208	29.56
W.J. Cronje	4794	155	39.95
M.D. Crowe	4704	143	38.55
S.T. Jayasuriya	4672	178	28.66
Aamir Sohail	4651	49	32.52
C.L. Hooper	4500	177	36.00
N.S. Sidhu	4414	36	37.09
G.R. Marsh	4357	17	39.97
G.A. Gooch	4290	125	36.98
K. Srikkanth	4092	46	29.02

Sri Lanka All One-Day Most Runs Scored

(Based on all matches played up to 30/03/1999)

Name	Runs	Scored	Matches
P.A. de Silva	8020	254	36.12
A. Ranatunga	7250	260	36.43
R.S. Mahanama	5026	208	29.56
S.T. Jayasuriya	4672	178	28.66
A.P. Gurusinha	3902	147	28.27
H.P. Tillekeratne	3303	176	29.23
M.S. Atapattu	1972	66	34.59
R.S. Kaluwitharana	1931	112	18.93
R.L. Dias	1573	58	31.46
L.R.D. Mendis	1527	79	23.49
D.S.B.P. Kuruppu	1022	54	20.03
R.S. Madugalle	950	63	18.62
H.D.P.K. Dharmasena	849	94	26.53
M.A.R. Samarasekera	844	39	22.81
J.R. Ratnayeke	824	78	14.98
R.S. Kalpage	810	82	21.31
S. Wettimuny	786	35	24.56
U.C. Hathurusinghe	669	34	21.58
R.J. Ratnayake	612	70	16.54
W.P.U.J.C. Vaas	506	105	12.97

Appendix 2

TEST MATCH CRICKET STATISTICS

P.A. de Silva Career Record
up to 30/3/99

Batting

Tests	M	I	NO	Runs	HS	Avge	100	50	Ct
Home	33	55	7	2586	168	53.38	9	11	18
Away	42	74	2	2566	267	35.63	8	7	20
Neutral	1	2	0	78	72	39.00	0	1	0
Total	76	131	9	5230	267	42.86	17	19	38

Record Against Specific Opponents

Opponent	M	I	NO	Runs	HS	Avge	100	50	Ct
England	5	9	0	339	152	37.66	1	1	5
Australia	9	15	0	611	167	40.73	1	4	2
West Indies	3	6	1	228	78	45.60	-	2	-
New Zealand	12	20	0	785	267	39.25	2	4	7
Pakistan	16	29	3	1212	168	46.61	7	1	8
India	19	32	2	1252	148	41.73	5	3	9
South Africa	5	9	0	391	82	43.44	-	3	3
Zimbabwe	7	11	3	412	143*	51.50	1	1	4

Record In Each Calendar Year

Year	M	I	NO	Runs	HS	Avge	100	50	Ct
1984	1	2	0	19	16	9.50	–	–	–
1985	6	11	1	418	122	41.80	2	1	1
1986	5	9	1	160	37	20.00	–	–	4
1987	1	2	0	29	21	14.50	–	–	–
1988	2	4	0	34	18	8.50	–	–	3
1989	2		0	314	167	104.66	1	2	1
1990	1	2	0	12	7	6.00	–	–	2
1991	6	9	0	603	267	67.00	2	1	4
1992	6	8	0	301	85	37.62	–	3	3
1993	8	14	1	656	148	50.46	1	5	2
1994	8	15	1	326	127	23.28	1	–	1
1995	6	12	0	282	105	23.50	1	1	2
1996	3	4	0	73	35	18.25	–	–	1
1997	11	19	3	1220	168	76.25	7	2	7
1998	8	14	2	682	152	56.83	2	3	5
1999	2	3	0	101	72	33.66	–	1	2

Bowling

Test	Balls	R	W	Avge	Best	5w	10w	S/R
	2065	1007	26	38.73	3-30	–	–	79.42

Appendix 3

Aravinda's All-Time World XI

1. Gordon Greenidge
2. Sunil Gavaskar
3. Allan Border
4. Viv Richards
5. Javed Miandad
6. Imran Khan
7. Richard Hadlee
8. Ian Healy
9. Dennis Lillee
10. Abdul Qadir
11. Michael Holding

On the basis that I had to have played against these best of the best, I am spared the selectorial conundrum of having to fit in Greg Chappell. Dennis Lillee I only faced during his bowling-clinics in Sri Lanka and even though he was well into retirement, the mind and carriage of a great fast-bowler evidently remained. There are so many with good claim to be in this XI; Desmond Haynes narrowly misses out, as does Sachin, as does Wasim, as do . . . But these cricketers, I dare any other XI to beat.

Aravinda de Silva